The Keys To Corfe Castle

Linda Sindt

Ink & Quill Publishers
2022

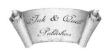

Henderson, NV 89002

The Keys to Corfe Castle
Linda Sindt
Copyright 2022

Line/Content Editor: Summer Gull Interior
Design: Jo A. Wilkins
E-Pub generated by: Richard Draude
Cover: Richard R. Draude

p. cm. — Linda Sindt (Biography)
Copyright © 2022 / Ink & Quill Publishers.
All Rights Reserved

ISBN: 978-1-948266-43-7/Paperback
ISBN: 978-1-948266-29-1/ E Book Part 1
ISBN: 978-1-948266-80-2/ E Book Part 2
1. Biography & Autobiography/Women
2. History/Modern/17th Century
3. History/Europe/General

www.mysticpublishersinc.com

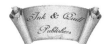

Henderson, NV 89002
Printed in the United States of America
1 2 3 4 5 6 7 8 9 10

TABLE OF CONTENTS

Table Of Contents
(Continued)

Table Of Contents
(Continued)

Table Of Contents
(Continued)

Corfe Castle, Key Family, Altham

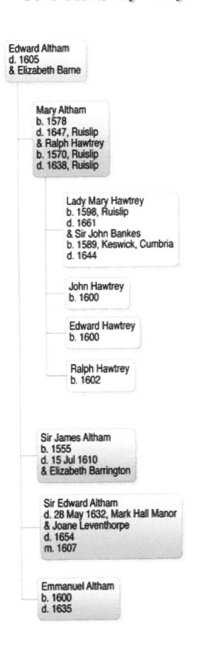

Edward Altham
d. 1605
& Elizabeth Barne

Mary Altham
b. 1578
d. 1647, Ruislip
& Ralph Hawtrey
b. 1570, Ruislip
d. 1638, Ruislip

Lady Mary Hawtrey
b. 1598, Ruislip
d. 1661
& Sir John Bankes
b. 1589, Keswick, Cumbria
d. 1644

John Hawtrey
b. 1600

Edward Hawtrey
b. 1600

Ralph Hawtrey
b. 1602

Sir James Altham
b. 1555
d. 15 Jul 1610
& Elizabeth Barrington

Sir Edward Altham
d. 28 May 1632, Mark Hall Manor
& Joane Leventhorpe
d. 1654
m. 1607

Emmanuel Altham
b. 1600
d. 1635

Corfe Castle Key Family, Hawtrey

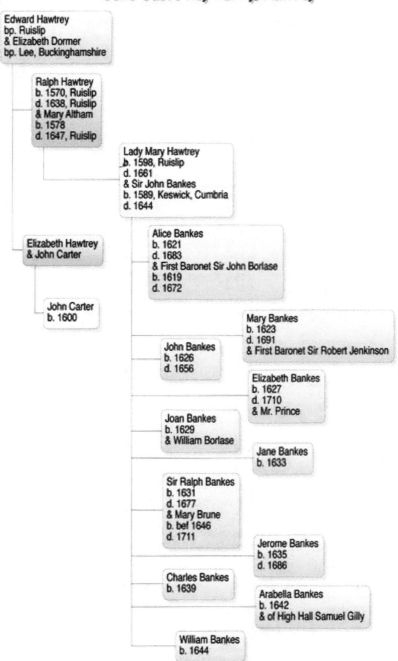

Edward Hawtrey
bp. Ruislip
& Elizabeth Dormer
bp. Lee, Buckinghamshire

Ralph Hawtrey
b. 1570, Ruislip
d. 1638, Ruislip
& Mary Altham
b. 1578
d. 1647, Ruislip

Lady Mary Hawtrey
b. 1598, Ruislip
d. 1661
& Sir John Bankes
b. 1589, Keswick, Cumbria
d. 1644

Elizabeth Hawtrey
& John Carter

John Carter
b. 1600

Alice Bankes
b. 1621
d. 1683
& First Baronet Sir John Borlase
b. 1619
d. 1672

Mary Bankes
b. 1623
d. 1691
& First Baronet Sir Robert Jenkinson

John Bankes
b. 1626
d. 1656

Elizabeth Bankes
b. 1627
d. 1710
& Mr. Prince

Joan Bankes
b. 1629
& William Borlase

Jane Bankes
b. 1633

Sir Ralph Bankes
b. 1631
d. 1677
& Mary Brune
b. bef 1646
d. 1711

Jerome Bankes
b. 1635
d. 1686

Charles Bankes
b. 1639

Arabella Bankes
b. 1642
& of High Hall Samuel Gilly

William Bankes
b. 1644

Prologue

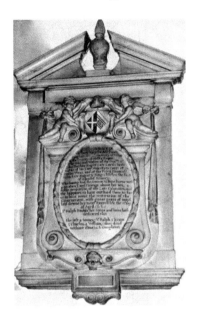

On the south wall of the chancel at St. Martin's Church, Ruislip, Middlesex, in England is a monument honoring Lady Mary Bankes. Some say the lavish tribute on her monument contains a deliberate lie. A 400-year-old April Fool's joke. The inscription reads:

> *"To the memory of LADY MARY BANKES, the only daughter of Ralph Hawtery, of Ruislip, in the county of Middlesex, esq. The wife and widow of the Honourable Sir Bankes, knight, late Lord Chief Justice of his Majesty's Court of Common Pleas, and of the Privy Council of his Majesty King Charles I, of blessed memory, who, having the honor to have borne with a constancy and courage above her sex a noble proportion of the late calamities, and the restitution of the government, with great peace of mind laid down her most desired life the 11th day of April 1661. Sir Ralph Bankes her son and heir hath dedicated this. She had four sons:*

1.Sir Ralph
2.Jerome
3.Charles
4. William
(since dead, without issue), and six daughters."

Sir Ralph, who commissioned this monument had an older brother, John (1625 – 1656), the original heir to the family fortune. Why was this one-time heir (who died without children) not even named on his mother's Monument? Why the emphasis that William, her youngest son died without having children? Why was the Monument not even erected until nine years after the death of Lady Mary? Coincident with the "death" of her youngest son? Is there something suspicious going on with this curiously worded "obituary?"

This "eulogy" lavishes the highest praise on Lady Mary. The words "... a constancy and courage above her sex..." nevertheless would wound delicate 21st Century "enlightened" souls. Did Sir Ralph intend to diminish his mother's courage by suggesting her bravery may have exceeded that of mere women, but possibly not that of most men? Should it matter that her monument records her sons' names but not the names of her daughters? Even though Sir Ralph's valiant younger sisters stood fiercely by their mother's side in face-to-face combat with enemy Parliamentary forces while Ralph and his brothers safely hid from possible harm?

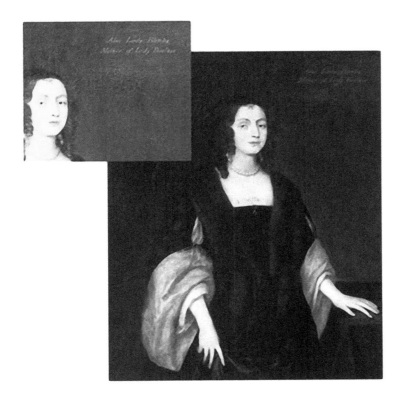

Four-hundred-year-old portrait of Lady Mary Hawtrey Bankes by an unknown artist. It is currently displayed at Sudbury Hall, National Trust, United Kingdom, titled "Unknown Lady."

AUTHOR'S NOTE: Final editing by the author exposed a previously invisible inscription clearly identifying this portrait to be "Lady Banks." The inscription reads in part: "Lady Banks Mother of Lady Borlase." (Our heroine's oldest daughter was Lady Alice Borlase. National Trust records show the portrait was acquired from the Vernon Trust which came from the Borlase family). Clear evidence that this is no longer an "Unknown Lady." As of the publishing date of this novel the National Trust had not yet changed its identification of "The Unknown Lady," but it was "under review."

The Keys
To
Corfe Castle

CHAPTER ONE
"Look upon thy death,"
Shakespeare, Romeo and Juliet
April 11, 1661

"Why did you lie to your children? And send them away?" Clodagh's tear-sparkled green-blue eyes hovered over my face. "They would want to be here, by your side."

I bade my nearby offspring and their families to depart from my bedside yesterday in a parade of gift-laden carriages. They needed to be at their brother's wedding—not tending to their ailing mother. I longed to go with them. To the grand wedding celebration of my now oldest son, Ralph, in Dorsetshire, so near to the home I once loved with such desperation. Corfe Castle.

"No," I said to Clodagh, "it is better this way. They will also remember the day of my death as a day of great happiness and celebration. My John lives on in his children. Our family must have ample means. I cannot meet my Maker in peace until I am certain my family's future financial welfare is assured. The enormous wealth of my son's bride will sustain our family for many generations to come."

"You always did insist on doing things your way. You will be stubborn until the end."

I glanced at the high window in my room. Gloomy clouds

dimmed the grey light that filtered through the curtains on that Spring Day—I could not judge the time.

"Surely the wedding vows between my Ralph and his bride, Mary Bruen, will have been said by now?"

Clodagh tried to distract me. "You did well when you arranged for this marriage with such a wealthy young woman," she said. "Even though her late father was a Colonel in the Parliamentary forces that so recently tried to destroy us all."

"You are right as always. There are indeed strange bedfellows arising from the ashes of the Civil War."

"And you are not grieved that she has recently declared herself to be a Roman Catholic?" Clodagh's usual mischief colored her speech.

I stifled a cough, hiding my smile from my long-cherished Irish Roman Catholic friend. I squeezed her hand with what strength I could. "If there is any positive side to the devastating times we have lived through, it is that those with differing faiths can, at last, begin to try to live openly and peacefully together in our land. I have left you a stipend, Clodagh. You will be able to live on your own wherever you wish. I am sure all my married children will beg you to join their households. They all believe they belong to you as much as to me."

Clodagh squeezed my hand back. "I love them all as if they were my own, you know that. But they no longer need me. It has never been a secret that something else has long been calling to me. My homeland fared so cruelly under the harsh rule of Cromwell. I know well I am no longer young. I have learned of a new order that endeavors to aid my countrymen who are now so impoverished and starving. This new convent desperately seeks help. They will take me in and allow me to help as long as I'm able. It will be comforting to know my coffin will lie near my courageous mother and the heroic father I never met."

"My dear, brave friend. My family owes you so much," was all I could manage to say.

Tears flowed freely down her cheeks.

I squeezed her hand again. "And now I think you must leave me alone for a while."

She bent to softly kiss my brow before she left my side. Predictably, she took solace in her music. I could not help but smile at the fierce way she attacked her harpsichord that stood near mine in the library. Her voice soared as the joyous madrigal she had sung at my wedding so long ago took wing, throbbing now more in a fierce lament.

My thoughts turned to "my John." As one sweet, too young daughter once worried when confronted so early with the death of her father, I hoped he would recognize me in Heaven "without my skin on." How would we speak in a heavenly realm? My whole being ached for the sheer joy of just being with him. I longed to hear once more the noise of our lively arguments.

Of course, I yearned, especially, for my brilliant eldest son, John, namesake for his father, struck down so early. I yet ached to hold the stillborn babies so cruelly denied to me. Also, of course, there will be my so wise father, Ralph Hawtrey. And my funny, amazing mother, "Mair-Mair" to all. There are already so many who await my presence. In the centuries to come, will I recognize my vibrant children and grandchildren, and those beyond my time? The flesh and bones that contained their spirits left behind?

Can our so mysterious Creator not send messages to me into eternity? Might my darling children find me there, so I can know what happened to them and to their children and to their children's children? Can I possibly peek down in my afterlife now and then and watch over all my dear ones wherever they may go as their lives unfold? Will I get to know all the answers to the universe? Will it all at last make sense? That is my prayer. That I will get to know all the answers to everything, past, present, and future. Is that too much to ask?

The last in a long line of beloved greyhounds, my latest Canute, dozed beside my bed. My heart delights in anticipation. Surely his much-adored predecessors await my arrival in the next realm?

The more than one hundred men whose deaths I directly caused lie heavy in my heart. And, of course, the six brave souls who died protecting me and my young daughters. I choose to believe all these needless deaths lie on that cruel monster, Cromwell. I know not how to rid my eyes of the vivid scenes of combat. I confess an angry coal in my heart yet flames to life when uninvited memories of the monstrous betrayal of those once trusted and dearly cared for persist in forcing their way into my introspection.

I will know soon how my so mysterious Maker judges my unforgiving heart. Shadows flicker against the wall. My eyes drift shut. A flutter tickles my cheek. Is that my love teasing me once more with an eagle feather from the New World? Or the dance of a white butterfly wing?

CHAPTER TWO

"So foul and fair a day I have not seen,"
Shakespeare, Macbeth
November 5, 1606

Remember, remember the fifth of November
Gunpowder, treason and plot
I see no reason why gunpowder treason
Should ever be forgot
Guy Fawkes, Guy Fawkes, 'twas his intent
To blow up the King and the Parliament
Three score barrels of powder below
Poor old England to overthrow
By God's providence he was catched
With a dark lantern and burning match
Holloa boys, holloa boys
God save the King!
Hip hip hooray!
Hip hip hooray!
A penny loaf to feed ol' Pope
A farthing cheese to choke him
A pint of beer to rinse it down
A faggot of sticks to burn him
Burn him in a tub of tar
Burn him like a blazing star
Burn his body from his head
Then we'll say ol' Pope is dead.
Hip hip hooray!
Hip hip hooray!
(Traditional English Rhyme - 17th Century)

My parents rarely argued. Father openly adored my mother, his "Mair-Mair," and generally quite happily yielded to her every whim. Yet, one of my earlier memories is of them having a real fracas, which my mother did not win (at least not entirely). I was seven. They had not yet noticed I had slipped into the room.

"I detest the very idea of this Guy Fawkes Day celebration that Parliament has ordered upon us!"

I edged a little closer, still without detection. My always merry mother was crying! Father, of course, was solicitous.

"You are thinking of your Uncle Thomas, aren't you?"

"He was so dear and gentle. My uncle suffered so much when he defied my grandfather and married a beautiful Roman Catholic girl who had come to England with her family from France. It hurt him so much when my grandfather disinherited him as the oldest son and gave Mark Hall to my father instead."

Mair-Mair dabbed at her eyes with her trademark lacy handkerchief and continued. "I know you did not have any choice about signing an Oath of Allegiance to King James and denouncing the Pope. But our children must not grow up to hate and possibly even hurt anyone as dear as my uncle and aunt and my sweet cousins."

"My darling wife. Your uncle suffered so severely for assuming his wife's religion. I am forever sorry about that. But I can't help being glad your father inherited Mark Hall!" Father always knew just how to sweet talk my mother.

"Otherwise, our parents might never have arranged our marriage, and I would not have missed having you as my wife for anything on this earth!"

"But the very idea that Parliament wants to make what amounts to a ghoulish children's party out of something so beyond abhorrent as this new Guy Fawkes bonfire is revolting! I won't make a game out of pretending to burn anyone alive," my mother said. "And especially not the Pope! Why can't we just stay home?"

"Now, Mair." My father moved closer and put a comforting hand on her shoulder. "You know how worried I am about the future of our family. Your kinsfolk at Mark Hall have always enjoyed the favor of Queen Elizabeth and now of King James. It has not always been so easy here at Eastcote. We simply cannot afford to incur the displeasure of the king. As Bailiff of Ruislip Manor, I am in the service of the king. My duties as the landlord for King's College demand that our family set an example for all here that depend on us and ultimately, on the king, for their livelihoods."

"But there were only a few Catholic rebels involved in this terrible plot," argued my mother, "and they have all been caught and tortured, and hanged."

Mair-Mair lowered her voice to a whisper, but I could still hear. "I heard that Sir Edward Coke, the Attorney General, also ordered that the genitalia of the conspirators be cut off while they were still alive and burnt before their very eyes. Isn't all of that punishment and deterrent enough? Must we encourage hatred for all Catholics, most of whom would never dream of harming anyone, much less the king?"

She did not say it out loud, but I am pretty sure my mother was also worried about her personal attendant (and dear friend), Roisin (you say it Roh sheen—the English translation is "Rose," or "Little Rose," but I much prefer the musical lilt of saying "Roh sheen") and Roisin's young daughter, Clodagh, my special playmate. They had somehow escaped ongoing turmoil in Ireland and were of the Roman Catholic faith, although they had never practiced it publicly. All of us children understood, without knowing exactly why, that this was a private, family issue never to be discussed in public. After the plot to blow up Parliament, my father insisted that the two of them accompany our family, along with our servants, to our Anglican church services on all Sundays.

"I am so sorry, my dearest Mair-Mair." My father's voice was uncharacteristically firm. "I know how upsetting this is for you, but I must insist. You and our Mary and the twins and Baby Rafe will all be at the ceremony tonight. My sister and her husband and their son and your young brother must all be there. And all our tenants. And all their children. It is a command performance. Roisin and Clodagh must absolutely attend, or people may gossip. And the cook can pack some special treats to share with all."

My mother was silent for a moment and then said, tightly, "As you like. Except for one thing." A defiant glint sparkled in her eyes. "I am certain Baby Rafe has suddenly developed the sniffles, and I find I must stay by his side to attend to him. And Roisin must, of course, assist me."

My father sighed, bent over Mair-Mair, kissed her forehead, and brushed a tear from her cheek. "So it will be, my dearest one."

I scooted over and grabbed my father's hand. "Father, what is genitalia?"

Startled, he said, "Crumpet, where did you come from?"

"Mary! Hush!" said my mother.

Father turned to Mair-Mair as he guided me from the room. "I promise you, my love, that our children who do go will not see this event as an endorsement of hatred, but as simply a jolly old romp in the dark with an exciting bonfire and festive treats."

And my father was right. I ran and screamed and laughed and danced with delight with Clodagh and my younger twin brothers and my cousin, John Carter, as well as my younger than me Uncle Emmanuel, and the other village children in the light of the magnificently flaming bonfire. The sweet treats provided by our cook added fuel to our revelry. Canute, my pet greyhound, romped with us. I adored the Guy Fawkes Day celebration for many years after and did not hesitate a moment to share it with my children and their children. Perhaps this annual festival called out to something ancient and pagan in my Celtic bones. I refuse to feel a bit repentant about this example of yet another failure on my part in living a godly life. To my knowledge, my blessed Mair-Mair never in the years to come graced a Guy Fawkes bonfire with her presence.

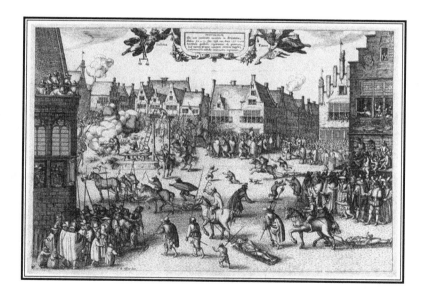

A 1606 etching by Claes (Nicolaes) Jansz, depicting Fawkes's execution

Linda Sindt

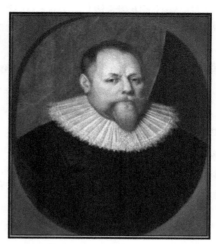

Ralph Hawtrey by 17ᵗʰ Century artist, Cornelius Janssens van Ceulen
Source: National Trust Images

This painting by Cornelius Janssens van Ceulen is of my adored father, Ralph Hawtrey. How can I describe him to you? Patient, demanding, stern, strong, gentle, and wise beyond words. As his oldest child and only daughter, we shared a special bond. Our family has had ties to Chequers, Buckinghamshire, since the 13ᵗʰ century. [Note: Chequers is currently a stately vacation residence of Great Britain's Prime Minister]. My father's family is actually quite ancient, dating back to the Norman times in the 11ᵗʰ Century and arriving in England at the time of William the Conqueror. For several generations prior to my birth, we owned the lease of the lands of the rectory of Ruislip. Shortly before his marriage, my father became bailiff of Ruislip Manor on behalf of King's College, Cambridge. I grew up in Eastcote Manor in Ruislip. In a word, during my childhood we were among the more fortunate, landed gentry of England's society, but definitely not (yet) on the level of aristocracy in our social position.

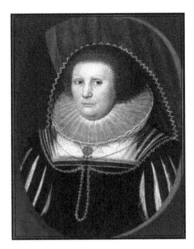

Mary Altham Hawtrey by 17th Century artist, Cornelius Janssens van Ceulen
Source: National Trust Images

This painting, also by the respected painter, Cornelius Janssens van Ceulen, is of my mother, my "Mair-Mair." Can you not see the pent-in merriment flashing in her eyes, the droll comments about to burst from her lips? As she often teasingly reminded my father, he definitely married "up" when he acquired her as his wife. Her childhood home was in Mark Hall Manor in Essex, where her grandfather entertained Queen Elizabeth three times. Definitely a higher social circle than my father's family! Do not be misled by the apparent sobriety of my parents' dress. They were not at all Puritans, as later defined by the zealous and hated "Round Heads." They were more like left over Elizabethans in their devoted, conservative religious beliefs, as well as their choice of apparel, very elegant in an understated way and were not at all comfortable with the flamboyant colors, bold sexuality, and ostentation of King James' Court, much less the excesses of the Court of his even more arrogant and pathetic son, King Charles I. I say this as a devoted Royalist.

AUTHOR ENDNOTES, CHAPTER TWO: *Guy Fawkes Day is celebrated on the 5th of November in the United Kingdom to this day, although the effigy of the Pope has been generally replaced with an effigy of Guy Fawkes or, sometimes, current political figures. Elaborate fireworks have augmented and often replaced the bonfires, and there is a generally accepted tolerance for the peaceful coexistence of many faiths. Following is a popular Guy Fawkes Day ("Bonfire") recipe that has been handed down through the generations. Shared by the owner of a lovely Bed and Breakfast in the village of Corfe Castle, whose grandmother gave it to her.*

Bonfire Cake
Serves 8
450g (3 1/3 c.) tart green apples, diced into large chunks and sprinkled with lemon juice
450g (3 1/3 c.) flour
3 tsp baking powder
230g (1 2/3 c.) unsalted butter
230g (1 2/3 c.) brown sugar
2 large eggs mixed with 5 tbsp of milk
2 tbsp brown sugar
1 tsp ground cinnamon
whipped cream (optional)

Heat oven to 175 degrees C. (350 degrees F.), Grease and flour a 10inch round cake pan. Mix flour, baking powder and butter in a large bowl until crumbly. Add the sugar, eggs, milk, and apples. Mix and put into the cake pan. Mix the 1 2/3 cups sugar and the cinnamon and sprinkle on top of batter. Bake for 50 mins. Sprinkle remaining brown sugar and cinnamon over the top. Serve warm. Top with whipped cream if desired.

CHAPTER THREE

"I...durst commend a secret to your ear."
Shakespeare, King Henry the VIII
October 1608

"Ouch!" **a tiny spot** of blood appeared on the finger I had stabbed with a needle. Mair-Mair was making me learn to "embroider like a lady." I was not quite ten.

"You mustn't attack the cloth, Mary," admonished my mother. She dabbed at the spot on my finger with her embroidered, lacy handkerchief. "There is a little rhythm that comes with practice. And you must try to learn it and take only the tiniest of stitches. Soon you will find that the needle fairly dances in your fingers as the lovely designs appear."

I compared my awkward stitches to those of the elaborate design on the pillow I was supposed to be copying. I was not certain my destiny included "embroidering like a lady." My pet greyhound, Canute, napped near the fireplace. Clearly, embroidery bored him, also.

My mother's real name was Mary, like mine. Although she seldom drank anything more potent than her breakfast beer, my father often declared, sometimes maybe with a gentle hint of exasperation, she was born with sweet wine in her blood. Her intoxicating delight with life, in general, could not be contained and just bubbled out, catching all within her happy spell. When they were first married, Father's pet name for his adored bride was "Merry Mary." When I, their firstborn, was learning to talk, and they were trying to teach me to say "Ma-Ma," I, according to the family legend, argued that no, she was "Mair-Mair." Apparently, my version of "Merry Mary."

The "pet" name stuck. Mair-Mair she was to all from then on. Even many years later my goodly number of grandchildren universally adored their great-grandmother, "Mair-Mair."

I glanced longingly at the October drizzled windowpanes. As much as I loved my own mother, I would have much preferred to be with my dear Clodagh and her mother, who were overseeing the delivery of the weekly supply of food and necessities to the special tenants who lived in the nearby Almshouses backing onto St. Martin's Church. As the Bailiff of the larger Ruislip Manor, one of my father's duties was to oversee the care for these unfortunate beings. Normally, I went with Roisin and Clodagh on these excursions. Ten of these churchyard cottages housed individuals in our community who had no other means of support. Some were ancient beings who had outlived the grown children that had previously cared for them and had nowhere else to go. Several were former soldiers, maimed or ailing with agues and fluxes from fighting in Ireland. Father often lamented that he couldn't help more of these now vagrant war veterans that roamed the countryside. Some were new mothers who had lost their husbands to accidents or to war and had no family to give them support. The mothers of the babies often encouraged Clodagh and me to hold and cuddle them. We loved teasing dimples into the babies' cheeks and making them laugh and kick. I was missing those babies, but mostly, I was missing Clodagh, who was nearly two years older than me, and her amusing chatter.

Setting my embroidery on my chair and edging up to the fireplace to scratch Canute's ears, I turned to Mair-Mair. There was a question that had been troubling me for some time, but I wasn't sure I should ask.

"What is in your mind, Mary?"

"It is about Roisin and Clodagh."

"What is it you want to know?"

"How did we get them? I know they are not exactly servants," I said, "but they seem almost like servants. Clodagh is my best friend in the whole world," I confessed. "I don't think I could live without her."

"Oh, sweet child," said my mother. "You are so perceptive to see this. I do not believe I could live without her mother, also. She is so very dear to me." Mair-Mair's fingers flew with emotion as she continued stitching the silken, intricate flower petals onto the linen cloth.

The door to our cozy room opened as Clodagh and Roisin returned from their duties. They carried baskets of mending and joined us around the fire.

"Roisin, my wonderful friend," said my mother. "Mary has asked to be told the truth of how you and Clodagh came to live with us. But that secret is rightfully yours to tell, only if you wish to do so."

Clodagh looked up, startled. It was a question she had often puzzled over with me in our private discussions. Roisin dropped her mending. Her hands flew to her mouth. Were those tears in her eyes? Clodagh rushed to her mother in alarm, but Roisin brushed her away. She answered Mair-Mair's question in her heavily Gaelic-accented English, "You are right, of course. I have been dreading this day, but if our daughters are old enough to learn to embroider and to do important grown-up chores, like caring for those who are less fortunate than we are, they are old enough to learn of grave secrets."

Roisin hesitated a few moments. "I do not know how to begin."

"Let me start with what I know. Then you can fill in as the story progresses," suggested Mair-Mair.

"But first..." Mair-Mair looked intently at both Clodagh and me. "...You must both, seriously, spit on your hands and promise not to say one word about any of this with anyone but me and Roisin and between yourselves. Ever. Not even with your brothers, Mary. Especially not your brothers. They have not yet learned how to not be chatterboxes and cannot know of this."

It was not in my mother's character to be so serious. Nothing laughing or merry lightened her face. Clodagh and I, of course, solemnly, and with questioning, wide eyes, spat on our hands and said, "I promise!" in unison.

"For their safety and also to protect our own family, the world must continue to believe that Roisin and Clodagh are simply our servants," continued Mair-Mair.

"Only we can know that they are actually from what was once a highborn, aristocratic family. In truth, Clodagh is from two highborn aristocratic families. In fact, they are technically both even higher born than we are," she said, catching my eyes with hers, so I felt her intensity.

Clodagh and I looked at each other in astonishment. Her fingers followed the outline of the homemade Catholic rosary I knew she wore under her dress. Her mother had lovingly crafted it.

"But," Mair-Mair said with mock sternness, "Mary, you must pick up your needle and continue stitching as you listen!"

"Before I became betrothed to your father, Mary, the young son of one of our servants at Mark Hall Manor, where I grew up, was pressed into the service of Queen Elizabeth. The war against the Irish rebels was going badly. Many thousands of brave, young English men had already died on the battlefields.

Queen Elizabeth ordered many more into service. You have

both met several unfortunate men in our care who suffered horrible hurt in that dreadful war. Thankfully, it finally ended just five years ago after nine devastating years of bloodshed. Many more died than came home. We were all distressed about our servant's son because we were very fond of him, but my father could find no way to spare him from this service."

"Clodagh and I owe him our lives," chimed in Roisin. "We would have died had he not been there." Roisin had glorious, long, curly black hair, which she pinned up in a fiercely tight bun every morning. By mid-morning, the stubborn curls always began to spring a bit free, forming a sweet halo of curly tendrils that danced around her face as she went about her work. Her bright eyes were an unusual shade of the palest green-blue turquoise and seemed to dance back and forth between bluish-green and greenish-blue in the changing October light. Clodagh's hair and bright eyes echoed those of her mother, except she attempted, also with charming ineffectiveness, to imprison her curls in long braids.

"There were two Irish chieftains," said Roisin in her lilting brogue. "Hugh O'Neill of Tir Eoghain and Hugh Roe O'Donnell of Tir Chonaill, who were exceptionally brave. They hated the English who governed them but despised even more fiercely English efforts to oppose and squash down our Catholic religion."

Clodagh asked her mother a question in Gaelic. She could not only talk to her mother in the Irish language, but she could also perfectly imitate her mother's brogue flavored English when she chose. And, of course, having grown up with me as my almost sister, her aristocratic English was indistinguishable from my own.

"Yes, I have met both Hughs," Roisin said, answering her daughter's question in her brogue flavored English. "Hugh O'Neill and Hugh Roe O'Donnell enlisted many Irish Lords in their service. My father and your father's father were two of those Irish Lords. My brothers and my husband's brothers joined their fathers in the fierce fighting near our homes in Ulster.

"We Irish were not so large in number compared to the English forces, but we got much financial support from Catholic Spain in arming and feeding our desperate Irish warriors.

"There were nearby skirmishes over time, with my Irish clansmen holding their own. Our Irish fighters won the terrible fight that killed my husband and his father and all of his brothers, as well as my own father and all of my brothers. But the English prevailed in later clashes and exacted vengeance for their losses.

"Following that horrendous battle when my dear ones perished, I continued to live in the castle of my husband's family with my mother-in-law and my husband's sisters."

"You lived in a castle!?" Clodagh and I exclaimed in unison.

Canute lifted his head at the sound of our surprise and decided to join the party. He wandered over and put his head in my lap for a pat, only drooling a little bit on my forgotten embroidery.

"Since I grew up in my father's castle, I have indeed lived in two castles," said Roisin, eliciting another gasp from Clodagh and me.

"You had not been inside me for very long, Clodagh. I missed your father so much it felt like I could not breathe. I was distraught with sadness. One morning, I awoke very early. Rosy dawn fingers colored the sky. No one else in the castle was up, not even the servants, who by then were mainly women. I felt ill, as I did most mornings in those days of feeling you growing inside me. I decided to go for a short walk to settle my stomach. I wandered some distance from the castle. There was a grove of trees. Growing weary, I found a soft, grassy mound and sat with my back to a tree to rest.

"I fell asleep. I awoke to the sound of many horses riding up to the castle. I started to run toward the castle to see what was happening and then I heard the sounds of women screaming. Many women, many screams. And then there were no more screams, only the sounds of men shouting and talking to each other. They were English voices. I waited, and waited, hiding, for several hours, but the English soldiers and their horses did not leave.

"I will not go into all the details of my journey, but I traded my linen dress for a peasant woman's clothing and coat, and begging food and water along the way, I cautiously traveled for three days on foot and made my way to my father's castle. However, there were English horses there, also, and I then knew my mother and my sisters were also gone.

"I slept on the streets of our village, along with many others who were dispossessed, sharing water and food as we were able. We were all so ravenously hungry. One morning I walked through a nearby woodland, looking for berries or edible leaves, or anything we could put in a communal stew to help feed my now homeless new friends and me. I found a wounded English soldier hiding. He was gravely hurt. He had run away from his regiment and wanted only to return home to England.

"The English had been among us, ruling us for many years. We all spoke and understood some form of English. It was and is mostly our Catholic faith the English continue to fear and despise. Until then, except for trying to destroy our religious practices, they had left our other institutions intact, allowing the Irish Lords to rule and care for their people as they always had. However, the Queen of England demanded that they pay her increasingly large sums of money.

"Now, after the insurrection of the two Hughs, the English invaders wanted to destroy everything Irish, leaving scorched earth and destroyed villages behind. I was so terrified and abandoned and lost. I loved Ireland with my whole heart. Now there was no place for me to go or any way even to stay alive.

"I secretly tended to this English soldier's wounds for many days and nights, watching over him until he could limp along somewhat. We developed a plan. I would help him get safely through Ireland and back to his family in England. He would plead with his family to provide shelter and food for me and for the baby that would soon arrive. We had many close encounters and adventures along the way, but eventually arrived at Mark Hall Manor in Essex.

"I hoped to find employment as a servant in the kitchen of the Manor where the family of this soldier worked. My new friend promised there would be space in his family's cottage where I might have a cot for my baby and me, but—"

"Mark Hall, of course, is where I grew up and where I still lived with my family." Mair-Mair intervened. "When I heard the story, I insisted that Roisin become my personal maid and live in my home, and she has been my dearest friend and companion ever since!" She reached over and patted Roisin's hand. "What happened to the servant?" asked Clodagh. "He seems very kind and brave."

"Indeed, he was," said Mair-Mair. "We were all so proud of him. His wounds had weakened him so much. Indeed, he would not have lived at all had it not been for Roisin's care of him on their long journey. His mother and father and sisters looked over him for many months. They rejoiced to have him back home in their care, but a bloody flux passed through the village. Many people got it and eventually healed, but in his weakened condition, he did not survive."

Clodagh walked over and threw her arms around her

mother. "You were so brave, too! Why didn't you tell me before?" Her already bright, green-blue eyes shimmered with tears.

"Listen to me, my dear one. It was not a child's game when our mistress, Mair-Mair, bade you spit in your hands. It was a most solemn promise. It would hurt all their family and both of us if whispers began that they harbored Roman Catholic Irish nobility. Especially someone whose family had led the fight against the English in the recent rebellion. It is much better and safer that we always be known as what we now are—impoverished Irish peasants with absolutely no social status who are servants living on the charity of this generous family." Roisin's customary iron composure was coming undone. Tears fell from her turquoise eyes.

Clodagh hugged her mother. "I want to know more about my father and all of my family!"

"Of course you do, my dear one. And so you shall in the years to come. You must try to understand how difficult it is just now for me to talk of these things. And you must always be grateful for the affection and comfort we have found in this wonderful English home." Dabbing at her tear-filled, green-blue eyes, she gathered her sewing into her basket in preparation to leave.

"But why do the English hate the Catholics so much? What business is it of ours?" I demanded of my mother in indignation.

"I wish I were wise enough to know how to answer that, child," said my mother, who always before in my life had known the answers to all my questions. "It is all very complicated, with much honor and villainy on both sides."

Canute walked to the door, signaling his desire to be let outside. Clodagh and I followed. I felt compelled to curtsy saucily at her and call her "My Lady" several times along the way. I cannot tell you what her cheeky response was because she deliberately spoke in Gaelic. Both our mothers called after us to not forget our coats as we danced together out into the October drizzle.

AUTHOR ENDNOTES, CHAPTER THREE: *Historians tell us the terrible famine and illness following the nine years of fighting in Ireland during this time caused more than 100,000 Irish to die. At least 30,000 English soldiers also died, some, of course, from devastating battle wounds, but most from the illness, hunger, and the general misery they encountered in Ireland. The costly war also put England on the teetering brink of bankruptcy, leading in part to the devastating English Civil War that followed. In 1605 Hugh O'Neill, Earl of Tyrone and Rory O'Donnell, Earl of Tyrconnell, fled to Europe with 90 family members and followers (the Flight of the Earls). This ended the power of Ireland's Gaelic aristocracy.*

CHAPTER FOUR

"Now, God be praised, that to believing souls
gives light in darkness, comfort in despair,"
Shakespeare, King Henry VI
January 1609

I turned ten years old several weeks before Christmas. Clodagh was now twelve. I was bored. Canute was bored. The weather was dreary. It was too chilly to romp outside. Mair-Mair suggested that I work at my embroidery skills, but that was boring, boring, boring. In truth, I could still barely even thread a needle, much less replicate beautiful flowers. I was also decidedly peevish. Mair-Mair and Roisin and Clodagh had a great secret they would not share with me. I would discover them whispering together, looking conspiratorial and even a bit frightened. But they stopped and started chattering about inane things whenever I came near. Clodagh avoided me and seemed preoccupied with private thoughts, staring off into space and fingering at the rosary in its hiding place under her dress. Finally, I cornered her. "What is going on that you don't want me to know," I demanded.

"Mary, you must remember that I am twelve. You are ten. I am now officially a grown-up, and you are still a child. There are some very grown-up things that you are still much too young to know about." Clodagh straightened her shoulders into a womanly pose. It was true that Clodagh had recently abandoned her pigtails and was now wearing her hair in a matronly, if curly-tendrilled, bun.

I rolled my eyes. "Clodagh, I am two inches taller than you, and I'm pretty sure I was born old. According to Father and our tutors, I am 'wise beyond my years!' Besides, I already know all that boring stuff about 'becoming a woman.' I thought that had already happened to you. Is that what all of this is about?"

Clodagh fingered her hidden Rosary again and crossed herself. "It is even much more wonderful and terrifying than that!"

"Then tell me!

"I promised my mother and Mair-Mair I would not!"

"Did you spit in your hand promise?"

"Well, no…"

"Then it doesn't count!"

"It felt like it counted!"

"Here I am. Watch!" I spat in each hand and rubbed them together. "I don't think there is anything more sacred than my double spit promise to keep this secret, whatever it is, compared to your no spit promise!"

"Mary, don't make me laugh. This is so seriously serious."

"Then what?!"

"You are going to keep at me until you find out, anyway, so I might as well tell you. But if Mair-Mair and my mother discover you know, they might not even let this amazing thing happen."

"You are just killing me, Clodagh—TELL me!"

"You know how Mair-Mair is when she gets an idea in her head and cannot let it go. And how sociable and fun she is, so that people tell her many things, sometimes even without meaning to."

"That is indeed my Mair-Mair," I agreed. "So?"

She lowered her voice to a whisper and leaned into my face. "Well, there is a Catholic priest who comes to Middlesex two or three times a year."

I was for once speechless.

"He is hidden away in secret hidey-holes in the homes of the wealthy. Only the husbands in these homes don't know. Only the wives. They arrange for their wealthy lady friends to come for an afternoon of tea and tittle-tattle, so there is already much noise and much coming and going of carriages to the house. In their carriages each mistress secretly brings one or two from her local neighborhood who need the services of a Catholic priest. They are mostly much-loved servants, but sometimes, shopkeepers and other villagers who remember the old days under Queen Elizabeth. In the cellar below, in a hidden cubby hole, the priest secretly conducts mass, hears confessions, and administers sacraments. Mair-Mair has been so sad that my mother and I cannot practice our faith. She has arranged for us to go to the next service!"

"But isn't this dangerous?" I felt compelled to whisper. "What would happen if you and Roisin get caught?"

Clodagh shrugged. "I am sure there would be some kind of punishment, but I'm pretty sure it has been going on for several years here and there. And no one has been caught— yet. I am surprised Mair-Mair did not hear of it before. My mother is so excited. She has taught me so much about our Catholic religion, but she had despaired of ever finding a Catholic priest to minister to us."

I did not ask the question that loomed even larger than my worry for Clodagh and Roisin—What would happen to my Mair-Mair if they were caught?

"I don't think it is fair that I don't get to go." I pouted. "It will be such a grand adventure! When is it going to happen?"

"That I am absolutely not going to tell you! And you must

completely, totally, forget this conversation ever happened!"

Roisin entered the room at that point, looking for Clodagh.

"Clodagh, there you are! I need you to help me sort through some bedding for a new arrival at the Almshouse. What are you two talking about that you seem so serious?"

"Mary was just complaining about the dreary afternoon and how bored she is."

"Well," said Roisin, "there is always embroidery to practice!" She gave me a commiserating pat as she and Clodagh left.

I could not quell my apprehension as I contemplated what Clodagh had just told me. I called to Canute. We marched off to find my father. He was in his library, working, as usual, on the tall pile of ledgers that helped him manage the affairs of Ruislip and Eastcote Manor.

"Crumpet!" he said. "What a dreary, boring afternoon this is. I am glad to have some company. What brings you to my door?"

I joined Canute in front of the cheery fire and settled on a low stool.

"Why does England hate the Catholics so much?"

"Ah, you are perhaps thinking of your friend, Clodagh?"

"NO!" I exclaimed—guiltily.

"It's just...why don't we allow Catholics to worship as they wish?"

"Ah, well, during my grandfather's time it was just the reverse! Did you know that at one time, all of England was Catholic? And those who did not serve the Pope were severely punished?"

"What happened?" I asked. My father abandoned his ledgers and joined me in his favorite chair by the fire. He reached in his pocket and handed Canute a treat. "I am sure this story goes back many centuries beyond the stories I have heard, but here is what I remember from the tales my grandfather told me as well as what I have learned from my association with Gray's Inn. It was during the reign of King Henry the VIII. The story begins when Henry's older brother, Arthur, who was heir apparent to the throne, married Catherine, the beautiful daughter of King Ferdinand of Aragon, and Queen Isabella of Castile. Queen Isabella descended from English royalty. Everyone in England considered her daughter's marriage to a future English King to be a most favorable union. So, this beautiful, red-headed, fourteen-year-old Spanish Princess Catherine, with her Royal English connections, married fifteen-year-old Prince Arthur. Their parents negotiated this marriage when they were toddlers. They married by proxy while they were still children."

"Prince Arthur," continued my father, "sadly, died of illness only a few months after he met Catherine in person. Prince Arthur's younger brother, Henry VIII, became king of England several years later. He took his brother's royal widow as his wife. The English people adored her. She was both beautiful and highly educated. She spoke several languages. She was a talented musician.   She even," he said with a wink at me, "was well known for her beautiful embroidery.

"You will be especially interested to know she was exceedingly compassionate, and greatly admired for starting a generous program in England for relief of the poor, a tradition we proudly carry on here at Eastcote Manor. She was also devoutly Catholic, as was all of England then. The Pope had immense influence over all of our affairs, which may not have always been a good thing for all our wellbeing."

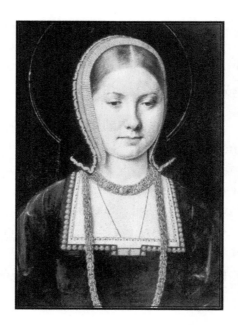

Queen Catherine of Aragon, painting by Michael Sittow, in the Kunsthistorisches Museum, Vienna

"Ultimately," continued my father, "King Henry and Queen Catherine had only one living child. A girl, who later became Queen Mary. But," my father added, "King Henry VIII, feared that his daughter, Mary, might not be able to ascend to the throne because there had never been a female ruler before. He longed for a son. He appealed to the Pope to annul his marriage, so he could legally marry again in the church in the hope of having a baby boy who would become King. This, the Pope refused to do. So—with various elements of religious reformers already breaking away from the Pope in Europe, King Henry broke all ties with the Pope and with the Roman Catholic religion. He declared himself as divinely appointed by God to be King of England, subject to no authority other than God. He named himself as head of the Church of England. And everyone in

England was expected to belong to this new church.

"King Henry sent away all the Catholic Priests from the cathedrals and established his own church leaders, who reported to him, rather than the Pope. Of course, this "new" religion closely resembled the old, barring the severing of ties with the Pope. He ordered the new church leaders to annul his marriage to Queen Catherine. He sent her away and married one of her ladies waiting, Anne Boleyn. This marriage did not produce a son, either, but resulted in the birth of another daughter, Elizabeth, half-sister to Mary."

Canute awoke from his nap and walked over to my father's side, staring up at him adoringly. My father obligingly reached in his pocket for another treat.

I had a million questions, but my father held up his hand. "You are so clever and inquisitive, Crumpet. I always forget how young you still are! I suspect your mother would say I have already gone way too far in discussing any of King Henry the VIII's amorous pursuits with you. The whole point was to try to explain the difficulties the current Roman Catholic generation faces in England. There was a great backlash against the Catholic religion under King Henry. Those who could not accept this revised religion into their hearts suffered cruel punishment. When his first daughter, Mary, ultimately became Queen, she was incensed at how cruelly her father had treated her devoutly Catholic mother. Queen Mary attempted, with limited success, to restore Roman Catholicism as the acknowledged faith in England. She demanded that hundreds of Protestants who by then found it difficult to go back to the Roman Catholic faith be burned at the stake. Her tyranny inflamed the hatred of one religion against the other and earned her the nickname "Bloody Mary." She was queen for only five years. Her half-sister, Elizabeth, daughter of his marriage with Anne Boleyn, succeeded her.

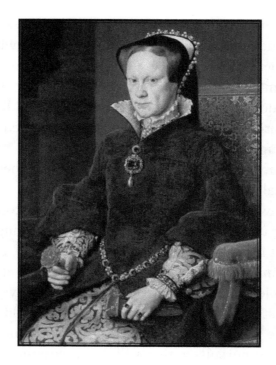

*Queen Mary I, Portrait
by Antonis Mor, 1554*

"Queen Elizabeth truly believed that Catholics and the Anglican Protestants were essentially the same faiths and that any differences were only disputes over "trifles." She worked very hard to promote tolerance and peaceful coexistence between the two closely related faiths. Unlike her older half-sister, she assumed the role as "Supreme Head of the Anglican Church," much to the dismay of the Pope, who quickly excommunicated her. Sadly, there were many outrages on both sides of the religious question during her reign. A Roman Catholic group conspired but failed to assassinate her. Her supporters killed many innocents as well as guilty Catholics thought to have plotted against her. This included many Catholic priests hidden in cubby holes in the mansions and halls of wealthy sympathizers." My father paused.

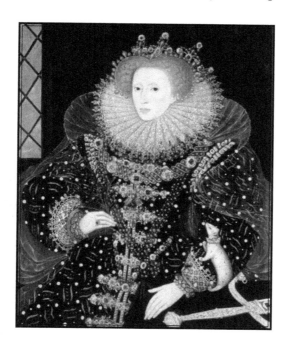

Queen Elizabeth, "The Ermine Portrait,"
William Segar 1585

"Catholic priests?" I tried to catch my breath. "In cubby holes?"

I could not help asking, "Do they still kill them if they find them?" My voice trembled.

"What if they find someone who is worshipping with them? Or...or...who brought them there to worship?" My voice had dropped to a whisper.

Father could not miss my stricken face. My heart pounded. I could not catch my breath, or scarcely look into his eyes.

"Oh, dear Lord," he said. He rushed from the room. Canute and I raced after him.

"I didn't mean to tell!" I sobbed as I pounded behind him.

Mair-Mair was with Roisin and Clodagh. My father grabbed Mair-Mair's shoulders and clasped her to his heart.

"Oh, my dearest one, your tender heart will be the downfall of us all!"

I wept loud and my body convulsed. "I didn't mean to tell!" I said over and over again.

Soon we all sobbed. Even my stalwart father had tears in his eyes.

"I know you had the noblest of motivations," my father finally said to Mair-Mair, "but had there been a discovery, you might all have lost your lives. The King would have removed me from my position and would have severely fined our family. We would have all fallen on hard times. We might even have been imprisoned and tortured in the Tower of London!"

"I did not think of that," said my mother. "It just seemed so unfair that Roisin and Clodagh must forever be denied the comfort of their faith."

My father, with great trepidation, did not turn in the sympathetic wife in the next village over, who harbored the priest. No one got caught. No one was killed or tortured in the Tower of London. Presumably, all who needed priestly sacraments got them, as would have Clodagh and Roisin had it not been for my interference. Even though Clodagh and Mair-Mair and Roisin ultimately forgave me for my role in the matter, my heart remained forever conflicted, but ultimately guilty in this betrayal by me of those dearest to my heart. As mandated by King James, Roisin and Clodagh continued to attend the Anglican services in our village. Along with our servants and all the other villagers. My father never learned of the forbidden rosaries they hid under their dresses.

But a worm of doubt about the ultimate supremacy of

my faith embedded itself forever in my heart. I liked Queen Elizabeth's (and Mair-Mair's) idea. Of course Clodagh and I would meet again in the same eternal Heaven! Any differences in our routes were only "trifles." If only we could have gotten the Pope and King James and later, his son, King Charles I, out of the way for our earthly stay.

AUTHOR ENDNOTES, CHAPTER FOUR: *There is much to admire about the remarkable Queen Catherine. She rode into battle in armor, leading the troops, when her husband, King Henry, VIII, was away on business. She nurtured the idea of the education of women, became the first female ambassador in the history of the world, and so much more. Readers who are intrigued by history should check out this fascinating and courageous, if ill-fated, Queen.*

While the persecution of Catholic priests had mostly died out under the regime of Queen Elizabeth I, there are documented reports of abuse of Catholic priests as well as the existence of "hidey-holes" in the homes of the wealthy continuing under King James I as late as 1609.

CHAPTER FIVE
"How beauteous mankind is!
O brave new world that has such people in it!"
Shakespeare, The Tempest
May 1609

My family and entourage were all at Mark Hall Manor in Essex (Mair-Mair's wonderful childhood home). With her father's death in 1605, Mair-Mair's oldest brother (my Uncle James) inherited the family home and fortune. Mair-Mair made sure we all visited Mark Hall several times a year. I was still ten years old, and Clodagh twelve.

Uncle James was knighted by King James at the King's Palace in Whitehall the year before. He and Aunt Elizabeth Altham had a darling new baby—Johanna— and Clodagh and I were swooning over the chance to coo and cuddle with her under Aunt Elizabeth's hovering eye. The twins, then eight, were with us, and our cousin, John Carter, also eight, son of my father's sister (also an Aunt Elizabeth). She and her husband (Uncle John Carter) did not join in this visit to my mother's family but allowed their son to accompany us for a holiday. The three eight-year-olds plus my eight-year-old Uncle Emmanuel were almost always together, anyway, and tutored as a group. Mair-Mair's youngest brother, my Uncle Emmanuel Altham, also eight, permanently resided at Uncle James's residence with his mother, my Grandmother

Elizabeth Altham.

Together, the four eight-year-old boys, with six-year-old "Baby" Rafe charging behind, formed a merry band of mischief and loosely controlled pandemonium. Uncle Edward, Mair-Mair's fun-loving middle brother between her and Uncle James, had promised to give archery lessons to the five boys as a special Spring treat. Uncle Edward, with his then wife, our Aunt Margaret, were also permanent residents at the elegant and sprawling Mark Hall Manor. Aunt Margaret was pale and ill with a difficult pregnancy, and seldom ventured from her room.

Officially, the home of Grandmother Elizabeth and Emmanuel was at Mark Hall Manor. They were more often at Eastcote Manor. Emmanuel tutored with the Twins and John Carter, as did Clodagh and I. I know, not only did my family have way too many Elizabeths, the added complication of late-arriving Emmanuel adds to the confusion! I seldom, except when I wanted to tease him, called him "Uncle," but considered him to be mostly just another younger brother/cousin to contend with, and I loved him and tormented him as much as I did my own three younger brothers.

Aunt Elizabeth Altham, wife to Uncle James, was probably why my grandmother Elizabeth and my "Uncle" Emmanuel preferred life at Eastcote Manor. Aunt Elizabeth was a bit of a conundrum. We tiptoed around her. I once overheard my parents whispering about this somewhat offbeat match, saying she had brought with her a generous bride portion to the family fortunes.

"I can't imagine why else my father agreed to this marriage for his eldest son and heir to Mark Hall Manor," Mair-Mair speculated. Father suggested it probably didn't hurt that Aunt Elizabeth's devoutly Puritan parents were enamored of the Knighthoods routinely bestowed upon eldest sons in the

Altham family. Her father was a Baronet in his own right, but the supply of eligible sons in the English gentry/aristocracy lineages was limited. Only many years later did I learn that Aunt Elizabeth's mother, Joan Cromwell Barrington, was an aunt to my later intensely despised personal enemy, Oliver Cromwell!

I confess—despite my early conviction that there must be many avenues to Heaven—I just never could get into the hearts and minds of the Puritans. Technically, by law, they mandatorily belonged to the Church of England and were bound to the king. But they held themselves apart as a separate group and were very critical of our traditional ways. My father said they feared we were too much like the Roman Catholics. They didn't like the beautiful gold and silver that adorned our cathedrals and, in my mind, added to the awe and reverence of our worship. It felt like their God—scary, judgmental, and punishing, bore little resemblance to the loving, forgiving, all-mysterious, magical Being my secret heart had communicated with throughout my life. All right, maybe we didn't need all that gold and glitter. Somehow, in my then still childish mind, the sparkle added to the wonder and essence of our devotion for this unfathomable, loving, mysterious presence that endowed our lives with purpose and a way forward, however problematic, amid all the chaos of living. Above all, and most unforgivably, the Puritans hated Christmas! That was especially hard to pardon.

Aunt Elizabeth, with her Puritan convictions, wore nothing but unadorned black. She pulled her hair back in a severe bun, from which no curly tendrils dared escape. The twins giggled that she looked like she had swallowed a lemon, earning a stern rebuke from Mair-Mair. We were all privately admonished to treat her with the greatest respect and affection.

On this bright Spring Day, from so long ago, the boys were

bustled outside to vent their energy prior to the elaborate mid-afternoon meal Aunt Elizabeth Altham had ordered. She alternately fussed over the setting of the table by the servants in the grand dining room between frequent checks on her darling new baby—even though a supremely competent nursemaid hovered nearby. Clodagh and I also leaned over the sweet miracle of baby Johanna, who grabbed our fingers with her tiny, perfect hands and laughed up at us. Roisin and Mair-Mair and my grandmother watched our play as they visited, busying their hands with the ever-present embroidery. Father and Uncle James and Uncle Edward would soon return after several days at Gray's Inn. Uncle Edward promised, with great mystery, to bring some amazing guests.

As the eldest Altham son and heir, Uncle James was a long-time member of Gray's Inn. Father, thanks largely to the influence of my mother's family, according to family legend, was admitted to Gray's Inn the year the twins and Emmanuel were born. Uncle Edward entered two years later. While Gray's Inn was officially a much-revered school of law, it also served as a long-term social club for the landed gentry—a place for eldest sons and others with noble credentials to hang out and make connections that served them well in service to the King. An exclusive venue for current students and older members, the elite of the elite, to mingle and further their various careers and financial endeavors. My father, while well-born and well-connected, was not quite yet in the upper gentry, "elite of the elite" category. However, his arranged match with my mother brought him close, and he was not above taking advantage.

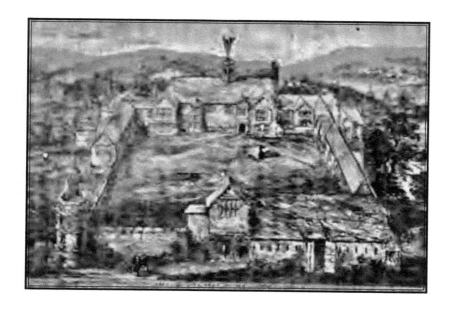

16th century Mark Hall from an old watercolour, reproduced from Essex Review 1908

The shouts of the boys from the courtyard rose several decibels, announcing the arrival of Father and the Uncles. Our two special guests indeed astonished us. One of the men was missing a hand! He was not the center of our attention, however. With him was a dark-skinned young man, almost a boy, wearing virtually no clothing, with red stripes tattooed all over his body. He carried a bow that reached nearly to the top of the large feather pinned to his head.

Linda Sindt

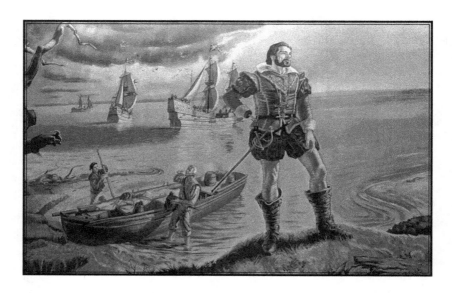

Excerpt from Christopher Newport Library Mural by Allan Jones, Jr., West Avenue Library System, Newport News, Virginia 1957

Captain Christopher Newport was a reformed pirate, who had lost a hand in his former life while capturing and looting a Spanish galleon. He had recently heroically helped establish a Colony for England in a place they called the Virginia Colony in a faraway new world. He returned to England to seek additional funding and supplies for this colony and had grand tales to tell of potential treasures for those who might choose to invest in this fascinating, far away realm. Hence, his visit to Gray's Inn. Captain Newport's partner on this fundraising trip was another colonist, Captain Gabriel Archer, a former law student and lifelong member of Gray's Inn. Where those with the wherewithal to gamble on such risky adventures were prone to hang out. Now, Uncle James—at the request of Captain Archer—promised to introduce Captain Newport to some of the gentry in Essex, who also had available assets to potentially invest.

With him, more amazingly, was a native from this new land. Chief Powhatan (a seemingly "royal" native leader) sent him to live among the colonists and learn about the English language and customs. His name was Namontack. Father said later his presence on this voyage was essentially a theatrical gesture to incite interest in this elaborate money-making scheme. Namontack spoke little but seemed to understand most of our conversation. His guarded, dark eyes followed every word.

The stories they told about the impish Pocahontas intrigued me. She seemed to be a "Princess" in this distant land. Daughter of Chief Powhatan, the local ruler with whom the English Colonists were attempting to deal. I could not help asking many questions about her.

"She is about the same age as you," said Captain Newton. "And also tender-hearted. And, also, a bit mischievous, perhaps also like you, I think!"

"Yes, Mary can be a real torment sometimes!"

"A real nuisance!" chimed in the disloyal twins, to the amusement of all, before being shushed by Mair-Mair.

"She often," Captain Newton continued, "turns cartwheels with young English boys in the dusty street of the settlement when she and leaders of her Algonquian people bring provisions to the English Colonists who often suffered much hunger."

"Of course, in Pocahontas's village," added Captain Newton, "girls your age do not wear clothing. Just a few strings of beads and many red tattoos."

Aunt Elizabeth choked on her tea. Uncle James solicitously escorted her from the room. Father and Uncle Edward quickly changed the conversation to the investment opportunities and fortunes to be made in this New World. I am pretty sure both

Uncle James and Father made generous investment in this bold potential money-making venture.

After our lengthy and filling meal, including much duly idolizing chatter with Captain Newton by the awed boys, Uncle Edward's face lit up with one of his roguish grins. Do I need to tell you I adored Uncle Edward?

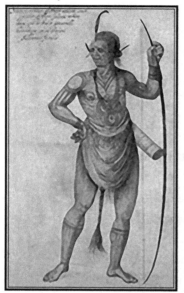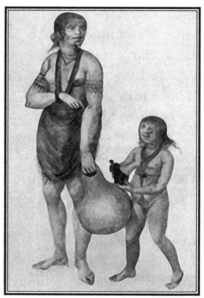

"Indian in Body Paint and Indian Woman and Young Girl"
John White (died 1593), early Colonist and Governor of the "Lost Island of Roanoke" famously made paintings and sketches of the native peoples and the lands, which are now displayed at the British Museum.

"I promised the boys a lesson in archery," he said. "I think this will be a lesson the ladies will also enjoy." We retired to our rooms to freshen up. When we arrived in the courtyard, the targets were all set up. An array of bows and arrows were on hand for our budding young archers. Namontack was not yet in sight. We chatted idly for a few moments while we waited and then sensed movement behind us. A blurred shadow flashed, crouching, dodging in and out among our chairs. And when the shadow stopped moving, seconds later, three arrows had lodged dead center in one of the targets before we could scarcely draw our breaths.

And then Namontack stepped in front of me. His face was expressionless. His eyes opaque.

"Your spirit is much like our Pocahontas," he said, in his strangely accented English. "You will think of her when you see this."

And he plucked off the tall feather attached to his head and placed it in my hand, bowing deeply. I later learned it was the feather of an Eagle, a bird unique to the new land, with fabled symbolism. It forever after remained by my bedside in a narrow vase. I considered it a talisman of great mystery and promise. It somehow comforted me in the dark days ahead.

AUTHOR ENDNOTES, CHAPTER FIVE: *It is important to distinguish between "Mark Hall Manor, Latton, Essex" and "Marks Hall Mansion of Colchester, Essex," which are two entirely different entities, but are often confused. To learn more about the Althams and Mark Hall Manor, you can visit the Harlow Museum and Walled Gardens located in the former Mark Hall stables. It is associated with the Mark Hall Manor House—visited on three occasions by Queen Elizabeth I and her retinue. The Manor has been demolished, but the Museum is surrounded by lovely "Walled Gardens" which were originally the kitchen gardens for the great house and the eminent families who lived there.*

Although Emmanuel's affectionate letters as an adult clearly indicate he considered Edward and Mary Altham ("Mair-Mair") to be his older siblings, there is speculation among some historians that because of the age distance, he might in fact have been an illegitimate son of either older brother James or Edward.

There are differing historical references as to Namontack's estimated age. A guess is he was just two or three years older than

Mary. He had been traded for Thomas Savage, a thirteen-year-old English boy sent by the colonists to live among the "savages" to learn their language and ways and report back to the colonists.

There is absolutely no evidence that Captain Newport and Namontack ever met with the Hawtrey/Altham clan during their visit. It is well documented, however, that Emmanuel Altham, Mary's young uncle, and her cousin, John Carter, both sailed to the New World as adults and John Carter and his wife settled there. It is also well documented that in December 1608 Captain Christopher Newport sailed to England from Jamestown, accompanied by the Native American Namontack along with Captain Gabriel Archer and another Native American, Machumps. And would have been there at an impressionable time in the young boys' lives.

On May 23, 1609, King James approved a second royal charter for the Virginia Company of London. It replaced the royal council with private corporate control and expanded the colony's borders to the Pacific Ocean. On June 2, 1609, the largest fleet England had ever assembled—nine ships, 600 passengers, and enough livestock and food and supplies to last a year—left England for Virginia. On July 24, 1609, a devastating hurricane blasted into the nine-ship fleet. The flagship Sea Venture, with Captain Newport and Namontack on board, became separated from the other vessels and was torn apart. The shipwrecked crew and passengers landed in Bermuda. John Rolfe (future husband of Pocahontas) and his pregnant wife were aboard. Shortly after, both his wife and by then newborn daughter (they named her Bermuda) died. Namontack reportedly also died there. The marooned crew and passengers built two new ships, The Patience and the Deliverance, from remnants of the Sea Venture and a lot of Bermuda cedar. On May 24, 1610, the surviving castaway colonists arrived in Jamestown.

The misadventures of those involved in the Bermuda shipwreck are thought to have inspired Shakespeare's "Tempest."

CHAPTER SIX

"Heigh ho! Sing heigh ho unto the green holly!"
Shakespeare, As You Like It
Christmas Eve 1610

I was twelve. There was nothing about the twelve days of Christmas I didn't hold dear. The mystery and delight of giving and receiving small gifts. The fragrance in the air that only Christmas brings spiced the air. Pungent evergreen branches adorned every banister and entryway at Eastcote Manor, along with sprigs of holly, bay, rosemary, and ivy. The Kissing Bush (two wooden hoops, passing one through the other, decked with holly, ivy, baubles) and baubles sparkled in the candlelight. Apples, oranges, and nuts hung from the ceiling. Father sometimes lurked near the Kissing Bush with mischief in his eyes, hoping to surprise Mair-Mair as she sped to and fro on her long list of Christmas errands. The savory aromas that emerged from the kitchen during the special days of celebration tantalized. Especially the plum pudding.

And always, there was Mair-Mair, fluttering everywhere, gay with laughter and merriment, with her trademark cheekiness that endeared her to all. The scurry of the servants in the kitchen and the delectable scents of the magnificent feasts to come in the twelve days ahead tantalized. Tomorrow, Christmas Day—the First Day of Christmas—would bring a feast to exceed all feasts.

John Bankes first appeared at Eastcote Manor on a blustery Christmas Eve in 1610. I always associate him with the smells and joy of Christmas. I had turned twelve a month earlier. He was then twenty-one, as far distant from me and my world as the silvery moon that peeked in and out in the wake of the rain-swollen clouds above. But he was still not fully grown—or at least not filled out. He was slim and tall as the birches on the grounds of Eastcote Manor. A bit awkward, even. He shook diamond sparkles of rain from frizzy curls of dark red hair that framed his pale, freckled face as he entered Eastcote Manor, accompanied by my father and Uncle Edward. He was taller than both of them. His initial smile upon being introduced to my large, lively, extended family was tentative—even a bit shy. Not at all hinting of the powerful barrister he would become in the next few years. We were, in retrospect, a bit blasé about meeting him. He was one of a long string of "interesting personalities" my gregarious father brought home from his frequent visits to Gray's Inn. John Bankes, of course, could scarcely hold a candle to Namontack or the roguish Captain Newport, as an intriguing guest.

Uncle James (oldest brother of Mair-Mair and Edward and Emmanuel), father of darling baby Johanna, but no male heirs, had sadly died a few months before, and Uncle Edward then inherited Mark Hall, my mother's childhood home. Uncle James' wife, the dour, but "saintly" Elizabeth, and their sweet baby girl, Johanna, immediately fled back to her father. She already had a new husband—a stalwart Puritan. We all hoped she would be much happier. Aunt Elizabeth had always put a damper on the Hawtrey and Altham merry Christmas traditions. Uncle Edward and my father were often together after Uncle James' death, attending functions and special gatherings at Gray's Inn. Aunt Elizabeth Altham married William Masham, protégé of her father, who later "purchased" a baronetcy from King James on 20 December 1621, and ultimately became a vociferous foe of my future husband.

Uncle Edward's wife and her new sweet baby and Grandmother Elizabeth and Emmanuel were already at Eastcote Manor for our Christmas festivities. With the recent death of dear Uncle James, this would not be a time of celebration at Mark Hall. We delighted in having Mair-Mair's family with us. Father's sister and her husband and our cousin John, who lived nearby and tutored with us, joined us for the evening's festivities.

Everyone finally gathered around the grand fireplace, where a decorated Yule log stood ready. The servants, with much laughter, dipped cups of cheer for all from the large Wassail bowl. With appropriate words of Christmas welcome, my father, with great drama, lit the Yule log with a carefully preserved remnant of last year's Yule log. It blazed gloriously to life. It would be gradually fed into the fireplace bottom first, sparkling and crackling over the twelve days of Christmas.

Clodagh and I sat at our two harpsichords that graced the room. We provided spirited accompaniment for a lively round of Christmas Carols before we adjourned for our Christmas Eve supper. Unleashed, Clodagh's soaring, joyful soprano caused all to catch their breath. The five boys could scarcely contain themselves in eager anticipation of the entertainments to come. The loud knock was, at last, heard just as we finished the sweet trifle that concluded our Christmas Eve meal. The Mummers were here.

We all hurried to the door, but I heard Mair-Mair whisper to my father, "I sincerely hope this year's antics are not as bawdy as they were last year."

"Do not fear, my dearest one," said my father, with a wink. "That has already been pre-arranged."

Clodagh and Roisin and all the servants joined us on the

expansive steps to Eastcote Manor to watch the hijinks of the Mummers. There were no women among the Mummers, but several men dressed as women added to the merriment. All the costumes were extravagantly colorful. They sang, they danced, they juggled. They made ribald commentary. There was much laughter.

My mother poked her elbow at my father. "I thought you said they were not going to be bawdy," she whispered.

He shrugged back at her sheepishly. "It appears I did not pre-reward them enough!"

The servants passed the large wassail bowl to the performers, and, again, to we watchers on the steps. My father handed out generous envelopes of appreciation in the spirit of Christmas, notwithstanding their occasional lapses into bawdiness.

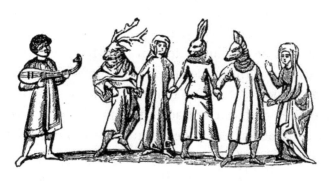

Mummers Museum, dedicated to the strange and extravagant costumes and memorabilia "Mummers mumming," streetsofsalem.com

After the Mummers departed, we returned to the great room with the blazing Yule log. The Wassail bowl was handy for any who cared to dip their cups. Dice and gaming boards appeared. Even all the children were given handfuls of cash and joined in the games of chance with great delight. The gambling games were on.

But that was not yet the end of Christmas Eve. In due time

there was another loud knock at the large entry door. The servants hauled out the large Wassail bowl yet again. And we rushed again to the outer steps. A large crowd of "Wassailers" serenaded us with the lovely, celebratory carols of Christmas. And again, our servants merrily passed the wassail bowl to all.

But even that was not yet the end. After the Wassailers left, those who wished dipped their cups in the wassail bowl for a last time. Then, with the Wassail bowl held aloft, we marched as a family with our guests and servants to the nearby orchard as we caroled.

> *"Here we come a-wassailing*
> *Among the leaves so green;*
> *Here we come a-wand'ring*
> *So fair to be seen.*
> *Love and joy come to you,*
> *And to you your wassail too;*
> *And God bless you and send you*
> *a happy New Year."*

We paused before the designated apple tree. We dipped pieces of toast in the wassail bowl and flung them into the branches. Our servants splashed the dregs of the Wassail bowl over the apple tree roots.

> *"Old apple tree we wassail thee and hope that thou shalt bear*
> *for the Lord doth know where we shall be come apples another year*
> *for to bloom well and to bear well so merry let us be*
> *let every man take off his hat and shout out to the old apple tree*
> *Three cheers for the apple tree:*
> *hip hip horray!*
> *hip hip horray!*
> *hip hip horray!"*

"Wassailing" of apple orchards was traditionally done either on Christmas Eve or on Twelfth Night, hoping to assure a bountiful harvest in the coming year. And then Mair-Mair shooed us all to bed.

AUTHOR ENDNOTES, CHAPTER SIX: *Mummery was exported to colonial America. The Philadelphia Mummers Parade on New Year's Day is the oldest continuous folk parade in the United States, with (pre-COVID-pandemic) ten thousand participants and hundreds of thousands of viewers. There is also a Mummers Museum in Philadelphia, dedicated to the quirky, extravagant costumes and memorabilia.*

CHAPTER SEVEN

"My Stars shine darkly over me."
Shakespeare, Twelfth Night
The Twelve Days of Christmas
December 25, 1610 to January 5, 1611

December 25, 1610. That Christmas morning the chilly drizzle abated. We walked, along with our Ruislip neighbors, in relative comfort, although under a darkening, cloud-covered sky, from Eastcote Manor to St. Martin's Church. We were all decked out in new Christmas clothes. We shouted out gay Christmas songs with great joy as we marched along. Uncle Edward's merry baritone belting the chorus of "Angels from the Realms of Glory" echoes in my memory. I can still recall every detail of the lovely church where the ancient stories of faith brought magic and hope and purpose. And, of course, the sacred music is embedded forever in my heart. On Christmas Day three masses were said. And the genealogy of Christ was sung while everyone held lighted tapers. I did not then fathom the dangers that were rapidly closing in on everything I held dear. It is only in retrospect that I ask the unanswerable questions. How could anyone declare such joy and happiness, and especially, denounce the glorious music of my worship as wicked? How could anyone want to physically harm the beaming, gentle rector who blessed us all with such fervent love and such grace?

Linda Sindt

Who could have guessed there were already dark forces at work in our world that would soon declare our joyful Christmas celebrations to be evil! Our recently departed Puritan aunt had certainly hinted at this. We had laughingly dismissed her. We had then no real understanding of the groundswell to come.

From a more decadent viewpoint, how can I explain the glories of our Christmas feast on the First Day of Christmas? Thomas Tusser in his "500 Pointes of Good Husbandrie" wrote, well before I was born.

> *"Good bread and good drinke, a good fier in the hall,*
> *brawne, pudding and souse, and good mustard withall.*
> *Beefe, mutton, and porke, shred pies of the best,*
> *pig, veale, goose and capon, and turkey well drest;*
> *Cheese, apples and nuts, joly Carols to heare,*
> *as then in the countrie is counted good cheare."*

I can only assure you that the sumptuous table set by my parents exceeded all that, beginning with a roasted boar's head with a lemon stuffed in its mouth, and concluding with a magnificent, flaming plum pudding. In later years, when my hated foe, Oliver Cromwell, outlawed plum pudding, proclaiming it to be evil, I could only shake my head in disbelief. Surely, no sane man could judge such a lovely, innocent treat to be wicked!

After Christmas dinner we withdrew to the Great Room with the Yule log. Father and John Bankes and Uncle Edward and Uncle John Carter engaged the five boys in a noisy game of Cherry Pit. The women pulled out the inevitable embroidery. My mother had by then all but given up on teaching me this art. My stitching had grown less clumsy, but my heart never truly welcomed this traditionally womanly pastime. I sat on a low stool by the Yule log. Canute curled beside me, his head cuddled on my lap, as I listened to the chattering of the women and watched the progress of the noisy games of the menfolk. John Bankes was a smash with the five boys, teasing and joking with them.

"Who is this interesting young man that your Ralph has invited to our Christmas celebration?" my grandmother asked Mair-Mair.

"Oh, Mother," she said, "he is quite clever. He is the son of a merchant in faraway Keswick. His family is successful, but not wealthy. His ancestors for many generations have held property in Keswick in Cumberland. Indeed, they have mining grants from the Crown that date back as far as Henry VI. When John's genius became apparent at an early age, they, at great sacrifice to themselves, arranged for him to enter Queen's College when he was only fifteen—only three years older than our Mary is now. He is such a brilliant scholar. Before he could even graduate from Queens College, the top legal minds at Gray's Inn snatched him up. They are grooming him for senior leadership positions in service to the king, so passionate and compelling is his legal acumen."

"Ralph is quite taken with him," she added. "I am sure John would much rather spend the Christmas holiday with his family in Keswick after being away so long, but travel is so difficult and very expensive at this time of year."

The boisterous Cherry Pit game came to a noisy conclusion. The gambling dice again came out. The womenfolk left for higher pursuits in the kitchen. Dishes from our Christmas feast had been washed and put away. A large pile of boxes and coils of bright ribbon sat on the countertops. Cook and all the servants, dismissed for the rest of the day, joined their families in celebrating their own Christmas. Now the ladies joined in preparing for Boxing Day. Clodagh and I chattered and laughed together as we filled the boxes with bountiful portions of the remnants of our Christmas feast. Mair-Mair added small gifts she had put together for the occasion. I knew my father would slip in generous envelopes the next day. Mair-Mair fussed, making sure the gaily beribboned boxes looked just right. The abundant boxes were not only for our personal servants and their families, but also for the tenants who leased our land. More gaily decorated boxes would delight those who lived in the Almshouses.

The Second Day of Christmas, *Boxing Day, December 26th 1610.* After a lazy morning of sleeping in and lying about, we had a light breakfast, put together by Mair-Mair and Roisin. All the servants had the day off to spend with their families. My brothers joined Uncle John and Aunt Elizabeth Carter and our cousin in their home for the day. Grandmother Elizabeth and Uncle Edward and Aunt Margaret and Baby Jane and Emmanuel set off after breakfast, with many goodbye hugs and waves, to return to Mark Hall for the rest of the Christmas season. That left Mair-Mair and Father and Roisin and Clodagh and John Bankes and me to make our rounds through the village, loaded with the generous Boxing Day boxes. We returned often to Eastcote Manor to get more boxes. My genial father was never at a loss for words as we chatted and laughed with families of our servants and tenants. Mair-Mair was the effervescent timekeeper, gracious and bubbly to all, but keeping us firmly to our schedule as we went about our merry errands.

We ended up at the Almshouses, where we lingered a bit longer. Clodagh and I, giggling, thrust a sweet baby into the unsuspecting arms of John Bankes. In a twinkle, after his initial consternation he made faces and wiggled his ears at the infant, compelling us all to laugh. Soon, he was down on all fours, giving "horsey-back" rides which delighted the toddlers who lived in the compound.

On the walk back to Eastcote Manor, Mair-Mair gave John's arm a squeeze. "You were so good to our special tenants," she said. "It must be difficult to be so far from Keswick and your family at Christmas."

"I miss them a lot," he said. "But I am most grateful for the opportunities that will be open to me.

"Thank you for allowing me to join your Boxing Day rounds," he continued. "I was most impressed with the Almshouses. Indeed, we have a great need to support a similar outreach in Keswick. But not the means to provide anything so generous that includes decent housing."

The Seventh Day of Christmas, *December 31, 1610.* I confess, we did not observe all the twelve days of Christmas with the same degree of fervor. Mostly, it was a time of rest from our normal routine, and for we children, a break from our lessons. We delighted in the friends and family who generally gathered about, enjoying the cheer and fun of visiting with dear ones. The Seventh Day of Christmas was also New Year's Eve. Another festive, but not so elaborate supper, with more family games and chatter, as we all tried to stay awake until the midnight hour to welcome in 1611. The Yule log still crackled away but was growing much shorter.

John Bankes was still with us on this Seventh Day of Christmas/New Year's Eve and by now a comfortable and easy "almost" member of our family. Mair-Mair had made it her mission during this holiday to fuss over him, trying to be sure he did not miss his own mother too much, plying him with special treats from the kitchen. He easily succumbed to Mair-Mair's charms, of course, and already clearly considered her to be his personal "Mair-Mair."

Father delighted in lively legal debates about current

issues with the eventually to be "my John." (Not to mention his destiny as the future Attorney General of England and Chief Justice to King Charles I).

One spirited discussion I remember particularly, from that New Year's Eve was "Dr. Bonham's Case," regarding practicing medicine without a license. Dr. Bonham earned a degree in "physic medicine" from the University of Cambridge. He was discovered practicing medicine in the city of London. This was technically against the law, as at that time, per order of the Parliament and with the consent of the king, only the London College of Physicians could authorize the practice of medicine in that city. Dr. Bonham was examined by the "censors" of the London College of Physicians and found to be "unfit." He was ordered to stop practicing medicine in London. He disobeyed this order and was arrested and placed in prison in the custody of the "censors" of the London College of Physicians. Dr. Bonham would not undergo additional examination, claiming that the London College of Physicians did not have jurisdiction over him and could not arrest or fine him. He claimed false imprisonment. He would not promise to stop practicing medicine in London. In arguing its case, the London College of Physicians cited the statutes under which it was established. This included regulating all physicians in London and fining and imprisoning those not licensed by the college.

The case was ultimately argued before the Court of Common Pleas under the court's Chief Justice, Sir Edward Coke. (Yes, the same one who had ordered the genitalia of the perpetrators of the "Gunpowder Plot" to be cut off and burned before their eyes). The real arguments, it turned out, had nothing whatsoever to do with Dr. Bonham's competency in practicing medicine. It was a fight over whether Parliament or the judicial courts of "common right and reason" were the ultimate deciding authority in settling disputes. The Court of Common Pleas was divided. Two Justices, Wamisley and Foster, argued that the statute clearly had precedent, and the royal charter was to be interpreted as granting the college a duty on behalf of the king. Chief Justice Coke (a fellow alumnus of Cambridge with Dr. Bonham) and Justices Daniel and Warburton, however, were the predominating votes in favor of Dr. Bonham. They argued, somewhat reasonably, "... no person may be a judge in his own cause...and one cannot be judge and attorney for any of the parties," further suggesting that the impartiality of a judge is compromised when the judge is also the plaintiff who will benefit financially from any fines imposed on the defendant, or the prosecutor who is the advocate responsible for seeking such fines.

However, that was not the most ultimately interesting part of the argument. The real twist was Chief Justice Coke's final pronouncement in also declaring the concept of judicial rule. The primary authority in interpreting common law rested with the courts and not the Parliament (or even, ultimately, the king).

Clodagh and I had been listening in on this discussion. We looked at each other in mutual skepticism.

"First of all," said Clodagh, "what if the physician truly wasn't educated enough to do a good job and he hurt someone? Shouldn't that have been the main issue?"

"Well, since Sir Coke also attended Cambridge, he himself attested eloquently as to the excellence of the education provided," Father reassured her.

"Well, then, it does seem a bit dodgy that any law could unfairly allow one university to have a monopoly and punish and fine those from different universities," she conceded.

"But how can an argument about whether a physician is qualified to practice in London end up changing the rules about how laws are made and who is in charge of deciding?" I asked.

Father and John Bankes both beamed.

"Ah, that is the true magnificence of the law!" said one.

"The absolute beauty!" echoed the other.

The long evening finally drew to an end. Midnight arrived. The church bells rang. Mair-Mair dramatically flung open all the doors to let the New Year in. Our Ruislip neighbors pounded loudly on pots and pans, shouting and laughing. 1611 had arrived. And then Mair-Mair sent us all away to bed.

The Eighth Day of Christmas, *New Year's Day, January 1, 1611.* Another lazy morning and a late breakfast of porridge, black pudding, beer, bread, and cheese. After which we gathered around the ever-dwindling remains of the Yule log and exchanged small gifts. I remember Father gave Mair-Mair a small, jeweled pin, and me one to match. John Bankes gave Father a book about law. To Mair-Mair and me he gave lacy handkerchiefs. I recall giving him a fragrant orange I had covered with cloves. Mair-Mair and Father gave him a pair of gloves. And the boys received small toys and coins from all.

And then there was a knock at the door. Mair-Mair's eyes sparkled. "I bet that is a tall, handsome, dark man!" She hurried to the door and returned with Uncle Edward. "Our 'first footer' is here!" she announced gaily. Uncle Edward's dark brown curls gleamed in the late morning light. He had brought Emmanuel back to stay with us for the Tutoring lessons that would soon resume after the Christmas holiday. He carried a gaily wrapped package that we already knew contained the traditional silver coin, a loaf of bread, a packet of salt, a lump of coal, an evergreen sprig, and a bottle of whisky, which, according to legend, represented financial prosperity, food, flavor, warmth, long-life, and good cheer respectively in the year to come. The rule of the tradition was that the gifts had to be presented by the first dark-haired man to step foot in the house in the New

Year. The catch was the dark-haired man could not have spent the night in the house the evening before. Mair-Mair and her dark-haired brothers always conspired to make this long-time 'first footer' tradition happen for us every year.

Twelfth Night, *January 5, 1611.* *Gray's Inn.* Twelfth Night, the final day of Christmas, would have ordinarily been the occasion for a final, elaborate family meal to end the Christmas season, but this year Father had arranged for a special treat. The boys would stay with Father's sister, Aunt Elizabeth, and Uncle John Carter at Ruislip and celebrate with them. Mother and Roisin and Clodagh and I were to enjoy Twelfth Night dinner at a grand banquet at Gray's Inn with Father and John Bankes. The featured play, "Twelfth Night," was reported to be wildly funny. The playwright, a William Shakespeare, was enormously popular with King James.

The outing was to be a special treat for me since I had turned twelve in late November. I was now deemed "a young lady." Mair-Mair was going, but only reluctantly. She could seldom be persuaded to go anywhere close to plague-ridden London. She hated the dirt and smells in the inner city and worried constantly about the ever-present specters of disease that could and often did strike with no warning

As we traveled, the bright January morning turned increasingly gray as we neared the city. The houses grew closer together, and larger and larger piles of refuse littered the streets. Mair-Mair covered her nose with her trademark lacy handkerchief. We could tell her head already ached. Father had reserved guest rooms at Gray's Inn for us. He and Mair-Mair would share one room. Roisin and Clodagh and I settled into the room next door to rest up for the evening. John Bankes took his leave, promising to re-join us at the banquet for the festivities.

Eventually, Father excused himself to visit with some of his Gray's Inn cronies. We "Ladies" proceeded to dress. Mair-Mair's plan was to magically transform Roisin and Clodagh into the "nobility" they were for this special occasion. We were far from home. Roisin and Clodagh would be introduced simply as "dear friends," should there be any introductions to make. Roisin was to smile graciously, but silently, to all and not disclose her Irish brogue. The secret of their Irish aristocracy had been shared with John Bankes. He gallantly promised to run interference if need be. He was, of course, by then totally under the sweet spell of Mair-Mair. He would gladly have slain fire-breathing dragons for her.

As was the tradition, Mair-Mair and I gave many of our cast-off dresses to be re-fitted to Roisin and Clodagh, anyway. The well-to-do in those days were harshly judged if their servants were not also elegantly dressed. Although, with their striking beauty, Roisin and Clodagh would have been entrancing, no matter what they wore. For this special occasion there were no hand-me-downs. We all had brand new dresses. Clodagh and I felt especially grown-up and lovely in our new frocks featuring full, silky skirts, adorned with ribbons, lace, puffy sleeves, and velvet "stomachers." Father beamed as he strolled with the four of us into the Great Hall. John Bankes met us at the entrance and raised his eyebrows in appreciation as he escorted us in. He graciously bowed and kissed both Mair-Mair's and Roisin's hands. And clownishly wiggled his ears at Clodagh and me, not at all appropriately impressed with our "grown-up" status.

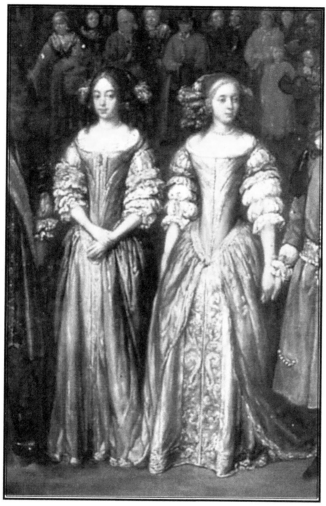

Women's Clothing in the 17ᵗʰ Century Showing Layered Stomachers, History of Dress

The Great Hall blazed with candles and flames from the fireplaces. Crystal and silver sparkled in the festive glow. Women and men in sophisticated attire already crowded the large room. I fear I gaped at the gowns of a few more avant-garde women. Having only recently acquired the age of twelve, I had yet to discern even a smidgen of personal bosoms. Clodagh, of course, at fourteen, already had a perceptible bust, of which I was most envious. Our non or preliminarily developing bosoms were camouflaged by generous fluffs of lace, thanks to Mair-Mair's prudence in overseeing our wardrobes. Mair-Mair and Roisin, of course, were most circumspectly, but elegantly, attired. Our relative modesty was definitely in the minority. Several of the female guests unabashedly displayed the full spectrum of their cleavage, down to the rosy tips of their nipples peeking out! There was certainly no denying the legitimacy of their endowment. Moreover, an abundance of makeup unnaturally brightened their cheeks and eyes.

"Well, I can see why you enjoy spending so much time at Gray's Inn," I overheard Mair-Mair whisper to Father as we made our way through the throng. Because our host was such a star member of Gray's Inn, we were seated at a table near the stage. I could scarcely eat. I was too excited by my first peek into a world other than Eastcote Manor or Mark Hall. Finally, the serving staff brought goblets of Wassail and slices of a dense, spicy fruit cake to end the meal. The much-anticipated performance began.

The play was a bit confusing at first and then got increasingly bewildering. Teenage boys dressed as women played all the female roles. Endowed with obviously fake bosoms and an abundance of makeup. The ship-wrecked heroine in the play had traveled with her twin brother. She (erroneously) presumed he died in the shipwreck. She survived, but took her brother's identity, dressing in male clothing to endure safely in a strange land. So...we had a male actor, in the role of a woman, who was pretending to be a man...who was seduced by a male actor playing the part of a woman. The action and sometimes ribald antics moved so quickly, Clodagh and I did not "get" all the jokes that caused the more sophisticated male students of Gray's Inn to hoot uproariously. But we followed enough of the plot to be wildly entertained by all the merry mix-ups and hi-jinks. Was this when the concept of a woman pretending to be a man as a means to an end became embedded in our thought processes?

There was a short intermission while the servers replaced the dying candles. Several of John Bankes' classmates stopped by our table to chat with him. One of them, who could not seem to stop looking at Clodagh, asked to be introduced. John presented Father, as a fellow Gray's Inn member, and Mair-Mair and me by name, and mentioned Roisin and Clodagh simply as "their dear friends." But John's classmate persisted.

"And their names?" he asked.

I held my breath. We had not anticipated any need to disclose Clodagh's unmistakably Irish surname. John didn't hesitate a bit, however. "May I introduce Mistress Rose Smythe and her daughter, Clotilde," he said with a slight bow. The classmate plainly wanted to continue the conversation, but the performers dramatically returned to the stage, indicating the performance was about to begin again. He left with a lingering, admiring glance at Clodagh.

The incident put a blight on an otherwise indelible holiday treat. What would happen to my "Clotilde," as I sometimes teasingly called her, after that? What reputable man in all of England would ever knowingly marry the impoverished daughter/granddaughter of Irish Catholic rebels?

We returned to Eastcote Manor early the next day with Mair-Mair clutching her handkerchief to her nose and vowing to never ever again return to "the filth" of London.

John Bankes and Father maintained their friendship over the next several years. He was a congenial, albeit infrequent, guest among the lengthy list of visitors to our home at Eastcote Manor as I progressed through my teen years.

AUTHOR ENDNOTES, CHAPTER SEVEN: *It is historically documented that Mary's father, Ralph Hawtrey, provided substantial financial support to residents of the Almshouses. Mary's future husband must have been especially impressed with this endeavor, and the critical need filled in the lives of the recipients. In his will he directed that a generous portion of his fortune be devoted to establishing a similar Almshouse program in Keswick (you pronounce it "Kessick") where he was born in the north of England. In the 1530s poet, John Leland, wrote of Keswick as "a lytle poore market town"*

King James I and Parliament were both unhappy with Justice Coke's ruling in the controversial Bonham case. The king ultimately removed Justice Coke from office and Coke's ruling was discarded. With the emerging power of Parliament, England eventually bestowed full authority for such decisions to Parliament, where it remains today. The Colonies eventually established the Supreme Court as the ultimate adjudicator of law.

Water was not safe to drink in those days and even children drank beer, ale, and wine at an early age.

You probably don't really want to know what is in a black pudding, which remains a popular breakfast treat in Great Britain, even today. Here is a recipe:

OLD ENGLISH RECIPE - BLACK PUDDING
Often eaten as part of a full English breakfast. Not sweet!

INGREDIENTS
    1 quart of fresh pig's blood
    1 quart of skimmed milk
    ½ loaf of bread cut into cubes
    1 cup of rice
    1 cup of barley
    1lb fresh beef suet, grated

2 or 3 handfuls of dry oatmeal
Pepper, salt, black pepper and dried mint (to taste)

INSTRUCTIONS

1. Bake rice and barley in water at 375 degrees for 30 minutes
2. Place the bread in a large pie dish.
3. Warm the milk in microwave for 30 seconds. Pour the milk over the bread.
4. Pour the blood into the warmed milk and bread.
5. Add the cooked rice and barley and the grated suet.
6. Stir in the oatmeal.
7. Season with pepper, salt etc.
8. Bake in a moderate oven until cooked through.

Christmas gifts at that time were indeed exchanged on New Year's Day.

The Inns of Court were, and continue to be, four law schools in London—the Inner Temple, the Middle Temple, Gray's Inn, and Lincoln's Inn. Gala performances of Shakespeare's plays were held in the halls of at least two of the Inns of Court. "Twelfth Night" on Twelfth Night in 1602 in the Middle Temple and "The Comedy of Errors" in 1594 in Gray's Inn. Shakespeare enjoyed the Inns of Court and made them the setting for "Act 2, Scene 4 of 1 Henry VI." There is no record that "Twelfth Night," one of Shakespeare's most celebrated comedies, was performed in Gray's Inn in 1611. It is set there for the sake of moving this tale along. Women were not allowed to perform in such public plays in those days, so young men were dressed as women to perform the female roles.

For those who love Shakespeare, the author shamelessly recommends the annual world-famous Oregon Shakespeare Festival in lovely Ashland, Oregon.

CHAPTER EIGHT

"I count myself in nothing else so happy
as in a soul remembering my good friends,"
Shakespeare, Richard II
May 1612

I was thirteen. Clodagh was fifteen. The Hawtrey family descended on Mark Hall, Mair-Mair's childhood home. Where Uncle Edward was now "Master" following the death of his older brother, my Uncle James. I had never known Aunt Margaret, Uncle Edward's first wife, really well. She died giving birth to her second little girl, who was also named Margaret in her memory. Jane, their first daughter, was still a toddler—a sickly child, and barely talking. Uncle Edward did not wait long to remarry.

Clodagh and I were a bit in awe of meeting Uncle Edward's new wife, Joane. Her father, Sir John Leventhorpe, of Shingle Hall, in Sawbridgeworth, Hertfordshire, was a Baronet, a member of Parliament, and sheriff for that county. My new Aunt Joane actually had ties to Mark Hall through her great grandfather, the 10th Lord Morley, a predecessor of the Altham family at Mark Hall. Even more dazzling in our eyes was the fact that royal blood ran in her veins. She was 12th in descent from Edward I, former King of England.

I overheard Mair-Mair and Grandmother Altham discussing Uncle Edward's re-marriage so quickly after losing Aunt Margaret.

Linda Sindt

"What were we to do, Mary?" Grandmother asked her daughter. "I am much too old to raise two such tiny girls. I have my hands full enough with Emmanuel. And you are not near enough to help. The nannies and the servants are wonderful, but the girls need a proper mother to oversee their upbringing."

"Well, honestly, Mother, I have never seen my brother look so tranquil," said Mair-Mair. "I think it will be a good match."

"The Bride's Portion was well beyond what we would have anticipated for a second wife for Edward," continued Grandmother. "The family seemed most eager to promote this marriage so quickly after they learned Edward had become available. Almost too eager. I hope that is not a bad omen. She is so much younger than he is. And also, quite...um... outspoken."

"Now, Mother, you'll have to admit my brother is quite a catch," Mair-Mair replied. "Not only is he pleasing to the eye, he's most engaging. Besides, who wouldn't want to live at wonderful Mark Hall? All indications are that the king will soon make Edward a Knight. Also, best of all," Mair-Mair added, "he seems quite taken with his new bride."

Only five years older than Clodagh, Aunt Joane was indeed much closer in age to Clodagh and me than she was to Uncle Edward. She was twenty. Uncle Edward was forty.

She was stunningly beautiful, with sapphire eyes, bouncy golden curls, and a mischievous grin. Somewhat surprisingly, in our eyes, for such a sophisticated and glamorous creature, she doted on her new stepdaughters, lingering many hours with them and especially entertaining the delicate and pallid little Jane. She adored Mark Hall, as we all did, and for now seemed content to allow my grandmother, her mother-in-law, to continue to run the household as she had resumed when Uncle James died.

"I am jealous of you, Aunt Joane," I confessed one morning when she stopped by for a chat in the lovely room Clodagh and I shared while visiting Mark Hall. She seemed a little lonely with no one nearby who was even close to her own age to talk to. Even the servants, who had been there forever, were older than Uncle Edward.

"When I was very young, I told everyone I was going to marry Uncle Edward when I grew up. I have always adored him." I confessed.

She laughed. "Well, you can't have him. I am still pinching myself. He is so handsome and fun. I was afraid I would end up with some ancient Baronet who could hardly walk. And for Heaven's sake, can you please not call me *Aunt*."

"Uncle Edward often refers to you as 'Her Ladyship.' Would you prefer we call you that?" I said, cheekily.

She tossed an elegantly embroidered pillow at my head and eyed me speculatively. "So have you started thinking about who you *will* marry?"

"Mair-Mair and Father say they can't possibly do without me until I am at least twenty-one. They promise to find someone nice. I wish they could find someone nearby. I will miss them both terribly if I have to live far away. However, I overheard Grandmother going down the list of possibilities once with one of her friends. There aren't any estates anywhere nearby with a firstborn son close enough to my age who is destined to inherit."

Aunt Joane regarded me speculatively, with the eye of an inveterate matchmaker. "Well, what about a second son? If he is amusing and with the Bride's Portion your doting father is sure to provide, you could still have an interesting life."

"I am pretty certain I don't have any choice," I said. "My father and the father of my future husband will decide. Although, I am sure Father will seek Mair-Mair's approval. I suppose it will all depend on how much my father is willing to pay to assure the position and legacy of his future descendants."

"Hmm, we shall see about that," said 'Her Ladyship.' A speculative glint flashed in her azure, ever compulsively matchmaking eyes.

Aunt Joane then turned her imperious blue gaze to Clodagh. "And you," she exclaimed. "Edward has told me all about your secret highborn Irish family. What are we going to do about finding a husband for you?" She echoed the concern I had never dared voice to my dearest friend. Clodagh had no highborn family members, other than me, conspiring to protect her future welfare.

Clodagh hurled another artistically embroidered pillow at 'Her Ladyship' and then one at me. "You are both overstepping your boundaries," she declared. "As one who has absolutely no standing whatsoever in the current peerage of the realm, I can assure you both that I am most happily in charge of my own destiny. Unlike the two of you, if I choose to marry, it will be to a mate of my own choice. It is a legal freedom I relish that neither of you enjoys."

'Her Ladyship' and I exchanged conspiratorial glances. No way could we see my aristocratically born almost sister as the wife of a shopkeeper or even a merchant. There were no other options open to her, even with Father's financial help. And then there were the added problems of her illegal Roman Catholic faith and her Irish heritage.

And so it was that the assertive, clever, a little bit spoiled, always pampered, often outrageous Joane Leventhorpe Altham came into my life. Known as 'Her Ladyship,' to all, even her eventually large passel of children, my erstwhile aunt, became my dearest confidante and ally, next to Clodagh.

CHAPTER NINE

"Ignorance is the curse of God; knowledge is the wing wherewith we fly to heaven."
Shakespeare, Richard II
1613

1613 was an eventful year in the life of the Hawtrey/Altham families, and in all of England. The Twins and Uncle Emmanuel and Cousin John Carter were all twelve. "Baby" Rafe was ten. Clodagh was sixteen. Which meant I was fifteen. To begin with, King James had been fighting with Parliament for several years. He sent them away the year before when they refused to fund his extravagant lifestyle in managing both his personal affairs and those of the kingdom. The King's main hopes for financial relief in raising needed revenue initially rested in negotiating with France for a substantial dowry for his oldest son, Henry, Prince of Wales. This idea of a potential Roman Catholic queen greatly distressed both the Puritan and Church of England factions of Parliament.

King James knighted Uncle Edward on 21 March at the "Palace" in Royston, Hertfordshire, which was essentially an elegant hunting lodge. Uncle Edward's and Aunt Joane's ("Her Ladyship's") first baby, Joan, was born in June. Even more momentously in the history of the world, the King James Bible was first published that year. It had been seven years in the making. Father brought home several copies. They cost ten shillings each in loose pages, or twelve shillings for a bound copy. King James commissioned this Bible in 1604. The scholars completed it in 1611. Publishing took two more years.

Father assigned the seven of us children, including Rafe, to read it through at our leisure. He did not compel Clodagh to participate in Biblical studies. She gamely joined in, anyway. since she was required to attend the Anglican Church whether she wanted to or not. The Roman Catholic Church did not then encourage its unordained members to study the Scriptures independently. There was no English translation of their Catholic version of the Bible.

Clodagh and I made much progress in plowing through the newly minted King James Bible. The boys…not so much. We took copies with us on our late summer visit to Mark Hall to meet new Baby Joan and check in with Grandmother Altham. Grandmother continued to relish her reincarnated role in managing the household at Mark Hall. She was no longer such a frequent visitor at Eastcote Manor, although Emmanuel continued to spend much of his growing up time at Eastcote Manor, tutoring with the rest of us rapidly growing children. We were all enjoying our summer fortnight at Mark Hall.

As was the custom when it was "just the family," Roisin and Clodagh joined us around the grand dining room table as the "sisters" to Mair-Mair and me they truly were. The new curate for Saint Mary at Latton Church also joined us for one of our meals during this visit. He would also serve as a part-time tutor for we children during our frequent visits to Mark Hall.

At sixteen, and with an uncertain future, Clodagh could have discontinued her studies. She was an eager and inquisitive student, however. Mair-Mair and Father encouraged her to continue on with me as my companion in joining with the boys for our tutoring. Roisin remained a silent observer at the meal with the new curate, not wanting to disclose her Irish brogue to a guest with a particular antipathy to her inherited (Roman Catholic) religion.

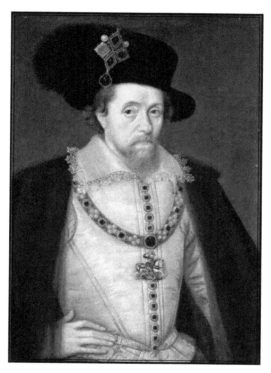

King James VI and I 1556 -1625
King of Scotland 1567-1625
King of England and Ireland 1603 – 1625
by John de Critz

The table conversation, of course, turned, to Uncle Edward's recent knighting ceremony.

Emmanuel asked his much older brother, "So, if you are a knight and our brother, James, was a knight, does that mean I will be a knight, too?"

Uncle Edward beamed a fond smile at his blond wife. "Well, that pretty much depends on 'Her Ladyship,'" he replied. "And whether she produces a brother for Baby Joan and her big sisters."

Everyone chuckled.

"Tell me about it," said my brother, Edward (we called him Ned to distinguish him from Uncle Edward). Ned was only minutes younger than the oldest Twin, John. "The oldest heir's oldest son gets everything!" he complained.

"I keep telling you, I will take care of everyone, just like father, does—even you," Twin John replied to more chuckles.

"Tell us about the ceremony when you were knighted, Edward," Mair-Mair intervened.

"I was so disappointed we had to go to Royston. It is a lovely hunting lodge, but not as much fun and not nearly as elegant as the Whitehall Palace would have been," 'Her Ladyship' said.

"Heaven forbid the king should interrupt his sporting events," said my Grandmother Altham. Her expression was not one of approval. "Being knighted today does not carry the same honor and distinction as it did in my day when both my father and my grandfather were knighted by Queen Elizabeth."

"Why do you say that, Grandmother?" I asked. Clodagh and I glanced at each other surreptitiously and smiled. One of Grandmother's ironclad rules for the correct decorum for women was that proper ladies were never ever to publicly express their opinions. It was a dictum Grandmother seldom obeyed herself.

"The mathematics are not that difficult," she said. "King James knighted 500 at his coronation and many more each year since then. Never in the history of this kingdom has there been so many knights. And what does a knight promise?

That he will constantly train and be ready for battle in service to the king. Are we presently at war or likely to be at war at any time in the future? No! Does it make sense for so many landowners and leaders in our realm to be constantly preparing for war? No! And what is the catch to all this? If a newly dubbed "knight" wishes to submit a "penance" instead of preparing for a non-existent war, he must pay King James forty pounds per year. Not a bad income, times more than 500 plus many more knights, even for a king, on top of everything else he gets, I would say."

"Well, I am happy to have my handsome knight. And especially if he does not have to train for war, it will be well worth the forty pounds a year." 'Her Ladyship' smiled with a toss of her blonde curls. Becoming a mother had not curtailed her sauciness. Or her extravagant ways of thinking.

"It is no secret the king desperately needs money," Uncle Edward said. We have all seen the prices of goods increase under his reign."

"Possibly due to the king's own mismanagement and extravagant ways of living," my grandmother whispered to Mair-Mair. Of course, we all heard.

Uncle Edward patted his mother's hand fondly but continued the discussion. "You are right, of course, as always, my dear mother. The king's financial affairs grow ever more dire. The king pinned his hopes on an alliance with France. He banked on a generous dowry from the betrothal of Prince Henry to the French Princess to see him out of his current financial difficulties. Sadly, the young prince's recent illness and death pretty much quashed that source of income."

"So sad it happened amid all the celebrations surrounding the marriage of his sister, Princess Elizabeth, to Frederick V of the Palatinate of Bohemia," Mair-Mair said.

My father chimed in. "The king has half-heartedly

continued to negotiate a marriage on behalf of Prince Charles, who is our Mary's age, but has been meeting with great resistance from some members of England's own Privy Council who would not welcome a Roman Catholic princess to the throne. These factions in our government also fear the growing political turmoil in France."

Grandmother Altham could not restrain herself from saying, "If he would simply reconvene Parliament, as he is technically required to do, perhaps they would assist with the failing finances of the kingdom, as they are technically required to do."

Father, ever the diplomat, especially when it came to dealing with his outspoken mother-in-law, chose to change the subject to the newly published King James Bible and inquired as to the progress of we children in reading it through.

"I'm only up to all the begats," complained Rafe. "That is so boring."

"Why did the king think we needed a new Bible?" asked Twin Ned. "What was wrong with the old one?"

"That is a very complicated question," my father answered. "You remember your Aunt Elizabeth who was married to your mother's brother, your Uncle James?"

"She didn't like Christmas," said Rafe. "And we were all supposed to be nice to her."

"Well, yes," said my father. "She was the daughter of a very powerful Baronet. And there are a growing number of members of Parliament who hold her father's Puritanical beliefs. They don't agree with all the traditions and ceremonies of the Church of England and want to change them. When King James came to the throne after the death of Queen Elizabeth, he became head of the Church of England. He was faced with this ongoing squabbling within the church family and had a meeting ten years ago to try to solve all this ongoing bickering within the church."

"But why don't the Puritans just start their own church?" asked Twin John.

"Right. I don't care if they hate Christmas, but they shouldn't get to tell the rest of us what to do," echoed Twin Ned.

"Perhaps the fact that King James demands, on pain of severe punishment, including possible death, that everyone in England must attend the Anglican Church whether they want to or not, has something to do with it," said Clodagh demurely. She ignored the warning glances both her mother and Grandmother Altham flashed at her.

Father rescued her. "Clodagh, my young friend, and my dear twins, I am happy to see you thinking about these things. Perhaps it would help to understand the theory of the 'Divine Right of Kings,' which in addition to this growing conflict also played a part in King James's thinking with this newest interpretation of the Word of God. Would our new tutor feel comfortable explaining how that works?" Father put the young Curate on the spot.

He brushed a lock of unruly hair from his eyes. "It is a complicated concept to explain. Perhaps it goes back to the story of Samuel where God anoints Saul?" he asked, a bit hopefully. "Where he appoints David as King over Israel, making Saul and David both the Lord's Kings. He in essence gives both Saul and David the "divine power of God." When Saul disobeys God's wishes in ruling his people, God takes that power from him. In this vein, King James claims all monarchs get their authority directly from God and that only God and no other can judge an unjust King. He is firm in his belief that any attempt to restrict a ruler's powers, especially by the people he governs, is contrary to this divine mandate from God. All the people of the world are expected to obey the orders of the leaders God has appointed over them."

I sensed Clodagh's growing discomfort with the direction of this conversation. Even I was taken aback when my normally self-contained and reticent friend actually spoke, with an icy calm, and in her perfect, aristocratic English. "So, suppose there is this kingdom," she began innocently. "It has long been a Roman Catholic kingdom. The king, by this definition, governs by the divine mandate of God. Nearby kingdoms are also Roman Catholic. Their rulers are presumably also divinely appointed by God. All the subjects of all these different rulers understand that their role in life is to obey without question the demands of these separate, but divinely appointed kings. So, if this one king decides that his kingdom is no longer accountable to the Roman Catholic God, but to a revised Anglican Church God and if that king declares war on the other Roman Catholic kings, does that mean that it is the divine will of God that all the kings of these nations force their people to take up arms against each other, all in His name and without questioning the wisdom of their leaders? Does He want all these kings He has individually appointed by His divine will to pillage and burn and destroy everything in each other's kingdoms in the spirit of the 'Divine Right of Kings'?"

This outburst brought an abrupt pause to the conversation. I glanced around the table. Grandmother Altham did not say anything (but clearly was already rehearsing the rebukes she would rain down on Clodagh and me at the first opportunity about proper ladylike decorum). Her mouth pursed and she stared at her plate. Her stern guidance as the family matriarch to me, her oldest granddaughter, and by association to Clodagh, my almost sister, echoed in my mind. "Proper" ladies ruled behind the scenes. We were not to speak out. If we played our roles discreetly and expertly, according to her, we could have great influence, but it was unthinkable for a "Lady" to express a public opinion. (Her own outspoken-ness notwithstanding). Mair-Mair, the (almost) expert behind the scenes husband manipulator extraordinaire, and accomplished diplomat, cast about for something amusing and distracting to say, but had not yet gotten there. Roisin held her breath, rigid and pale with trepidation about the possible consequences of her daughter's uncharacteristic public outburst in questioning the divine authority of the king. 'Her Ladyship,' who habitually and blithely and with no adverse consequences whatsoever routinely broke most of Grandmother Altham's rules regarding the proper decorum for "Ladies," looked at our young curate with a charming expectation, anticipating his response to this impossible to answer question. Our fledgling curate was palpably flustered and reached for a sip of ale to calm his nerves.

It was the boys who innocently came to Clodagh's rescue. They were accustomed to dealing with their two bossy older "sisters" (cousin/niece/almost sister) in the more informal confines of the classroom. They simply ignored all and changed the subject. "Our tutor told us the king was getting tired of all the arguing with the Puritans. He wanted the best scholars in the kingdom to get together. They were supposed to make sure the English translation accurately told the original messages from God," said Emmanuel (by far the most curious and studious of the boys).

"There were six committees," said Cousin John Carter, a close second to Emmanuel in his academic prowess. "When the groups finished their translations they shared their work with the other committees, until they finally had something they all agreed was the most accurate translation."

"That's right." Uncle Edward welcomed this diversion in the conversation. "There was even a committee of scholars appointed from Gray's Inn."

"So," asked 'Her Ladyship,' "Does this new Bible mean that the Puritans will stop being so critical of the rest of us?"

"I wish that were so, my dear one," said her adoring husband. "Unfortunately, at Gray's Inn the Puritans remain as vocal in their opposition to this new version of the Bible as they were to the way the king interpreted the Geneva Bible. Overall, they still prefer the Geneva Bible. The king has banned the printing of any more Geneva Bibles, but the Puritans have made it clear they are clinging to the ones they have, even in the face of his ban against them."

Mair-Mair, the ultimate proper "Lady," hoping, I am sure, to take her mother's attention away from Clodagh's indecorous outburst, said sweetly and with an innocence that only I could detect as counterfeit. "Why is that I wonder?" She turned her serene gaze to the increasingly flustered curate.

After another quick sip of ale and with a nervous glance at Clodagh, our plucky curate stepped back into the conversation, possibly hoping to reassert his authority as a budding religious scholar "Well, perhaps it goes back to the question that was originally raised—the 'Divine Right of Kings.' The Geneva Bible contains explanatory notes in the margins that could be interpreted to imply that the current church hierarchy is unnecessary. And, notionally, challenge the necessity of a king as a head of the church. These marginal notes are deemed to also encourage members of individual congregations to select their own leaders rather than looking to the church hierarchy for religious leadership. The Puritans, indeed, challenge the role of the current Bishop structure in managing the affairs of the Church." Our curate's face was flushed. He hesitated, as if not wanting to tread further into treacherous intellectual territory.

Where this interesting conversation may have led, I cannot

tell you. Mair-Mair, the ultimate arbiter of family decorum, notwithstanding her mother's seniority, and with her ever so innocent sweetness, stepped in to rescue the fledgling religious scholar. She signaled to the servants that the pudding should be served up. The conversation quickly turned to more mundane things. The long adoring servants at Mark Hall, of course, always acknowledged "their" Mair-Mair's inherent authority, even though she was technically outranked in that household by her own mother, as well as 'Her Ladyship.'

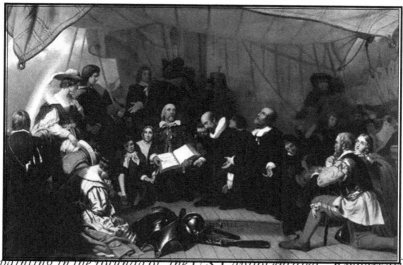

A painting in the rotunda of the U.S. Capitol entitled, "Embarkation of the Pilgrims" by Robert Weir. The Pilgrims are shown kneeling on the deck of their ship in 1620, nine years after the initial publication of the King James Bible and one year before Parliament issued a Protestation of King James's excessive financial demands, as they begin their own voyage to the New World. William Brewster holds an open Bible, while Pastor John Robinson leads Governor Carver, William Bradford, Miles Standish, and the Pilgrim families in prayer. The open Bible is NOT the King James version of the Bible, but the Geneva Bible, favored by the stern-hearted Pilgrims

as early Puritan settlers escaping to the Colonies. The last known publication of the Geneva Bible was in 1644, despite King James's initial ban many years earlier.

AUTHOR ENDNOTES, CHAPTER NINE: *A Curate, normally a young man just beginning his career, served as an assistant to the Vicar or Rector in serving and managing the religious needs of the Parish in the then Anglican church. He was not always paid much and often needed to augment his income.*

Despite the patently "un-divine" and personal political motivations of King James and his ignoble moral interventions in directing the interpretation of the "Divine Word" to his own advantage, the King James Bible ranks as a monumental literary masterpiece. Its genius, elegance of expression, and incomparable poetry not only shaped religious thought, but the very language and communication processes of the emerging world. It remains the most widely printed book in all of history. Regardless of the glaring failings and arrogance of the monarch who directed the translation, who is to say the faithful, highly educated scribes were not somehow Divinely inspired by the overarching, transcendent spirit of a mysterious Being who sought to convey via this document a beacon of light and hope to the future generations of the world in the emerging language of the day?

CHAPTER TEN

"The web of our life is a mindful yarn, good and ill together."
Shakespeare, All's Well That Ends Well.
1614

I perched as usual on my favorite corner stool in Father's study, working my way through his library of books. A cozy fire warmed the room. My charming new greyhound puppy dozed in a basket by my side. I named him "Canute the Second," but just called him "Canute." I missed his grandfather terribly. After nearly fifteen years, which is the normal life span for a greyhound, my beloved Canute had lived out his earthly stay. My sweet new Canute encouraged me to break often for walks in our gardens as the hours passed. Sometimes Father invited me to saddle up and join him on his rounds with the frisky new Canute.

I would be sixteen in November. I finished with my formal tutoring last year. Now I was to learn the art of managing a large household. In preparation for my matronly duties when I would be married off to a yet-to-be-determined "peer of the realm." I took to managing menus and organizing the domestic chores of the staff about as readily as I did to embroidery. In truth, Mair-Mair did not care all that much about endlessly ordering the servants about, either. She had turned over most day-to-day responsibilities for running our busy home to her "almost sister" Roisin along with my "almost sister," Clodagh. They were by then the behind-the-scenes forces that kept our household running on a perfect keel. With their caring hearts and velvet-gloved approach in dealing with any problems that arose, they easily and lovingly dealt with any issues, and the servants adored them.

Their chatter and frequent laughter filtered in from the distant kitchen as they bantered with each other and with the staff. When I finished the next chapter, I would think about seeking them out for another "lesson" in being a "lady of the realm." While my mind grew numb at the monotony of the never-ending meal planning and ordering of supplies and tending of the gardens, and on and on, I never tired of their amusing company.

In the far corner of the library Father's large desk, positioned to take best advantage of the light from the large windows overlooking one of the gardens, dominated. Always, the desk displayed a disarray of the large ledgers essential to administering the affairs of Ruislip and Eastcote Manor, as well as King's College. Currently, a debate crescendoed between Father and one of his agents. Mostly, they all seemed to forget I was there as they debated the pros and cons of various financial matters. I could not help soaking up many insights into the overall management of our family affairs.

Father was inordinately proud of my apparently unusual skill in summing up long lists of numbers and often had me double-check his entries in his ledgers. He sometimes lamented that the twins had not inherited my mathematical skills. I knew he was deeply concerned about the future welfare of our family when he was no longer able to care for all of us. By law, our family's holdings would pass to the oldest twin when my father died. Twin John would then be responsible for the overall management of our family's financial wellbeing on behalf of current and future generations and in general seeing to the welfare of all of us.

It is not that the twins were dullards. They listened carefully to the verbal explanations of our tutors and were able to think aloud through complex problems and develop logical, even brilliant solutions. They simply could not read or write or correctly do mathematical sums, often reversing letters and numbers. Even when they attempted to sign their names, their messy scrawls were illegible. They excelled at horsemanship, hunting, archery, and all outdoor activities. They identically inherited Uncle Edward's classical Altham good looks and charm and Father's sunny personality and quick wit. On the other hand, "Baby Rafe" could read satisfactorily, and do basic mathematics, but had not yet shown any aptitude for or interest in higher-level scholastic achievement, preferring to join the twins, his revered "big brothers" in their outdoor games.

And then there was me. Grandmother Altham increasingly pressured Mair-Mair and Father to negotiate a suitable mate for me, her oldest granddaughter. She made long lists of the peers of the Kingdom and all the male progeny that might be suitable mates and were anywhere nearly compatible in terms of age. Both Mair-Mair and Father pleaded with her to stop. They promised to secure a proper mate for their only daughter before I was in danger of being declared a social outcast or even, possibly, a witch were I not married by the time I was twenty-one.

Atop those worries there was the increasingly financially strapped King James adding to Father's stress. From my quiet perch in the library, I often heard Father lament about the adverse effects on the financial wellbeing of those in the extended community he managed because of the ever-increasing "impositions" levied by the King.

Grandmother Altham and Uncle Edward stopped by Eastcote Manor for a couple of days to check on the progress of "Uncle" Emmanuel in his studies. With her ever-growing tribe of children at Mark Hall, Aunt Joane did not accompany them. The conversation at dinner was lively.

Grandmother Altham, ever the incorrigible matchmaker, observed the offer King James had finally received from France to marry the French Princess to Prince Charles had fallen through.

"Her sizable dowry could have shored up the King's dwindling treasury," Grandmother lamented.

Uncle Edward chimed in. "Unfortunately, by now the French political elite are so divided along the Roman Catholic vs. Protestant lines they seem to be verging on Civil War. England mustn't vault into this quarrel. Thankfully, the King tabled this quest for now."

Roisin and Clodagh, of course, were present at this family dinner. Mair-Mair glanced meaningfully at them. She loyally and a bit disdainfully remarked that King James's own religiously battling factions in Parliament (Puritan versus Traditional Anglican) remained united on one thing—England still banned the worship of Roman Catholics.

A few weeks later, the dinner conversation distressed even more. Uncle Edward and Grandmother Altham weren't there, but Father's nearby sister and her husband joined us. Father's face reflected his worry at the reports he shared.

"King James finally decided to call another Parliament as a last-ditch means of easing his financial woes," he said. "The first since he arbitrarily dismissed the last Parliament two years ago. In a delusion of hope, he fancifully labeled the 1614 Parliament 'the Parliament of Love.'"

His sister, one of several of my Aunt Elizabeth's, chimed in. "There seems, as always, to be an atmosphere of deep distrust by all sides."

"Rumors of secret skullduggery do abound," said her husband. "We now know that the chancellor of the duchy of

Lancaster unduly influenced the outcome of the parliamentary election in Stockbridge, which only adds to the general distrust of the ultimate fairness of the pending proceedings."

Father agreed. "Tempers and distrust have risen to such a level that the chairman of one committee was physically jerked from his chair by two of his fellow committee members, who accused him of unfair bias."

Even Mair-Mair had an opinion. "I heard at one of my ladies' luncheons that the Earl of Northampton not only opposes the meeting of Parliament and the French marriage discussions. He advocates a marriage alliance with Spain instead, suggesting that a Spanish dowry alone would enable the king to exist without Parliament?" She looked at Father.

He responded. "That is hopefully not likely to happen, but many have expressed your mother's outspoken belief that the king's extravagant lifestyle is the cause of his own financial distress and all he needs to do is just cut back."

Several days later I overheard Father telling Mair-Mair that the Bishop of Lincoln religiously declared that any impositions by the king were matters of royal prerogative alone. Any opposition would amount to religious mutiny and sedition. Angry, Puritan leaning members of Commons responded by refusing to continue discussions until the Bishop of Lincoln was punished. Under intense pressure, the bishop ultimately reacted with a tear-filled apology. Furious with the ongoing dissension, the king impatiently announced that unless the House of Commons turned its attention to resolving his financial woes, he would again dissolve the assembly.

Father read to Mair-Mair the text of the House response:

"until it shall please God to ease us of these impositions wherewith the whole kingdom doth groan, we cannot without wrong to our country give your Majesty that

relief which we desire."

Three days later the king sent four of the most outspoken members of the Commons to be punished in the Tower of London. The king also dissolved the "Parliament of Love," which was forever after remembered as the "Addled Parliament."

This turmoil in the land paled in the face of the larger calamity that enveloped the Hawtrey family in September. Father fell ill. It started with worrisome coughing and progressed to a form of pleurisy. At one point he faded in and out of consciousness, breathing with frighteningly loud rasps. Mair-Mair and Roisin stood by in an anxious vigil. A local physician arrived with a large jar of leeches swimming in water and applied them to suck out Father's blood to "restore a better balance to his blood." Concerned with Father's overheated brow, this physician promised to return the next day with a spider for father to swallow to ease his fever.

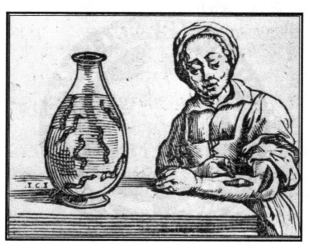

Woman standing at a table has placed a leech on her left forearm; on the table is a large jar containing leeches. Illustrated In: Bossche, Guillaume van den, Bruxellas, Typis Joannis Mommarti, 1639 Historia medica, in qua libris IV. animalium natura, et eorum

medica utilitas esacte & luculenter Image is in the public domain

Uncle Edward and 'Her Ladyship' arrived along with Grandmother and Emmanuel to support Mair-Mair. All of us hovered by Father's side. And then came John Bankes. He had learned of his longtime friend's illness and brought with him an esteemed physician, a Dr. William Harvey. I overheard John reassuring Mair-Mair as to the physician's superior credentials. He studied under the most learned European medical minds. At twenty-four he earned a Doctor of Medicine from the University of Padua. He accepted a position as Physician in Charge of St. Bartholomew's Hospital, agreeing to serve the poor who came to him without compensation. He lived then only on a small stipend.

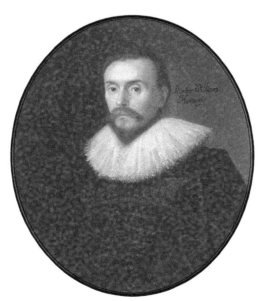

Dr. William Harvey, attributed to Daniel Mytens, oil on canvas, circa 1627
(image from Wikipedia)

Dr. Harvey's almost black eyes penetrated. His manner was direct—even gruff. He frowned at the marks of the leeches on Father's arms and demanded to know when, and for how long the leeches were applied.

He felt Father's forehead and wondered, "What was done for his fever?" His eyes flashed fiercely when he heard that the local doctor would return the next day with a spider or two for Father to swallow for the fever. But he merely said, a bit curtly, that wouldn't be necessary. He directed Mair-Mair to have the servants prepare damp, smelly poultices from powders he provided to be applied to Father's forehead and chest and changed often to help his fever and breathing. Soon Father seemed to be breathing a bit more easily.

Roisin and Clodagh consulted with Mair-Mair at one point and prevailed upon the kitchen staff to produce a special company meal to thank John Bankes and Dr. Harvey for coming to Father's aid. At dinner Mair-Mair announced that Father breathed more comfortably with less distress.

Tears sparkled in her eyes when she thanked "her John" and Dr. Harvey for their extraordinary kindness in arriving at such a critical time. And then she said she had an important announcement. John Bankes had just been "called to bar" at Gray's Inn. There was a general chorus of congratulations. 'Her Ladyship,' who had not before met John Bankes, had taken measure of his cool intellect and take-charge demeanor. She brashly asked how a merchant's son had come to study law at the "elite of the elite" Gray's Inn.

John shrugged. "That was not my parents' intent when they sent me to Queens College."

Uncle Edward intervened and boasted, "He was a child prodigy. When academics of Gray's Inn became aware of his brilliance, they were eager to recruit him, even before he graduated from Queens College."

"And why aren't you married?" asked my ever-outrageous Aunt Joane.

She blissfully ignored Grandmother Altham's glare of severe disapproval. Mair-Mair, initially astonished at her sister-in-law's temerity, temporarily allowed curiosity to win out as she looked quizzically at John. A quick flash of understanding overcame her.

"Of course," she exclaimed. "You are destined for great positions of leadership in the legal courts of England, but there is no peer who would ever betroth his daughter to the son of a merchant. Even if he is fated for great wealth and influence."

"Well, I do seem to be a bit of a 'fish out of water.'" He shrugged.

"It would be difficult at this point to expect a merchant's daughter to be comfortable in a lawyer's realm in today's kingdom. It appears I am destined for a celibate bachelor's life unless I choose to return to a merchant's realm."

'Her Ladyship,' my much idolized and usually outspoken Aunt, uncharacteristically said not a further word, but I could almost hear the cogs of her devious brain thumping. Even Grandmother Altham seemed to take pause as she fully considered the possible impacts of the eminently eligible, destined to be wealthy, socially difficult bachelor status of John Bankes. And then all eyes turned to me as if in a sudden "Aha!" moment. Startled and nonplused by this sudden scrutiny, I inelegantly ran from the room to check on Father.

He was awake and raised his hand in a drowsy welcome. I could not help weeping in relief to see his smile and hear his whispered, "Hello, Crumpet."

"I was so worried about you when you wouldn't wake up." I sobbed. "John Bankes is here. He has brought an important doctor to care for you."

"John Bankes, eh! A brilliant young man," said Father.

"Aunt Joane thinks I should marry him," I blurted out. "I am pretty sure Mair-Mair does, too. Grandmother just snorted when the idea sort of popped out of nowhere at dinner, but then I swear I saw her smile."

Father visibly shook off his drowsiness. "So, the Hawtrey/Altham women seem to have spoken out in their always astounding, devious ways. And what does John Bankes think of this idea?" my father asked.

"Nobody asked him," I said, "but he seems to be in need of a wife as he embarks on his career."

"And what is your opinion?" Father pushed.

"I—I have not had a chance to think about it," I stammered. "It feels like we have known him for a long time, but he has always seemed more like a distant but familiar cousin who occasionally pops in, not someone I really know well. The boys have always thought he was jolly. And you know how Mair-Mair is; he adores her along with the rest of the world."

A broad smile of relief slowly appeared as Father considered my somewhat incoherent outburst. The worried tension that tightened his face in recent months visibly eased.

"Well, I think I should have a few words with this young man," he said as a spasm of coughing overwhelmed him and left him gaspingly wheezing.

"I'm getting the doctor," I cried out as I sped back to the dining room.

Mair-Mair and John and Dr. Harvey hurried from the table to Father's room. Despite my 'official' adulthood, I was shooed away as the physician plied his skills. I hovered for a while outside Father's door, although I could not hear their words. The low murmurings went on and on, punctuated by Father's fits of coughing. Clodagh and Roisin finally steered me to my room and to my bed.

An insistent knocking lifted me from sleep. Clodagh slipped into my room, retrieved my cloak from my wardrobe, and urged me toward the door. "John Bankes is leaving," she whispered. "He wants to talk to you." I looked out the window. It was barely dawn. Shoeless, but wrapped in my cloak over my nightdress, I remember feeling the morning dew on my toes as I slipped out the front door on that beguiling, beginning of Fall morning. John paced restlessly as one of our servants saddled his horse. He stopped when he saw me. I could not help noticing how tall he was. Or how brightly his blue eyes sparkled. His reddish curls gleamed in the morning light.

Several vocal nuthatches in the nearby woodland repeated their cheery "dwip-dwip-dwip" calls.

"Where are your shoes?" he asked.

"Why are you leaving?" I replied.

He ignored my question, as I had his, and just looked at me with a bemused expression.

"I have always considered you a child up until now."

"I recall you once used the term 'bratty big sister' in discussing me with my brothers."

"Well, you obviously used your more experienced intellect to best them at a game."

"They needed to learn to try harder. I felt I should set a good example."

"I fear you have inherited your Grandmother Altham's tendencies toward plain speaking."

There was a pause as John Bankes looked at me intently. "I hope I know what I may be getting myself into. I had a long discussion with your father and with Mair-Mair last night. Your father has offered me an amazing Bride's Portion if I will take you off his hands." His teasing, but intently observing blue eyes negated any sting I might have perceived in his words.

I was nevertheless wounded. How could Father and

Mair-Mair have made this momentous decision without even consulting me? Contrarily, a wave of tremendous relief washed over me. This sudden resolution to the problem of my future marital status with someone somewhat familiar—even if he wasn't born a "peer of the realm"—was not unwelcome. He was invariably entertaining company, notwithstanding his superior intellectual status. I clearly understood that John Bankes was a brilliant scholar. It did not then occur to me to have any qualms as to where that brilliance would lead him.

John Bankes, it seemed, did have some personal qualms. He grabbed my hands and held my eyes with his own. "You are so very young."

I was obligated to argue. "You are only nine years older. Uncle Edward and Her Ladyship are seeming to manage. And she is twenty years younger."

"Ah, yes, 'Her Ladyship,'" said my future husband. "The Hawtrey/Altham families do embrace some compelling female figures, including your lovely Aunt Joane."

"Just don't expect me to be another Mair-Mair," I worried aloud. "She is her own magical self without even trying. No one else can ever be just like her."

"My contradictory Mary, you do have a challenging way about you. You must promise not to change a thing about who you are. But if we could get back to the subject of age. It is your parents who want to keep you longer. One of their conditions is that you do not marry until you are eighteen. That is why I have called you out in this early morning. I have urgent business in London that cannot wait, but I wanted to assess your response to this unexpected, but exceedingly interesting marriage proposal. And I mostly wanted to assure you that since I have no claim at present to higher levels of nobility, if at any time you become uncomfortable with this somewhat unusual agreement before we are wed, I will terminate it immediately. Indeed, part of the agreement that I demanded is that no part of your Bride's Portion is to be transferred until after we are wed."

"You may be the one who wants to back out," I retorted. "You may as well know. I detest embroidery. And…and…I absolutely will NEVER expose my nipples to public scrutiny."

"WHAT!"

"I just can't sit still that long, and I am always poking my fingers and bleeding all over everything."

"Ah, my ever-restless Mary—I am not in the least concerned with your embroidery skills, but why on earth would you think you would ever have to display your breasts?"

"There seemed to be plenty of pink nipples peeking out at the "Twelfth Night" performance when you took us there. When I was twelve."

My future husband burst into laughter. "I can see you have much to learn about the various kinds of women you will meet in London! You have been much protected here in the country. I do hereby give you my solemn oath that I will never ask you…" He paused for a moment and then continued. "No, I absolutely Forbid you ever to display your bosoms to anyone other than me!"

Reins jingled as the stable hand walked the saddled horse to John Bankes. I chose to let the word "forbid" slip by unchallenged.

"When will I see you again?"

"I wish I could stay—we have so much to discuss! But I have urgent business that cannot wait!"

He turned to me after he had mounted. "Don't let Mair-Mair be misled by the fact that Dr. Harvey is currently the Physician in charge at St. Bartholomew's Hospital for the poor in London. He is possibly the most brilliant physician in all of England and destined for great things. Mair-Mair must follow his guidance regarding your father's care exactly, and especially not allow any more bloodletting. And absolutely no swallowing of spiders!" With that he gave spur to his horse, and all too quickly vanished from my sight. The nuthatches continued their morning song as I slipped back into my room.

Over the years, I was to become ever resigned to the ache of my John's constant leaving—before I finished everything I wanted to say to him—for very legitimate "urgent business" that "could not wait."

And so it was that I became betrothed to John Bankes. I was to be wed on my 18th birthday in November in the year 1616.

AUTHOR ENDNOTES, CHAPTER TEN: *Despite intensive studies at learned Universities, the practice of medicine in the 17th Century was a thoroughly unscientific combination of superstition and misinformation. The common belief was that there were four fluids (called "humors" in the body—blood, phlegm, yellow bile and black bile—hence the focus on bloodletting (via leeches and other incisions) as a means of getting the "humors" back in the correct "balance."*

Dr. William Harvey had also been elected a Fellow of the Royal College of Physicians. He later enjoyed a lucrative career serving various aristocrats, became a Lumeian Lecturer, a 'Physician Extraordinary' to King James I, and then as 'Physician Ordinary' to King Charles I. He is credited with being the first physician to describe in detail the circulation of blood in the body, although his contemporaries did not accept his theories. He would have been a peer of Sir John Bankes. Of course, all his possible meetings with the Hawtrey/Bankes families are entirely fictional.

In the 17th Century and before, birthdays were not generally celebrated. Weddings were discouraged during Advent and Christmas, so late November, prior to the first Sunday in Advent was a favored time for a wedding. After St. Hilary's Day, the 13th of January, weddings began again.

CHAPTER ELEVEN
"Get thee a good husband…"
Shakespeare, All's Well That Ends Well
1614—1616

The following two years passed in a blur of busy-ness. John, true to his word, became a more frequent visitor. I became increasingly infatuated. He had a dry, quiet wit that I found hilarious. With young children he was downright clownish. He made me laugh. I came to treasure his profoundly caring heart and commitment to "doing the right thing," endearing traits often masked by his efforts to express himself in a thoroughly scholarly manner. All too frequently he would gallop away sooner than I wanted on "urgent business," "that could not wait," but true to his promise, he returned when he could, which was never as quickly as I wanted. During the course of his visits a perverse spirit often prompted me to argue with him endlessly, causing Mair-Mair to occasionally look up in alarm from her endless embroidery as the heat of our debates flamed up.

Father slowly recovered from his illness, coughing less and less and bit by bit regaining his strength. He gradually began to take back the reins of managing his business affairs, but often deferred from taking on more complicated business matters, saying, "Ask Mary— she will know what to do!" I expressed concern to John about my father's new hesitancy in fully managing our family's affairs and my worry about how things would go when I was no longer there to help out.

John appeared on his next visit with a studious young man who was the son of a merchant friend of his father's in faraway Keswick. I spent several days introducing him to my father's high stack of ledgers and was pleased with his quick grasp of the issues involved. Soon, he was fully adept in helping move along Father's business affairs, deferring always, of course, to Father's wisdom, but relieving him of the most tedious bookkeeping demands. The new clerk and his wife and three small children soon moved into a nearby vacant cottage (with much fussing over by Mair-Mair, of course). Over the course of the years, he would not only be completely responsible to Father, but would periodically check in with me wherever I was so that I could be prepared to step in should something untoward happen to Father. I need not have worried. Father's financial affairs continued to prosper with him fully in charge, until his death in 1638—just six years before I ultimately lost my John.

"My" John eased my worries about the long-term financial welfare of my family by imposing on a trusted lawyer friend to compose a carefully worded will for my father. It left the bulk of his estate to the oldest twin, John, as required by law, but stipulated that his son-in-law, John Bankes, act as "supervisor." Ultimately, as John pointed out, that "supervisor" would in reality mostly be me, but the technical legalities of the time precluded a woman from officially being assigned to such duties. Twin John, all too painfully aware of his scholastic limitations, was delighted to forego long hours with complicated ledgers. He welcomed this arrangement in managing the Hawtrey holdings for the benefit of all.

As he, little by little, continued his recovery, Father increasingly called on "his girls" (meaning Clodagh and me) to "play" for him. We were both proficient on the harpsichord and often enjoyed practicing and playing together. What comforted him most was Clodagh's lilting soprano, with her amazing voice set free, singing the sacred songs of a faith that did not comfort her heart as they comforted mine and Father's. And doing it with an intense devotion for a man who did not fully understand her, but who she understood cared for her with a deep, fatherly tenderness he did not know how to fully articulate.

Mair-Mair immersed herself in preparing my trousseau, determined that I would fit in respectably with London's high society. She even braved the "filth of London" on several shopping trips to elite London shops to check out the current fashions, returning with bolts of silks, satins, and lacy trims, as well as various baubles and furbelows and drawings of the latest fashions.

She was as dismayed as I was by the flagrant display of deep cleavage bared by plunging necklines that were the high London fashion, and shamelessly displayed by even the highest female nobility, including, ultimately, Queen Anne. Mair-Mair firmly instructed the seamstresses she employed that my necklines would be "fashionably low," but stop short of even any hint of cleavage. I never told her of the vow I had inelegantly blurted out to John on the day we became betrothed.

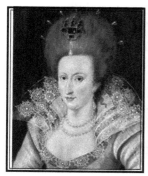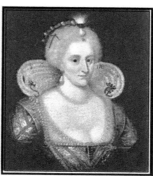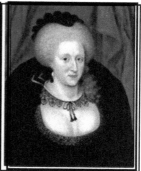

Various portraits of Queen Anne of Denmark, wife of King James I of England in the "highest society" fashions of the day. At far right she is in mourning for the death of her oldest son, Henry,

Linda Sindt

Prince of Wales, attributed to Marcus Gheeraerts the Younger, c. 1612, National Portrait Gallery. The center painting is by John de Critz circa 1605 Weiss Gallery. The portrait to the left is by Paul Van der Somer 31 Dec 1616, the same year Mary and John were wed, confirming the ultimate "high society" "haute couture" of the day. Queen Anne was famous for her extravagant—and costly—wardrobe.

As the wedding day grew near, Mair-Mair and Roisin busied themselves with planning the wedding feast, seeing to the store of wines and ales. They sent to London to order the live peacocks, which, when cooked, would be one of several main dishes served (resplendent with iridescent tail feathers and severed head with a gilded beak added back decoratively in the serving dishes). There would be many other savory meats, assorted cheeses, and a sumptuous array of special breads and sweetmeats. They plotted how the Bride's Pie, a sweet, minced meat pastry, would be prepared and cut to assure that niece Jane (Uncle Edward's and the late Aunt Elizabeth's oldest daughter, then six), would get the glass ring that would be baked into the pie). The legend was that the lady who found a glass ring in her slice of pie would be the next to marry, and the good ladies were conniving to make sure the right "lady" got the ring. They had quietly ruled out Clodagh, not wanting to call undue attention to her difficult marital prospects.

Shy little Jane, then six, and her-five-year-old sister, Margaret, would be my bridesmaids, along with, of course, Clodagh. 'Her Ladyship' had already produced an heir for Uncle Edward (James, then two). He would remain at Eastcote Manor with his Nanny, along with his lively three-year-old sister, Joan, who sported her mother's famous golden curls and was already giving off hints of her mother's trademark "attitude.". Aunt Joane ('Her Ladyship') already burgeoned with her third child (soon-to-be second son, John).

My John's growing law practice demanded increasingly huge chunks of his time, but each Saturday, three weeks before our wedding date, he made the long ride from London on a galloping horse to attend Sunday Church services at St. Martin's for the required "Crying of the Banns," and then, after a hurried Sunday lunch with my family, galloped back to London on Sunday afternoon to attend to his clients in the week to come.

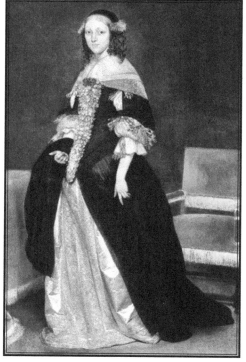

A 17th Century wedding dress might well have looked like this. Silver and black would have been considered an elegant choice for a bride of "gentry." Lady Mary's November wedding dress might have resembled this typical 17th Century "dress up" gown, with threads of silver and gold. Which would have served well for many other "dress up" functions and not have been tucked away, never to be seen again, after the wedding.

Finally, the day arrived when I would leave my childhood home. It was a grey day, as most November days in Ruislip were. Clodagh and the girls and I wore our hair down in long curls. There were no November flowers to adorn our tresses, but we made do with pretty ribbons and sprigs of evergreens from the gardens. My Bridesmaids and I led the way, holding hands from my home to the church through the November drizzle, followed by my groom and my merry family and the guests residing at Eastcote Manor.

John's parents understandably found the long, arduous, twelve-day round trip from Keswick in difficult weather to be insurmountable, but we were planning a trip to Keswick to see them in the Spring. If John's practice permitted him to be away that long. Grandmother Altham and Emmanuel came to my wedding, of course, as well as Father's sister and husband and my cousin, John Carter. Several mutual friends of John and Father and Uncle Edward from Gray's Inn came with their wives to lend support to my John. Family and friends, our wonderful servants, our neighbors, and townsfolk all joined the laughing parade to the church. Father hired a small contingent of players of flutes, viols and drums to follow us all and add to the gaiety of our procession.

At my request, and with Father's glad blessing, Clodagh sang a joyous madrigal as a part of my wedding service, causing all to smile as she perfectly hit the high notes. And so, with loving hearts, my community and my family celebrated my wedding vows and sent me away from their midst.

Finally, the elaborate wedding feast ended. I retired to my childhood room one final time to collect the small bag I would need for the trip to London with my John. We would leave that very afternoon. John, of course, had urgent business to attend to the next day. Most of my belongings now waited for me in John's London home. I packed a few last things in my reticule.

I could not leave behind Namontock's eagle feather that stood in its vase by my bedside. I smiled when I saw that Mair-Mair had slipped in earlier and tucked a charred remnant of our last year's Yule log in my bag. A starter for my first Yule log in my new home.

There was much to discuss on the three-hour trip to London, but eventually, perhaps encouraged by the flask of excellent wine Mair-Mair had included in a generous picnic basket to sustain us on our trip, our lively conversation lulled. My newest Canute traveled with us and snoozed at our feet in our carriage. John grew drowsy, but my internal disquiet grew as I considered the major event that loomed just a few hours ahead—my first night with John!

Grandmother Altham was the only one who had given me actual (unsolicited) premarital instruction. Her words echoed sternly in my head, although I did not really have a clue as to what she meant.

"Only the most common of women exhibit enjoyment in the conjugal act!" she said. "Ladies of culture and proper upbringing must remain stoic and unresponsive, lest you be considered immoral."

"The doctrine of our faith is that acts of procreation may be engaged upon only for the purpose of bringing forth children. To do otherwise, would be an ultimate sin against God and Church and a path to eternal damnation!"

After these dire, if confusing, warnings and upon inquiring of Mair-Mair as to what to expect and how I should behave, she would only smile and say mysteriously "You are both sensible and caring people, my dear. I am wagering you will figure out how everything works on your own terms between just the two of you—as it should be."

Even my ultimate, quintessential, and all-knowing confidante, 'Her Ladyship,' would also only smile (did she actually blush?) and say, also mysteriously, "I am sure you can always trust what your divine Mair-Mair tells you!"

Well, of course I am not going to tell anyone what happened in my marital bed! I will only tell you that I awoke with a smile on my face. Was it remembered bliss? Or—wait —something tickled my nose, making me smile. Did something flutter against my cheek? I swatted at my face. My eyes flew open. Bright blue eyes smiled down into my own. My love teased me with Namontack's feather.

"Why do you keep such a strange feather by your bed?" he asked. Eventually, after another tender intervention of marital delight, which I couldn't help enjoying out loud, contrary, of course, to Grandmother Altham's sternest admonishments, and possibly to the eternal damnation of my soul. I shared with my John as we nestled together the long-ago tale of my meeting with Namontack. And of Namontack's and the exuberant (former pirate) Captain Newton's accounts of the playful young girl, Pocahontas, in the far away New World, who had reportedly met the strange, struggling newcomers to her land with much kindness and charity. Notwithstanding the fact that she had also reportedly playfully, if nakedly, as a young girl, turned cartwheels in the dusty streets of the struggling settlement with the young sons of the Colonists.

"Pocahontas! I know that name!"

"What?"

"She has been in England with her English husband and small son for some time and is quite the celebrity! The king has welcomed her as a royal princess! A number of her countrymen came with her. The Virginia Company sponsored them to encourage further investment in the Colony at Jamestown in the New World. She has been converted to our Anglican faith and goes by Rebecca now. She is touted as an example of the positive influence of the colonists in converting the native savages to the Anglican religion. Several of my clients have entertained her and her husband, John Rolfe, who is a successful tobacco farmer, and will soon be promoted to a prominent position back in the Colonies."

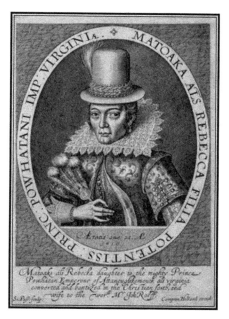

Society woman: Pocahontas by Simon van de Passe, 1616
The inscription reads: Matoaka Rebecca daughter of the mighty
Prince Powhatan Emperor of Attanoughkomouck at Virginia
converted and baptized in the Christian faith, wife to the worthy
Mr. John Rolff.

John continued his story, "She came to London as another fundraising scheme by those invested in the "New World." She is supposed to reassure investors that native, "heathen" tribes can be educated and converted to Christianity in promoting the interests of England. According to one observer, "She 'accustome[d] her selfe to civilitie' and 'still carried her selfe as the daughter of a king, and was accordingly respected [by] persons of Honor, in their hopefull zeale by her to advance Christianitie."

And so, the New World, with all its mysteries, perils, and ultimate promises of possible new wealth for England and its citizens in resolving its current financial woes—as well as just the plain, dramatic adventure of the whole idea—intruded itself on my marital bed. The very concept of this far away land still felt surreal—as if England might as well have been adventuring to the moon.

CHAPTER TWELVE
"All the World's a Stage..."
Shakespeare, As You Like It.
Twelfth Night, 6 January 1617

I HATED London! Piles of garbage lined the streets. The air choked me. My husband worked exceedingly long hours—no big surprise there. His supremely competent and business-like steward supervised our servants and made it clear he understood how the Master liked things. He plainly needed little help from me, even though customarily, it should have been my duty to supervise the household staff. Which, considering my then comparative lack of skills or even interest in such things, was just as well. I was already beyond homesick for Clodagh, and, of course, for Mair-Mair and Father and Roisin, and even all the boys. We dined often with engaging clients and friends of John. I had as yet found no real female friends to ease the increasing boredom and, yes, abject loneliness, of my days. My John's small library included mostly dry legal tomes that did not catch my fancy as a way to pass the hours.

Our servants attempted to adorn our household with appropriate Christmas décor. Despite the abundance of aromatic boughs, their decorating attempts missed the mark in terms of a customary, colorful, joyous Christmas celebration. There wasn't even a Kissing Bush! I lit our first Yule Log with dramatic ceremony for just John and me with the remnant of last year's Hawtrey Yule Log. And then we went out to share

Christmas Eve with business acquaintances of John, leaving the log to burn merrily alone, without witness or further celebration. No bawdy Mummers or serenading Wassailers graced our doorstep. There were no nearby apple trees to bless with prayers for abundance. I recall it was a pleasant enough evening as I tried to fit into my new world as John's wife. But nothing memorable remains in my heart of that long ago Christmas Eve.

A big event of this first holiday season of my marriage threatened to overwhelm me. Twelfth Night! We were invited by King James ("summoned" I think would be the more proper term) to Whitehall Palace for a production of a special Masque, "The Vision of Delight," composed by one of Queen Anne's favorites—Ben Jonson. I was in an agony of nerves.

I would not be presented to the King and Queen, of course. We would be seated based on our social rank, which was, then, very small compared to the royalty and aristocracy who would (also compellingly) be present. The very fact of our presence at all, was a significant regal nod to my John's already acknowledged intellectual prowess and potential for future service to King James.

The stress of preparing to get married seemed naively simplistic compared to preparing to attend a masque at the King's beckoning. Despite my fatigue and nausea, I got myself together for the big event. I hoped my wedding dress with its velvet cloth, silver and gold threads, and silken, embroidered white lace discreetly covering my bosom, would be elegant enough for an up and coming, but "not yet quite gentry" lawyer's wife. I was too fatigued to deal with seamstresses and fittings in concocting an elaborate new dress. At last, the Twelfth Night of Christmas arrived.

The night air, dampened by cloud-covered drizzle, assaulted—more than usually redolent of the refuse rotting on the streets. I held a perfumed handkerchief to my nose. After an eternity the long parade of carriages ahead of us discharged elegantly attired occupants at the entry to Banqueting House at Whitehall Palace.

Finally, we made our way inside and found our seats in the elegant hall that shimmered with crystal, candle-studded chandeliers and flaming fireplaces. An abundance of gold and silver dazzled everywhere. I could not help but recall my long-ago staunchly Puritan Aunt Elizabeth and the outspoken scorn and shame she would have cast upon this opulent display.

Waiting for the masque to begin, we visited with those seated at our table. John knew them all, of course. My stomach churned, and I continued to feel faint. I kept my scented handkerchief handy. In the distance I saw the figure of the king on his grand dais, complete with throne, with assorted attendants around him. The queen had her separate, also throned, regal dais with her own regally attired attendants.

"Why aren't the king and queen sitting together?" I asked.

"It is my understanding they haven't actually lived together for many years," my husband answered, a bit enigmatically.

My table mates exchanged knowing glances. I did not understand their meaning. I would have to ask my John about that later.

One of our companions said, somewhat obscurely, "I believe the king promoted George Villiers to Earl earlier today." More enigmatic, suggestive glances passed over my head.

"I hear he will be dancing especially for the king during the masque," someone said. Yet again an exchange of arch looks.

Gossip about his royal highness continued. "Stories from his tenure as King of Scotland before he also became King of England have followed him," ventured one of my table mates. "They say he wrote a book condemning witchcraft and that at his direction more than 350 young women were burned to death as witches under his rule in Scotland."

I looked at John for corroboration. I remembered Grandmother Altham's dire fear that I might have been labeled a "witch" by English society had I not married before I was twenty-one.

Ever the diplomat (and potential royal advisor), John only replied, noncommittally, something to the effect that the king apparently considered England to be a 'more developed' society and, so far, issues surrounding witchcraft had not surfaced during his tenure in England. And then noted that the king was specifically known for his personal elevated academic studies and admired by many in the academic world for his scholarship.

Not far from the king and queen was a separate, ornate dais, also visible to all, occupied by a dark-skinned, dark-haired couple sitting in regal chairs surrounded by their equally dark attendants. All were dressed in the most stylish, aristocratic, formal English attire.

John nudged my arm with his elbow, nodding toward this prominent dais, deliberately changing the course of this conversation.

"That is your famous Princess Pocahontas!" he whispered.

"But who is that dark man with her? I thought she was married to an Englishman?"

"I believe that is a top holy man of her native tribe in the New World. He goes by Tomocomo, but I seem to remember he also has another, more complicated native name. His wife, who is among the attendants in the dais with him, is half-sister of your Pocahontas, or Rebecca, as she is now known, since she has converted to the Anglican religion."

As always, I marveled at my scholar husband's perfect recall of seemingly trivial details.

"But where is the English husband of this Princess Pocahontas-Rebecca?" I persisted.

"The king specifically did not invite him. It is whispered that the king is displeased with John Rolfe for daring to marry a royal princess in another land without first asking for the personal blessing of the king," explained one of my table mates. "Also," he added, "the king despises tobacco, and John Rolfe is known in the New World for his acumen in growing and marketing tobacco."

At last, the Masque of Delight began. It was written by Ben Jonson, a favorite playwright of Queen Anne. John told me another court favorite, Inigo Jones, had created clever movable scenery that used ingenious shutters that slid in and out on grooves cut into the floor. He even made scenery appear to fly from above. The creative contributions of this Inigo Jones also included the intricate and often suggestive costumes of many of the participants.

Finally, the lovely music started. I continued to feel nauseous and a bit faint. The memories of this long-ago event are blurred. I do vividly recall the opening scenes of the "Masque of Delight" when a breathtakingly gorgeous young man, (identified by those at my table as the newly dubbed Earl of Buckingham), with astonishing grace and agility, danced, primarily before the king. There was a certain intimacy and blatant seductiveness to his movements that palpably troubled me, as though I were unwillingly peeking in on someone's private moments, adding to the discomfort I felt in my increasingly churning stomach. My table mates again exchanged knowing glances and raised eyebrows.

One of them audibly whispered, "It is told our king lavishly dotes on very young, very attractive men, even publicly kissing their mouths and pinching their cheeks and showering them and their families with many favors, but this young man is his absolute favorite and he and all of his family have been handsomely rewarded."

Another responded, "It is indeed known that the young Villiers and all his family continue to become exceedingly wealthy, solely based on his intimate relationship with the king."

Someone else asked, "Does anyone think the resplendent baubles dangling on the Villier's person are made of paste, or are they are real jewels?" No one said they were paste.

I do remember my main thought was regret that my musically gifted Clodagh was not there to hear the lovely music. There were lutes, viols, wind instruments, drums, and others I could not identify. The air swelled with a chorus of delightful voices, more entrancing than anything I had ever heard before (other than possibly Clodagh's joyous madrigal at my wedding).

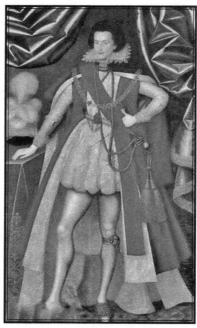

George Villiers, then Earl of Buckingham, eventually 1st Duke of Buckingham, attributed to William Larkin, oil on canvas, circa 1616—just before his legendary performance before the king on "Twelfth Night" (January 6, 1617)
On display at the National Portrait Gallery. Image from bing.com

After the newly dubbed Earl of Buckingham disappeared from the stage, the music changed, and members of the audience moved to the main dance floor. I gasped when I saw that many were apparently, by their dress, high-born young women, but with their breasts completely bared! Pink nipples bounced to the rhythm of the music. I tugged the lacy top on my modestly attired bosom an inch up. My John, of course, noticed and failed to suppress a grin. He then tormented me by nudging me frequently with his elbow and dramatically, casting his eyes at this, that, and the other well-endowed bosoms of the otherwise elegantly clad, clearly aristocratic young women swaying dramatically on the dance floor to the rhythmic music of the masque.

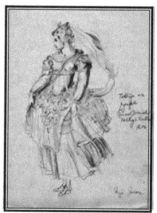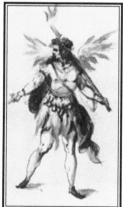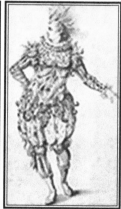

Masque costumes designed by Inigo Jones. Outraged Puritan (Parliamentarian) leaders loudly denounced these Royalty sponsored Masques as indecent, vulgar displays, and proof of lack of moral restraint.

And then I threw up all over my John's shoes and fainted. I awoke to vaguely familiar, piercing, black-brown eyes peering fiercely down into my own. I was in my own bed. My panicked

John, it seemed, had fled from the banqueting hall, carrying me in his arms, to our carriage and sent a frantic summons to his friend, Dr. William Harvey. (Yes, the same one who had attended my father.)

Dr. Harvey turned to John, who was hovering nearby, and said, gruffly, "Congratulations, my friend! You are going to be a father!"

John's shoulders sagged in relief, and he pulled my hands to his mouth in a wordless embrace. "Thanks be to our dear Lord," he whispered.

I so verily wish I could tell you that we all lived happily ever after from then on out, but that was, of course, not to be.

I lost our baby in March. Drenched in grief and misery and the pervasive stench of London, I learned later that Pocahontas, who had hovered for so many years on the edges of my imagination as a sort of mystical sister in my heart, symbolic of the strange New World that was filled with such mystery and adventure and hope, had died on the same day as my unborn baby. It is said she, too, had often complained of the vile London air. Pocahontas's and John Rolfe's ailing young son did not return to the New World with his father, but stayed in England with John Rolfe's brother, returning to the New World only many years later as a grown man. Pocahontas is buried in Gravesend, England.

I was numb with grief and loss. The poisonous London air continued to choke me. Father and Mair-Mair and Roisin and Clodagh came for a short visit, which cheered me immensely, but all too soon they returned to Eastcote Manor. I moped around the house. There was really nothing to keep me occupied amid all this grayness of life. I longed for a good gallop down a country road with Father as he tended to his "rounds."

And then another tragedy. The excellent clerk who had

maintained John's financial accounts fell ill and died, suddenly, of the ague. John, busier than ever, but also increasingly worried about my ongoing listlessness and depression, had a sudden inspiration.

"My love," he said one morning as we breakfasted. "I recall your uncommon skill in overseeing your father's financial affairs when he became ill. My practice demands so much of my attention—I need someone I can trust to oversee our own private financial affairs. Would you consider taking this on?"

"You may hire as many staff as you think you might need," he added by way of enticement.

It was just the therapy I needed to help fill the long days. I was astonished at the wealth my ambitious, up-and-coming husband had already accumulated. He was much in demand by the aristocratic elite in London, and most generously rewarded. A singular honor for one so junior was his appointment as a Deputy Reader (a senior lecturer to budding law students) at Stapleton Inn.

Despite his growing success and reputation, those early years of our marriage were tinged with a pervasive sadness. I became pregnant with ease but lost my unborn babies within a month or two of conception. I despaired at my ultimate failure as a wife. During this interim time of recurring grief, we received word of another loss.

Adding to my grief—news came that Uncle Edward's always frail and ever ailing oldest daughter, Jane, who received the glass ring in my Bride's Pie, and held my hand as we paraded joyfully through Ruislip to my wedding, had died.

Finally, my John called his longtime acquaintance, Dr. Harvey, for another consultation regarding my health. Noting my pallid skin, slumping shoulders, and constant cough, it did not take the good doctor long to proclaim with his characteristic, gruff directness, "I think it is safe to say that our dirty London air does not agree with her. I recall her lovely home in Ruislip as a fresh country village. I prescribe a month or two at her childhood home with her esteemed parents to see if that does not bring a bloom back to her cheeks. Then, if she does return to London, she should get back to Ruislip the instant it is suspected she may be with child and remain there for the duration of the pregnancy."

Also, during this time, Queen Anne, who had never really recovered from the early loss of her oldest son and had suffered from failing health for many years, finally died from "dropsy" in March 1619. King James ignored her during her long illness, apparently preferring to spend his time and affections with his bevy of much younger male court favorites.

AUTHOR ENDNOTES, CHAPTER TWELVE:

Tomocomo's official name was Uttamatomakkin. As an interesting aside, it is reported that Powhatan, the father of both Pocahontas, and Tomocomo's wife, Matachanna, had directed Tomocomo as his emissary, to count the number of people in England. Tomocomo reportedly picked up a stick on which to carve notches to keep count, but soon became "weary of the task."

CHAPTER THIRTEEN

"When I was home I was in a better place..."
Shakespeare, As You Like It
1620—1625

And so, I returned to my old room at Eastcote Manor. I missed my John wildly, but he came most weekends when he could get away. It was a bit like our two-year courtship, except now he got to sleep in my bed and not a distant guest room.

I did rejoice to be again with Father and Mair-Mair and, of course, chattering endlessly with Clodagh. And also, with frequent visits from Grandmother Altham and Uncle Edward and 'Her Ladyship' and their ever-growing family.

The twins were both married, and growing families of their own. "Baby" Rafe still lived at home but was now a gangly teenager with a fondness for fast horses and eager to get out into the "real" world.

My cousin, John Carter, son of my father's sister, my Aunt Elizabeth, and her husband had not only married, but also, astonishingly, made his way across the ocean to settle in the ever-beguiling New World—in Virginia.

Beyond envious of his "cousin" (with whom he had shared the Ruislip Nursery), "Uncle" Emmanuel Altham was agog with dreams and schemes of also adventuring to this fabled, unexplored corner of our earth. Much to the horror of his mother, my Grandmother Altham, now visibly aging, but still hanging onto her spunk. Emmanuel yearned for the daring exploits and promised fortunes that beckoned. Mostly, I think, he was simply alive to the thrill of exploring fascinating, alien lands and meeting unfamiliar people that lived so far from England's shores.

Emmanuel did not sympathize, nor did any of us, with the rigid, judgmental beliefs of the stern Puritans who hated Christmas so much. He could not tolerate the intolerance of those who would deny the mystery and hope and comfort of the established Anglican Church of England to all. While impatient with those who wished harm on adherents to the ancient rites of Roman Catholicism, he was giddy with the news that a group of these dissident Puritans now prepared to head for the New World to start a new colony. He hung out as often as he could where their ship, "The Mayflower," now anchored in preparation for its long voyage. He pestered all the crew and workers who would spare him the time of day for details about how the ship was structured, navigated, manned, supplied, armed, and anything else about sailing a ship he could tease out of them.

Slowly, the bloom returned to my cheeks. And then I was pregnant—again! I did not return to London. Our first child, Alice (sweet enchantress of her adoring father), was born in 1621. Our thought was that I would remain at Eastcote Manor until our precious baby Alice was safely through her first year before returning to the perils of London. Alice, of course, thrived in the glow of her doting grandparents. But no one pampered her more than her adoring father. They shared the same reddish, chestnut curls and merry blue eyes and were inseparable, even when she was a tiny babe in arms, whenever they were together.

We made a trip to Keswick to show John's parents their totally amazing, beyond adorable new granddaughter. Mair-Mair and Father joined in this family vacation and enjoyed socializing with my in-laws. While we were there, Father and John conspired together and jointly invested in the black lead mines in Borrowdale in the lovely Lake country. This lucrative joint investment between John and my father was long a source of income for both our families.

I soon learned that while my John was adept at making loads of money—he also very much enjoyed spending it. Mostly, I admit, to provide for his growing family's security, but also for generous indulgences for his family (many of which my inborn frugal nature worried we could just as well have done without). Except, I have to admit, the Borrowdale black lead investment, which initially troubled me turned out to be—over the long term—in retrospective light of the terrifying instabilities to come—a most lucrative and dependable acquisition.

In late 1621, after a lengthy illness, we lost my Grandmother Altham. I was glad she had lived long enough to meet her incredible granddaughter, Alice.

In late April 1622, Father received a letter from my cousin, John Carter, who had been a constant companion of the twins in their growing up years. John Carter was a recent adventurer to the New World and had returned to England from Virginia for much-needed supplies. He left his wife in the Colonies to oversee their holdings in the New World. Now he asked for help. Cousin John was in dire straits. The Company he represented and who had promised return passage had fallen on hard times and could now not pay for his passage to return to Virginia and his wife.

Of course, my generous father could not have denied support to one who had been almost a son to him.

In 1623 my bold "baby uncle," Mair-Mair's youngest brother, Emmanuel Altham, with whom I had shared my growing up years, achieved his lifelong dream. He invested enormous sums in the New Plymouth Company and became one of the "merchant adventurers" to faraway lands. Uncle Edward fretted at his younger brother's recklessness with his share of the family fortune. Emmanuel's mother, my late Grandmother Altham, would have been aghast at what she would surely have deemed "irresponsible foolishness." In one of his boldest early adventures, he sailed to Virginia in the New World as captain of the "Little James," the pinnace the company sent to Plymouth for fish and fur trading, alongside its companion ship, "The Anne." Emmanuel could not contain his delight at his exploits. Following is an account of one voyage, as relayed to his older brother, my dear Uncle Edward.

The marriage of William Bradford and Alice Carpenter Southworth is recorded in a letter written by Emmanuel to our uncle (Sir Edward Altham) in September, 1623.

> *Upon the occasion of the Governor's marriage, since I came, Massasoit was sent for to the wedding, where came with him his wife, the queen, although he hath five wives. With him came four other kings and about six score men with their bows and arrows—where, when they came to our town, we saluted them with the shooting off of many muskets and training our men. And so all the bows and arrows was brought into the Governor's house, and he brought the Governor three or four bucks and a turkey. And so we had very good pastime in seeing them dance, which is in such manner, with such a noise that you would wonder...*
>
> *And now to say somewhat of the great cheer we had at the Governor's marriage. We had about twelve pasty venisons, besides others, pieces of roasted venison and other such good cheer in such quantity that I could wish you some of our share. For here we have the best grapes that ever you say—and the*

biggest, and divers sorts of plums and nuts which our business will not suffer us to look for.

Emmanuel further wrote in that same letter which we all read over and over again.

And now to come more nearer to that I intend to write of, and first of the situation of the place. I mean the plantation at Patuxent [Indian name for Plymouth]. It is well situated upon a high hill close unto the seaside, and very commodious for shipping to come unto them. In this plantation is about twenty houses, four or five of which are very fair and pleasant, and the rest (as time will serve) shall be made better. And this town is in such manner that it makes a great street between the houses, and at the upper end of the town there is a strong fort, both by nature and art, with six pieces of reasonable good artillery mounted thereon; in which fort is continual watch, so that no Indian can come near thereabouts but he is presently seen. This town is paled about with pale of eight foot long, or thereabouts, and in the pale are three great gates. Furthermore, here is belonging to the town six goats, about fifty hogs and pigs, also divers hens. And lastly, the town is furnished with a company of honest men, that do, in what lies in them, to get profit to the adventurers…without our pales dwells one Hobomok, his wives and his household (above ten persons), who is our friend and interpreter, and one whom we have found faithful and trusty…so let my love be remembered to my sister Mary [Note: Mair-Mair!]. And I pray merrily tell her it will be no tarrying for me because I know not when I shall come

> *into England. But pray likewise tell her that I could*
> *give her much land if she will come and live among*
> *the wild scene of Indians. I hope this will make her*
> *smile…I have also sent to my sister…six ears of corn*
> *and beans to sow in her garden…*
>
> *[Sidney V. James, Jr., editor, Three Visitors*
> *to Early Plymouth (Plymouth, Mass.: Plimoth*
> *Plantation, 1963), p. 29-30."]*

Most notably in 1623, less than eighteen months after the amazing, awesome, Alice Bankes was born, her equally magnificent, marvelous, miraculous sister, Mary, safely arrived. The two sisters soon became as inseparable as if they had been born twins. Everyone was blossoming with good health and John was reluctant to have us move back to his London house and the dirty London air.

In 1626 our oldest son, John, was born. Although he bore his father's name, he favored me, with his dark curls, and mostly his features were reminiscent of Mair-Mair's Altham clan, with an uncanny resemblance to my very handsome, much idolized Uncle Edward.

It was time for us to find our own place in the country. And so we moved to an estate John purchased in Lincolnshire, which was 156 miles from my family home in Ruislip Manor and 146 miles from London. It was then up to John, of course, to do most of the traveling, divvying up precious hours between his blossoming career and his ever-growing family. He continued to fill the family coffers with the income from his ever more successful practice. In 1624 he was named as a Member of Parliament from Wootton Bassett.

I was no longer bored. Absolute joy consumed my days as I cared for my exuberant, ever-growing family. Countered by the always present anguish and worry of waiting for my John to safely gallop back to us from his London affairs. By then our Alice was old enough to delight in her own pony. One of my happiest memories of our life in those halcyon early days is of John cantering with me around Lincolnshire on our horses. Alice merrily followed on her pony. Little Mary, clutched tightly by her doting father, bounced with him in his saddle. We savored the fresh country air as we chatted and laughed with our Lincolnshire neighbors. The newest in the growing line of much loved "Canutes" chased joyfully alongside us with several of his brother and sister greyhounds. The then two smallest Bankes babies slumbered safely in their nursery, guarded by their Nanny. More (and more) darling babies were to come.

I missed my dear Clodagh in those luminous days. I wanted so much to share my amazing children with her. I was beyond homesick for her banter. But she felt compelled to remain with Mair-Mair and Father to keep an eye on her increasingly ailing mother.

Ultimately, the news from Eastcote Manor in Ruislip was heartbreaking. Roisin was perilously ill. Mair-Mair despaired about her lifelong friend. Convinced of her imminent death, Roisin begged to return to her beloved Ireland. She wanted to lie beside her brave husband in his grave. She longed to receive the long-banned Roman Catholic sacraments once more before she died from forbidden priests who reportedly yet persisted in the tenaciously rebellious Irish underground.

And so, compelled by Mair-Mair's grief about her lifelong friend, the three dearest men in my life, my John, Father, and Uncle Edward, conspired secretly to grant dear Roisin's dying wish. At possible dire peril to all of us, should they be discovered. And deliberately contrary to the orders of King James, to whom they had all mandatorily declared their allegiance. I will not go into all the details of the intricate scheme they devised.

Linda Sindt

My whole family traveled to Eastcote Manor to say farewell to our dear Roisin. How could we do without her? Mair-Mair contrived to make it a family celebration. I caught her several times sobbing into her ever-present lacy handkerchief when she hoped no one would notice. The sorrowing kitchen staff, without any prompting, prepared their much-loved Roisin's favorite treats for her farewell dinner.

An inconsolable Clodagh demanded that she accompany her mother. Reminiscent of the plot of William Shakespeare's "Twelfth Night"—the one we had enjoyed so many years ago at Gray's Inn—she disguised herself as a shabby, impoverished young Irish man, resplendent with a droopy fake mustache and a wispy goatee. And, of course, an authentic Irish brogue. She would drive her ailing mother in a rude cart behind two strong, but disreputable-looking horses. Two trusted servants, who had grown up in our household adoring Roisin, volunteered to attend to them. They would travel by horse, also incognito, as simple peasants. Riding at a discretionary distance, they were armed separately with funds and weapons should they be needed.

An endless month had passed since Clodagh and Roisin departed on their sad quest. John was away for several days attending to London business, as usual. At home in our Lincolnshire estate, I entertained my small children. My disquiet increased. Even my darling children could not distract me. Why hadn't we heard from Clodagh? Where was my "almost sister?" When would she return from this dangerous journey? Mair-Mair had promised she would send a messenger the instant Clodagh and the servants returned to Eastcote Manor. No messenger arrived. I already bloomed with soon-to-be Elizabeth. Our oldest, Alice, was six. Mary was four and baby John was just learning to walk.

I am even now ashamed to confess my complaints. My

husband's practice was beyond successful. A river of cash flowed in. I had plenty of excellent servants and nannies at my beck and call. Yet I fretted in abject misery for my absent lifelong friend.

Suddenly, both my parents were at my door, unannounced. After a few moments of ungluing themselves from their adoring oldest granddaughters, who had pounced on them, they led me to a private room.

Tears already flowed from Mair-Mair's eyes. Father enveloped me in a bear hug.

"We didn't want to just send a messenger." Mair-Mair sobbed.

"Our servants returned from Ireland yesterday," my father said.

My heart stopped. I could barely whisper her name. "And Clodagh?"

A fresh torrent of tears from Mair-Mair.

Father hugged me closer. "She did not come back with them."

"She is going to become a nun," Mair-Mair wailed. "In the secret convent that cared for my dear Roisin in her final days."

I was beyond devastated. How could I go on without this loving sister in my life and in my heart?

I tried to wish her well. I wanted to be happy that she had at last connected to the religion that was for so long denied to her. Yet I mourned for her as if she had died. And worried about her incessantly.

I continued to tend to my growing brood.

Less than two years later I was pregnant again with our wonderful baby Joanne. John, of course, was away, as always, tending to his London practice.

On a late fall afternoon, a foggy swirl dimmed the afternoon light. In the nursery I played with toddler Elizabeth.

A maidservant came to the nursery door. "I am so sorry to disturb you, madam," she said. "There is a filthy beggar at the door. He will not accept any food and leave, but says it is urgent that he talk to you personally."

Curious, I accompanied the maidservant to the door, where a slender, dirty, ragged man stood. The green-blue eyes gave her away. I screamed and grabbed Clodagh into my arms.

"The English slaughtered my convent sisters while I was out searching for food," she sobbed. "I did not know where else to go. Can I stay with you?"

And so my dear "almost sister" returned to me and accompanied my family into the heart of the English Civil War.

AUTHOR ENDNOTES, CHAPTER THIRTEEN: *John Carter's letter to his uncle, Ralph Hawtrey, begging for funds to return to his Virginia holdings and his wife.*

> *To the right worshipful and my very good uncle and friend, Mr. Ralph Hawtree, Esqre., at Rislip, give these.*
>
> *Good uncle, my humble duty remembered unto your worship and your wife, with my prayers for your healths and prosperities, so it is. May it please your good worship that by my long stay here in England, hoping and still expecting some relief from Virginia to defray the charges for my voyage thither again, I gave way to all the means I had here and am now quite disappointed of my expectation, only I hear that my wife is very well, and that our business there doth profit well, thanks be to God. But no supply comes over, so that now, I having wrought means for my passage*

over thither, have no means to defray the charge thereof. My humble request unto your worship is, that as you have been always my most especial friend, so you would still continue your love to me, and at this time extend your goodwill to me so much as to lend me so much money as will pay for my passage over, or otherwise I shall be disappointed of my voyage, which may turn to my undoing, for in this necessity I have no friend but your worship to fly to for succour, and my wife stops my supply thither only for expecting my coming over thither. I cannot give you such security as I could wish, but if your worship will do me this great courtesy, I will not only truly pay you again, but also be ever ready to do your worship what service I am able, with many thanks. Thus, desiring your worship's answer hereof, and hoping this favour from you, which may raise me a greater fortune than yet I have ever had, I leave your worship the safe protection of Almighty God.

Your poor and humble suppliant and kinsman,
John Carter
Southwark, this 25 day of April 1622
(Son of Lady Mary's father, Ralph Hawtrey's sister, Elizabeth)

P.S.—I would desire your worship not to be offended that I do write to you and not come and speak with you myself, for it is not any pride or presumption that prompts me to it, but only that I cannot so well declare my mind to you by my words as by writing.

CHAPTER FOURTEEN

"...the spring, the summer, The chilling autumn, angry winter change Their wanted liveries, and the mazed world by their increase, now knows not which is which."
Shakespeare, As You Like It
1625—1635

On 27 March 1625, King James died. Leaving our land in growing turmoil following his seventeen-year tenure. My John was among those left trying to deal with his inept management of England's finances. King James's son, Charles I, succeeded him, and England, Scotland, and Ireland, entered a new era.

Fifteen-year-old Henrietta Maria, a devout Roman Catholic, married Charles at Notre Dame in Paris by proxy on 1 May 1625, shortly after he acceded to the throne. Many in Parliament, of course, were deeply offended by her Roman Catholic faith. Her huge dowry, however, was greatly welcomed by all. The Puritans in Parliament were outraged when they learned King Charles had promised to allow Henrietta to practice her religion freely and that she was to have full responsibility for the upbringing of their children until they reached the age of thirteen. When the new king was crowned on February 2, 1626, at Westminster Abbey, Henrietta was not there, refusing to participate in a "Protestant" religious ceremony.

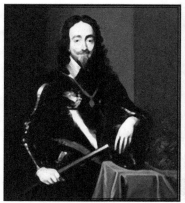 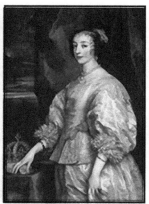

King Charles I, 1635　　　*Queen Henrietta Maria, 1632*
Both portraits by Anthony Van Dyck

It is now 1629. My dearest ones are all gathering at wonderful Mark Hall Manor. A flash of *deja vu* overwhelms me. Aunt Joane, 'Her Ladyship', Mair-Mair, and Clodagh busy their hands with the ever-present embroidery as we all visit. The latest Canute slumbers at my feet. My cousin, Joan, fifteen (Aunt Joane's eldest daughter), bends over the cradle of our wonderful new baby, Joanne, cooing and teasing dimples into her rosy cheeks. (Baby Joanne was, of course, named for both her saucy Great-Aunt Joane and Aunt Joane's equally pert blond daughter, Joan.)

Clodagh also remembers that long ago day when she was twelve and I ten and we both marveled at another tiny baby in this same drawing-room in this same family cradle. She winks at me and says, "We've done this before."

It suddenly strikes me! That long-ago baby, sweet daughter of my late Uncle James and his sternly Puritan wife, had been named Johanna. Also, a namesake for this new tiny bundle of Joanne who has invaded my heart. I do a quick calculation. Uncle James's Johanna would now be twenty. How could that happen? I resolve to send this long-lost cousin a letter giving her news of those in her Altham heritage and especially, of this newest darling arrival who also bears a version of her name. I had heard this lovely young heiress had married earlier this year, reportedly despite the opposition of some in her family, to an up and coming, brash young lawyer, Oliver St. John (you say it s*injin*).

Noisy children play outside while we await the arrival of our men from Gray's Inn. The little ones scream with delight as they chase the amazing new gift sent by Emmanuel, who has now sailed to a faraway land called Mauritius. It is called a Dodo Bird and runs with a jaunty, audacious gait that makes everyone laugh.

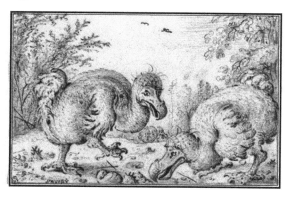

Sketch by early ornithologist Roeland Savery of two (soon to be extinct) dodos from c. 1626, Crocker Art Gallery

We all continued to read and re-read the latest letter to Uncle Edward from Emmanuel that had accompanied the Dodo Bird, along with other gifts from distant lands.

Right…loving brother, we were ordered by ye said councell to go to an island called Mauritius, lying in 20d. of south latt., where we arrived ye 28th of May [1628]; this island having many goates, hogs and cowes upon it, and very strange fowles, called by ye portingalls [Portuguese sailors] *Dodo, which for the rareness of the same, the like being not in ye world but here, I have sent you one by Mr. Perce, who did arrive with the ship William at this island ye 10th of June. Of Mr. Perce you shall receive a jarr of ginger for my sister* [Mair Mair!]*, some beades for my cousins your daughters, and a bird called a Dodo, if it live.*

The noise level of the children peaked, bringing me back to the present, as the three most adored men in my life—my husband, my father, and my uncle (not counting my then three-year-old son, John, of course!)—galloped into the courtyard.

Conversation around the dinner table was made even livelier by the fact that my John was just awarded yet another, rare accolade while at Gray's Inn—he had been named as a "Bencher," a step above that of honored "Reader" or acclaimed senior lecturer for Gray's Inn.

The discussion eventually turned—no big surprise—to the politics of the day. King Charles had recently dissolved Parliament and ruled by himself without consent of Parliament, which he would do for the next 11 years. My John was seated as a Member of Parliament for Morpeth in 1626 and served until being dismissed by King Charles along with the rest of Parliament in 1629. None of the men at the dinner table supported the king in this arbitrary action. This was countered by their wariness of the threat to overall peace and stability imposed by the increasingly clamorous Puritan factions. All were aghast that the king was abandoning the long tradition of input from the people he ruled, no matter how unruly or distasteful.

One thing led to another. Eventually, we were re-hashing life in the kingdom since the death of King James. And of the even more recent and scandalous death of the Duke of Buckingham, George Villiers.

"The whole business with that beyond handsome Duke of Buckingham, was so troubling," said 'Her Ladyship,' sapphire eyes flashing.

"Everyone was uncomfortable with his seemingly undue influence over King James," replied Uncle Edward.

"Best not discuss at this table just how he got that influence," was Father's gruff input, with a meaningful glance at the younger ones at the foot of the table.

"John and I saw him dance for King James," I said, trying not to be overly 'arch,' "but how did he come to have so much influence over King Charles?"

"There is so much gossip it is hard to know what is really true." I could tell my always discreet John was uncomfortable with where this conversation was heading—and sided with his father-in-law in trying to alter the course of the discussion.

Uncle Edward and Aunt Joane's fifteen-year-old Joan, bright golden curls bouncing, jumped in. "It did seem so romantic when the duke secretly took Prince Charles to Spain to try to win the hand of the beautiful Infanta Maria Ana."

"But my darling daughter, they both absolutely bungled it. And made a laughingstock of all of England in the process," admonished her mother. "Especially when the Spanish princess made it publicly and abundantly clear how much she detested our Prince Charles."

Uncle Edward intervened. "Of course, Buckingham's blundering and offensive comments led to the total collapse of the marriage negotiations. The Spanish Ambassador demanded that Parliament order the execution of Buckingham for his offensive behavior in Madrid. Then, of course, our newly crowned King Charles felt compelled to declare war on Spain."

"Without benefit of Parliament, of course." This from my husband, the now former Member of Parliament. King

Charles in fact, dismissed Parliament in a tizzy when they had instigated proceedings to impeach the ever-outrageous Duke of Buckingham. My "by the book" and straightlaced husband, had of course, for the moment, contrived to maintain good relations with both the Parliamentary and Royalist factions.

Uncle Edward chortled. "The Duke of Buckingham was such a dunderhead in even thinking he could lead a fleet of unseasoned English sailors to Cadiz to intercept Spain's experience-hardened crews who were bringing back treasure from South America. England's troops, forced to go ashore in Cadiz to find food, because they were so ill-provisioned, became so drunk they could barely stagger back to their ships. They came home in absolute disgrace."

"That was atrocious enough," added Father, "but then our king allowed the thoroughly incompetent duke to lead 100 of England's ships in attacking French forces. We needlessly lost more than 4,000 out of 7,000 brave English forces. Outrageous!"

"Don't forget—Parliament did attempt to impeach Buckingham before King Charles came to his rescue and dismissed Parliament," my husband said.

"It does seem that the infamous duke was overall a thorough scoundrel, no matter how charming. But still sad that he was ultimately murdered, as a result of his ill-conceived military escapades, by a disgruntled naval officer," Mair-Mair murmured.

"I notice King Charles had no compunctions about marrying a Roman Catholic French princess, or in cozying up and attempting to fill his empty coffers from the treasure chests of devoutly Roman Catholic countries," Clodagh said—increasingly emboldened by the reality that she no longer had her mother or Grandmother Altham to censor her words. It had not escaped Clodagh's notice that King Charles was trending toward an increasingly pro-Catholic attitude and was intent on relaxing many anti-Catholic punitive laws. This, of course, enraged the "Puritan" leaning Parliament, bent on "purifying" the Church from any "taint" of Catholicism. My "moderately" inclined husband balanced precariously between the two mutually exclusive ideologies, alternately attracting the affections and abhorrence of both sides.

Mair-Mair gave Clodagh a quick hug and deftly changed the subject. "Let's have some of Cook's lovely pudding," she ordered. The always adoring staff at Mark Hall, of course, again "jumped to" at the words of the legendary and forever loved former daughter of Mark Hall Manor.

Politics, naturally, continued to dominate the discussion after we retired to the drawing room. "With the Duke of Buckingham no longer stirring up trouble, we still must deal with the infamous duke's very close ally, the Archbishop of Canterbury," worried my father.

I still missed Grandmother Altham's biting observations. In my mind's ear I could hear her response, "Close ally, my foot!" The gossip of the day was that the sanctimonious Archbishop of Canterbury might also have succumbed, at least in his secret heart, to the seductive, forbidden, ever enticing allure of the ever-beguiling Duke of Buckingham.

Uncle Edward agreed with Father. "The most reverend and right honorable William Laud seems to take great pleasure in dreaming up new ways to stir up and offend the Puritans. Surely there are reasonable ways to allow those with Calvinistic leanings to co-exist with the rest of us."

My usually thoughtful and vocal John didn't add anything to the conversation, but I was struck by how worried he looked. "Laudianism" was soon to become something of an epithet as we all despaired against the open antagonism and scorn the archbishop imposed against the increasingly outraged

Puritans. Indeed (according to my John's later expressed opinions), Laud's peevish moods and obsession with points of ritual deliberately (with the full support of King Charles) provoked much of the disastrous discord that was to come.

During this politically troubling decade my ever-growing family flourished. Baby Ralph joined us in 1631. I basked in the delights of my expanding brood. Yes, I relished (albeit a bit guiltily) the many luxuries provided by John's flourishing law practice. He remained bonded close in heart with Father and Mair-Mair. There were also many lively and blissful family visits with Uncle Edward and 'Her Ladyship.' During these exuberant years with our growing children our families remained close.

In 1630, John was appointed by King Charles I as Attorney General to his son, the infant Prince Charles II. In retrospect, should that not have been honor enough? It does no good to fantasize about what "might" have happened had my John not become so closely aligned with King Charles I, but the thoughts persist. Had he not accepted the increasingly prominent leadership roles thrust upon him, might I have kept him by my side for more precious moments?

John's accolades continued to pile ever up and up. He maintained his close relationship with Gray's Inn. In 1630, he was named as Lent Reader. In 1631, he was honored as a "Bencher" for his contributions to the life of the Inn and to the law. He served as Treasurer to Gray's Inn from 1631 to 1635.

Most significantly for our whole family in 1631—King Charles himself knighted John in a lovely ceremony at St. James's Whitehall Palace on 5 June. I was now, officially, by default, a "Dame!" (Although I much preferred the title, "Lady Mary.")

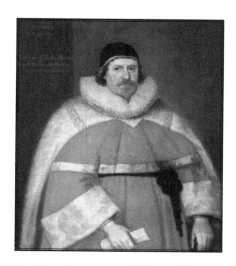

Sir John Bankes, portrait by Gilbert Jackson
National Trust Images

A crushing ending during this interim period was the sudden loss on 28 May 1632 of my dear Uncle Edward after a brief illness. The entire family sorrowed—my heart forever stricken. No family gathering would ever be the same without his mischievous teasing, his merry baritone, his hearty laugh and all the ways he was "there" for our entire family. Who now would shore up our hearts when we were sad, or make us laugh at comic antics? His adoring and grief-stricken family erected an elaborate marble monument in his memory at St. Mary at Latton Church.

The King's demands on my husband did not abate during this time of grief. That same year King Charles appointed a Council of Superintendents over Virginia in the New World. John was one of the commissioners responsible for overseeing this ambitious venture in service to the King. That was when we met most dear kindred spirits—whose friendship would sustain us in the trying times ahead. Sir Dudley Digges was also a Knight and a fellow "Bencher" at Gray's Inn. He and John had been passing acquaintances for years. King Charles also appointed Sir Digges as a commissioner to the Council of Superintendents over Virginia in the New World. My John and Sir Dudley soon found themselves in the course of these duties to be not only fellow voices of moderation and reason in an increasingly fractured government, but valued friends and allies. He and his sweet wife, also a Mary, were a little older than my John and me, but we valued their friendship and often socialized with them at mandatory functions of King Charles's court. Their younger children were generally of an age with our older children. I treasured her tranquility and calm and tips on child-rearing in our fast-paced world. Their second son, Edward Digges, eventually became Colonial Governor of Virginia in the New World (a much loved and trusted family connection.)

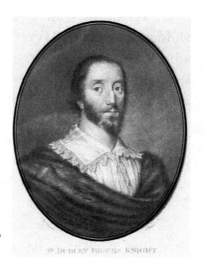

Sir Dudley Digges,
National Portrait Gallery,
UK English diplomat and politician.
Sat in the House of Commons between
1610 and 1629.
Invested heavily in the Virginia Company
of London. Son, Edward Digges, became
Governor of Virginia in the "Colonies."
Did this long-time family friend help rescue
the youngest Bankes son from youthful folly?

Our sweet baby Jane also diverted us from our ongoing grief following the death of my Uncle Edward. A most welcome new beginning, she joined us in 1633. Our ever-growing brood now numbered seven.

With printing presses now handy, pamphlets exploded into our daily reality, inflaming, rightly or wrongly, the opinions of the masses—becoming devastating political weapons, true or not. These pamphlets fearlessly attacked the bishops of the Church of England. The bishops responded by claiming the pamphleteers had overstepped all boundaries and infringed on royal prerogative. In those days the Church and State were intertwined. Any criticism of the bishops of the Anglican Church automatically translated as an attack on the king.

Sometime in 1633, John brought with him from London a particularly vicious pamphlet written by no less than a fellow lawyer, who was also a militantly zealous Puritan—William Prynne. The pamphlet strongly criticized parties, masquerade balls, fairs, mixed dancing, feast days, and many more customarily entertaining activities. In particular, Prynne condemned all theatrical performances and those responsible for them. He claimed they were "…the chief delight of the Devil… immoral displays of debauchery…filled with amorous smiles and wanton gestures, lascivious complements, lewd, adulterous kisses and embraces, lustful dalliances…they are the very schools of bawdery, real whoredoms, incests, adulteries, etc." As to those who regularly attend the theatre, he condemned them as "…adulterers, whoremasters, bawds, panders…profane and godless persons." His disparaging words extended to actors and actresses, cursing the male actors as "Sodomites" and actresses as "Notorious whores."

Mair-Mair, who was with us visiting her grandbabies, laughed when she read the vicious diatribe. "My gracious, what a lot of naughty words. My mother would have washed my mouth with soap for just thinking them. I know another woman who is sure not to be pleased with these complaints! Everyone knows how fond Queen Henrietta is of her "theatre." I do believe I heard that she is planning another of her galas in the near future in which she actually wears a costume and has lines to recite…which I presume could define her as an 'actress.'"

Mair-Mair was right. Queen Henrietta was not pleased. Which meant King Charles and his top religious leader, the infamous Archbishop Laud, were not pleased. Prynne was charged with "seditious libel" against the queen and others and found guilty. He was fined 5,000 pounds, stripped of his academic degrees, given two days in the pillory, and sentenced to have the tops of his ears cut off with shears. While he was in the pillory, hundreds of copies of his pamphlet were gathered up and burned while he watched. He was then imprisoned for life in the Tower of London.

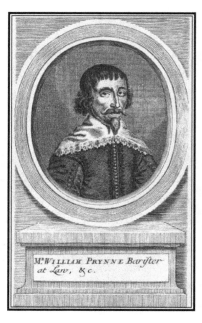

Sir William Prynne, English lawyer. Imprisoned for his scathing, wildly popular pamphlets criticizing the king. Credited with pioneering the idea of freedom of the press. On display at National Galleries, Scotland.

September 1634 saw my husband's highest accolade to date—he became Attorney-General to King Charles. My John was well known for keeping his scholarly legal arguments void of political expediency and based only on the legal merits. He sided often with causes of the Royalists, but just as often with issues of many Parliamentarians. For the moment, he had the cautious trust of both sides of the emerging opposing political forces. Archbishop Laud, wanting to impose mandatory autocratic domination of the political scene, argued passionately against the selection of John as the top legal advisor to the King, but was overruled. It was said of my darling at the time of his appointment that "—he exceeds Bacon in eloquence, Chancellor Ellesmere in judgment, and William Noy in law."

At my insistence our family moved permanently from Lincolnshire back to John's London estate. I missed him terribly when he was not with us and the two-day round trip to see us was taking its toll, along with his ever-increasing responsibilities. We needed more time together and there was only one way to make that happen. Besides, I thought— remembering the earlier cruel effects of London's foul air—We already have enough children. (Ha!)

John continued to drive himself hard. Freed from the lengthy round trip by galloping horse (or bouncing carriage) to see us, he delighted in spending more time with his all too quickly growing children.

The money continued to flow in. I kept a close eye on our finances, of course, but now had a highly qualified manager to oversee most of the more tedious bookwork. In a word, the humble merchant's son from the faraway, inauspicious town of Keswick, was now officially "wealthy," by any standard.

The vile London air had not improved. I suffered another miscarriage. John's dismay and grief at yet another loss matched my own.

Linda Sindt

AUTHOR ENDNOTES, CHAPTER FOURTEEN: *With
the invasion of adventuring sailors from several parts of the world
into Mauritius, the fragile, interdependent eco-system was quickly
overwhelmed and the Dodo Bird, along with several other species
were soon extinct.*

*In 1844 in Alexandre Dumas's famed "Three Musketeers," a
fictionalized Buckingham starred as one of the characters. Dumas
wrote, "At thirty-five, which was then his age, he passed...for the
handsomest gentleman and the most elegant cavalier of France or
England. The favourite of two kings, immensely rich, all-powerful
in a kingdom which he disordered at his fancy and calmed again at
his caprice, George Villiers, Duke of Buckingham, had lived one of
those fabulous existences which survive, in the course of centuries, to
astonish posterity."*

CHAPTER FIFTEEN

"This Castle hath a pleasant seat; the air nimbly and sweetly recommends itself unto our gentle senses."
Shakespeare, Macbeth
1635

My John (most mysteriously) beamed for weeks. His London work demands remained onerous. Yet, he disappeared for days at a time on mysterious missions to an undisclosed location. We, his adoring family, were not invited to accompany him. Try as we might, his children and I could not worm from him the secret of these uncharacteristic disappearances. He could not, however, repress the merry twinkle in his bright blue eyes. Never could we have guessed the surprise that awaited us.

It was late April. I longed for the fresh Spring air and blooming flowers of my childhood home. The always dank London air did not smell of Spring. And then, at long last, my darling surprised us with the news that we were all going on a fortnight vacation in late April to a surreptitious location. And my John was going to be with us, his adoring family, exclusively, for the entire two weeks. A parade of carriages and horses were made ready. John would only hint that the ocean would not be too far away. The children and their tutor tried to puzzle out on various maps of England just where our mysterious destination could possibly be. Sir John himself just beamed enigmatically, reddish curls bouncing above bright blue eyes, as he oversaw our happy preparations. Even I, his devoted wife, could not tease out the surprise that awaited. I did rejoice in this most welcome distraction from the tedious burdens of the law that typically purloined away his time.

At last, the long-awaited day arrived. We headed south. Alice, then fourteen (how did that happen so quickly!) and her "twin," Mary, already an also too grown-up twelve, "almost thirteen," joined their father and me in one carriage along with nine-year-old John. Ralph, four, (my dear father's namesake, of course), Elizabeth, eight, and Joanna, six, along with two-year-old baby Jane, followed in a separate carriage and were delighted to be entertained on the journey by their much adored "Aunt Clodagh."

The day grew warmer. We delighted in the sweet air and dazzling spring sky. Our caravan stopped near the road for a merry picnic, packed by Cook, below a ruined castle at Southampton. The sea sparkled nearby. A salty breeze crinkled our noses. Our children romped, shouting and laughing, in the seagrass and sunshine.

Not long after our seaside picnic, the racket of wheels on cobblestone streets assaulted our ears as we entered an ancient village. We had gone inland a bit from the ocean, but whiffs of briny sea air trailed after us. Woolly clouds frisked in the shimmering air above. It struck us a bit odd that no woolly lambs frisked in the passing sun-dazzled meadows. Sir John informed us we were now on the "Isle of Purbeck" in Dorset.

"How did we get on an Isle?" asked our precocious son, John. "We have never passed over any water."

"Excellent observation." His father beamed. "It is not really an island at all, but a long, very narrow peninsula. It is just called an Island."

My husband's delighted grin set my heart dancing. He had seemed so long distracted from his devoted family by the demands of England's legal worries. I smiled to see him so relaxed and happy. He soon pointed out the window of our carriage at a huge castle that loomed on the hill above the village. Astonishingly we did not stop at the village but passed over the moat and through the lower gates and proceeded up the hill to the towering castle. The gurgling croaks of flocks of ravens who nestled in the high reaches of the castle welcomed us.

The children were agog as they scrambled out of the carriages when we finally stopped. "Father, do we get to have our vacation in a castle? This is so amazing," cried nine-year-old John.

His father responded, "You don't have that quite right, my son." He dramatically reached into the satchel he carried and pulled out a ring of very large, very old keys. Bowing at the waist, and then ridiculously, dropping to one knee, he dramatically handed the ring of keys to Corfe Castle over—to me.

"Madame, welcome to Corfe Castle—your new home." He broadly beamed.

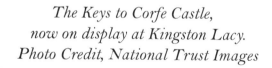

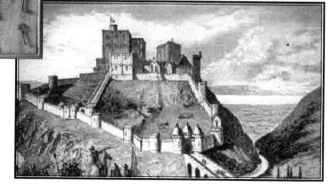

The Keys to Corfe Castle,
now on display at Kingston Lacy.
Photo Credit, National Trust Images

There was a moment of shocked silence. Then all pandemonium erupted as our children shouted questions at their beaming father.

"I want to see my room."

"Are there ghosts?"

"Can Mair–Mair and Grandfather visit us here?"

"Are there any children in the village for us to play with?"

I, too, had plenty to say, but was saving my comments for the later privacy of our bedroom. Had my genius husband completely lost his mind?

We toured the Inner Ward, where the living quarters of the castle were located, and then gathered in the elegant Hall for the welcoming dinner prepared by the castle staff. I could not help but note the gaunt appearance and worn clothing of the small staff who served us. The meal, while carefully prepared, was a bit sparse compared to the plenty to which we were accustomed.

John related a little of the history of the centuries-old Castle.

"It once belonged to Queen Elizabeth. She 'sold' it to one of her favored courtiers, a Christopher Hatton." He winked at me. "I understand he could dance very well."

I darted a warning glance at my dearest. What was it with monarchs of England and handsome young courtiers who can dance well? And were our innocent young babies old enough to hear of such tales?

My Love tormented me by continuing with this bordering on salacious tale.

"She gave him many more great treasures of the realm and named him her "Lord Chief Chancellor," the highest position in the land next to the queen."

John continued with his narrative to our children about Corfe Castle.

"Sir Hatton spent a small fortune restoring and improving the castle and making it a prestigious home with the fine furnishings, tapestries and silks that you see here today. The late Sir Coke's widow seldom enjoyed her castle and recently found herself in need of added funds. Since she never had any interest in actually living in Corfe Castle," said my beaming spouse, "I was able to purchase this wonderful castle for our family for practically nothing. Indeed, we now own the entire 'Isle of Purbeck,' which is not, as mentioned earlier, an actual island, but a very narrow, sea-surrounded, peninsula."

"Not the same Sir Edward Coke who was England's former Attorney General who presided over the Dr. Bonham case so many years ago?" I asked. "The one who earlier ordered the severe punishment of those who plotted to blow up King James?"

"The very one," England's current Attorney General replied.

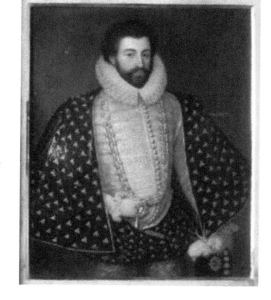

Sir Christopher Hatton,
National Trust,
Artist William Henry Mote

Photo Credit, National Trust
Images

Later that night, when our children were safely tucked in their beds, we sat in our private quarters in a cozy sitting room just outside our bedroom door. A fire in a charming little fireplace warmed the chill. I "examined" my lawyer spouse as to just how much "practically nothing" was.

"The cost was not so much," John assured me. "As castles go, Corfe Castle seemed a bargain."

"But I thought we agreed we no longer wanted to be parted for such a distance, I cried.

My husband argued back. "You can't deny our lovely castle is nearer to London than Lincolnshire and the road is much better. I can now more easily and quickly travel by carriage with a driver and several horses to speed things up and I'll be able to work as I travel."

I continued the quarrel. "I know your practice has already been eminently successful, but are you taking into account that we have to date five daughters to endow with generous Bride's Portions and two sons, so far, to provide for?

"And possibly even more than that in the not too distant future?" My husband tightened the arm that I nestled into and planted a tender kiss on the top of my head.

From above the fireplace the portrait of an incredibly handsome, youthful, gentleman, resplendent with much gold gazed down at us.

"I presume that is the erstwhile Lord Hatton?" I asked. "The former Lord Chancellor of England? Who was second in command in all our land only to Queen Elizabeth herself? Who gave him this castle that we have just bought?"

"Ah, that reminds me!" John stood and retrieved a packet of what looked to be yellowed, very old papers from a nearby chest. "Wait until you hear this!" Written by the Lord Chief Chancellor to the Queen herself!"

He read the words aloud. "My spirit I feel, agreeth with my body and life that to serve you is a heaven, but to lack you is more than hell's torment unto them. Would God I were with you but for one hour. My wits are overwrought with thoughts. I find myself amazed. Bear with me, my most dear sweet Lady. Passion overcometh me. I can write no more. Love me, for I love you."

I grabbed the fragile letter from my husband's hand. "He signs himself her 'most happy bondman, Lyddes.'" I said.

My husband grinned down at me. "It is noted that the queen herself called Sir Hatton her "mutton," her "bellwether," her "pecora campi."

"What do you think?" he asked. "Were they lovers?"

"That is none of our business,' I said, firmly.

My John snuffed out the candle by our sofa and led me into the bedroom.

"I wonder if Queen Elizabeth ever accompanied him to Corfe Castle?" I asked.

My husband again kissed the top of my head as we approached our bed.

"To quote my darling wife, that is indeed none of our business!"

I forgot the gist of all my arguments when my husband sweetly engulfed me in his arms. I think I may have murmured," My Mutton."

I was tickled awake the next morning. Of course my dearest did not forget to tuck in Namontack's feather from the New World that I superstitiously kept by my bed. However, this time he did not have more snuggling in mind.

"Awake my darling. It is Sunday. We don't want to be late for church."

We did not have far to go. We could look down on the roof of the church just below the Castle.

A stooped, diminutive man with wispy white hair and an obviously worn, but scrupulously clean surplice, paced in the doorway. His worried demeanor transformed into beaming smiles as he noted our family's parade toward the church. He trotted out, albeit a bit unsteadily, to greet us. Just how old was our diminutive new vicar?

"Ah, I was so hoping you'd join us," he cried out. "It is far too long since our congregation has had residents from Corfe Castle in our midst." His voice cracked and a tooth was missing from his aging smile. "Welcome, welcome."

He ushered our family ceremonially to the front of the church. The already gathered congregation stood in the rear as the pint-sized vicar led us all through the comforting litanies of worship. At the close, he curiously dismissed the rear of the congregation first. The purpose soon became clear. They raggedly lined up outside the door to the church, bowed their heads, and whispered shy words of welcome to us as we passed by them on our departure in our elegant London apparel. It was impossible not to notice their haggard appearance and shabby clothing. When we drew to the end of the line of humbly welcoming parishioners, led by the beaming vicar, the "Mair-Mair" in me finally kicked in.

"Our dear friend," I queried. "We are positively delighted to be with you on this lovely day. We would be most blessed if you would accompany us to the castle for our mid-day meal."

Our new religious leader looked as if he might weep in relief. "It would be my absolute pleasure."

The same few attendants who had provided our meal the night before served our Sunday midday repast. They looked weary. Did I previously say gaunt? I mentally noted to ask Clodagh to find out more about them. And about any other staff who might now be in our employ.

As we made more intimate family introductions, eight-year-old Elizabeth, our avid reader and always challenging inquisitor (surely, she got that trait from her father?) piped up.

"So why is the Corfe Castle Church named Saint Edward

King and Martyr? Who was he? I don't understand how he can be a saint and a king and a martyr all at the same time."

"What a wonderful question!"

Storytelling is, of course, a gift of any vicar worth his surplice. And so, he told us the ancient tale of the horrendous deeds that led to the name of his lovely church. He promised us it was a true story and we all believed him.

"Born seven centuries ago, it is guessed around the year 962. King Edward was the oldest son of King Edgar the Peaceable. King Edward's mother died when he was still young. His father later married AElfryth, who became his queen. Their son, AEthelred, was born in 968—about six years later. When Edward was only thirteen his father died. Edward became the rightful king. His stepmother, AElfryth was enraged. She wanted her much younger son, AEthelred, to be king. King Edward forgave his stepmother for her opposition to his reign. He settled his stepmother and his young half-brother into the first castle, then made of wood, on this very site.

When young Edward was sixteen, he stopped in at this wooden castle on the site where Corfe Castle now stands for a visit with his half-brother. A small band of men accompanied him. His stepmother met him at the gate of the old Saxon castle that preceded the Corfe Castle we now know and offered her stepson a drink to quench his thirst after a long ride. And then she—according to the legend—personally stabbed her stepson in his back as he drank. Thus, he became a martyr. The story goes that the young King Edward's stepmother first hid his body in the home of a blind woman. When the woman discovered the body her sight returned—the first of many miracles attributed to the dead young king. It is said that the church now stands on the site of the formerly blind woman's house.

After a period of investigation when it was considered

whether her son, AEthelred, was the rightful heir to the throne, AEthelred (also known as "Ethelred the Unready") was ultimately crowned as king. The late, teenaged, King Edward became revered as a saint and martyr. AEthelred himself championed his brother's memory, moving his bones to a new shrine at Shaftesbury Abbey in 1001. A grant that year to Shaftesbury Abbey, stated that the gift was being made to God and to "his saint, my brother Edward, whom drenched with his own blood, the Lord has seen fit to magnify in our time through many miracles."

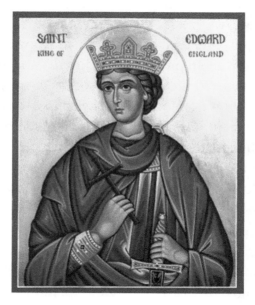

Edward the Martyr, King of England, bing.com

All right, then—I wasn't sure I wanted to hear any more tales of terror about our ancient new home.

Nine-year-old son, John, of course, gloried in the gory account. "Wow, 700 years ago. What happened after that?"

"Soon after," continued the vicar, "England was overwhelmed by the Norman invasion of William the

Conqueror. He recognized the strategic importance of this location and rebuilt the castle into a pretty much impenetrable fortress as you more or less see it today, taking advantage of the Purbeck marble and limestone in this area. It has had, as you can imagine, a checkered history over the years."

He again warmed to his tales of terror and villainy surrounding our new home. "Corfe Castle has been for most of its life a favored residence for England's Royalty—especially John, brother of "Richard the Lionheart," who made it his home, treasury, and prison. Wanting to consolidate his power in the third year of his reign, King John used Corfe to imprison his politically suspect niece, Eleanor, the sister of John's rival, Prince Arthur of Brittany. King John imprisoned twenty-five French knights loyal to Lady Eleanor at Corfe Castle. When they tried to escape, twenty-two of the knights were re-captured. The vindictive king locked them in the Corfe Castle dungeon, and they starved to death."

In a whisper, our esteemed Vicar added. "Some say the moans of the starving knights can be heard in the dungeons today."

I could not help glancing around the table for the reactions of my "babies" to this new horror story. Son, John, of course, was rapt.

"I can't wait to see the dungeon," he declared.

"Totally and absolutely off limits," ordered his father. "After so many years it is much decayed and not safe and has long been sealed off."

I introduced Clodagh as my "sister." Intuitive as ever, she deftly turned the conversation. "Tell us about your parishioners—what do they do to support themselves?"

Our new friend looked embarrassed and a little sad. "I am afraid our little village has been suffering for many years. When Corfe Castle was maintained as a royal castle there was income for many. When Sir Hatton acquired it, he also invested in many improvements and relied on our local workmen to make them happen, so they were again well employed. He even fortified it with the cannons you see today when the Spanish Armada threatened the forces of Queen Elizabeth so many years ago. Since he died there has been little interest by his heirs in Corfe Castle. There has been only a small caretaking staff. And their future remains in your hands."

"Well, of course we shall see they are well compensated," assured my husband.

"Oh, my dear sir, I was certain of that. Nay, the problem is a bit more troubling in the current political climate. There is work to be found in our neighboring Parishes. And even markets. But Corfe has always been a royal province and dedicated to the service of the reigning king or queen. Because of that loyalty, we are now something of a pariah by our fiercely Puritan neighbors. Most of the surrounding Dorset parishes are aligned with the Parliamentarians who now so ferociously oppose King Charles's financial demands.

"Several years ago, when King Charles dissolved Parliament, he attempted to shore up his income by imposing forced loans from the 'Gentry.' Sir Walter Erle, from nearby Charborough, is a most outspoken foe. He refused to pay this 'loan.' King Charles ordered that he be imprisoned for a year. Sir Walter finally got a court to hear his claim of unlawful imprisonment and a sympathetic judge released him. I fear Sir Walter Erle is one of the most fanatical of the Puritan factions within our larger church community. He especially despises the archbishop Laud and all the new rules of worship he has imposed." Our elfin, ancient vicar, paused. "Even I find many of the edicts of the archbishop annoying, and often outrageous in unnecessarily stirring up divisions in our religious community."

I refrained from assuring the dear man that our family also bore little affection for Archbishop Laud, who had so outspokenly opposed my John's appointment by King Charles as Attorney General. But then, our family absolutely did not support the stern and cold-hearted, puritanically dominant Parliament who wanted to deny Christmas to everyone in our world.

I cast an anxious glance at John. Did this darling, diminutive leader of the religious community in our new home expect our family to now singlehandedly provide financial support and jobs for an entire village?

"I sense you might have some suggestions for how we might best lend backing to these villagers who will now be our neighbors?" my husband ventured.

"Well, no guarantees, but I might have a few suggestions." A timid, if hopeful, gap-toothed smile illuminated our vicar's elfin face. He then proceeded to cast us under his spell and give us our marching orders. Clodagh later confided to me he evoked the magical leprechauns her mother had so often described in her tales of Ireland.

"None of these neighbors are going to welcome the fact of your position as Attorney General to King Charles. However, it is also well known that you now control all Manorial rights to Corfe Castle, including some of the best hunting forests in all of Dorset. And that might be the key." His look was anxious.

He sipped his ale, and continued, "For many years on the first day of May it was the tradition that the Gentry from the lands surrounding Corfe Castle were invited to an annual May Day hunt in the forests that belong to Corfe Castle. Of course, the wives and even the older children were all invited. It was a lovely, much-anticipated gathering."

"Oh, I don't think I could kill a deer, but the ride would

be exciting! I am glad I brought my riding trousers!" our fourteen-year-old-Alice chimed in.

"I have never learned the civilities of hunting, nor I believe, has my wife. Is there anyone who can guide us in the protocols?" my husband asked, a bit timidly.

A relieved smile brightened the vicar's face. "Of course, there are several villagers who are well-schooled in this sport. They can even ride with you and your party on the day of the hunt. My goodness, it has been so long since the villagers had red meat. It will be a lovely treat for them."

"I don't understand," I said.

"Oh, my Lady, it is the long tradition that a deer from the hunt is given to the villagers to share."

"But if they are hungry, why don't they just go hunt for themselves?"

"Oh, my goodness, no! To hunt in the royal forests is strictly forbidden on the threat of absolute pain of death!"

"Well, my John will certainly will give anyone in our Village who is hungry permission to use our forest!"

"Dear Lady Mary, you are so tender-hearted and generous, but I wonder if that might not be a mistake. It could encourage others in nearby villages who are not so desperate as those in Corfe Castle, to also harvest meals from the forest and the game would soon be depleted."

John's legal mind, of course, clicked in. "What if I provide a written order appointing a specific trusted villager as my forest manager, and giving him, and him only, the authority to selectively permit thinning of the herd as necessary to keep it from becoming over-populated?"

Our guest beamed. "And perhaps occasional hares and pheasants, also, as necessary?" he negotiated.

The vicar hesitated, a bit apologetically. "Will you bring your household staff from London, or perhaps employ some from the village?"

John and I exchanged glances. There was so much we had not had time to discuss since his huge surprise of an enormous castle the previous evening. He shrugged, turning this decision over to me. I raised my eyebrows at Clodagh, the one who would oversee such potential staff. She also lifted her shoulders into a consenting shrug.

"Well, of course," I heard myself reply. "John will be maintaining a full household in London. We'll bring some of our closest staff with us, if they are willing, and, of course, tutors as necessary for the children, but yes, we will indeed need extra help from the villagers. Can we count on your aid in identifying the ones best suited to specific jobs?"

I could not believe I had just heard those words coming out of my mouth. I glanced at John suspiciously. Had he engineered this? How could I have just tacitly agreed to his outrageous plot to again send me away from London? And also from him. Even with the most loving intentions. I hated living apart from my husband.

And then the conversation turned to plans for the coming hunt and our schemes to try to win over a harmonious relationship with our ill-disposed new neighbors. Invitations went out the next day. All were encouraged to remain for a late midday meal following the morning hunt. Clodagh was already planning the menu and had zoomed in on the castle's lovely gardens as the perfect, informal setting for amicable discourse.

Clodagh, who shared my love of riding, joined in the fun of our instruction in the correct comportment for a royal "hunt." All the children cantered along with us. We treasured this all too rare time of family togetherness. The latest Canute along with a pack of his greyhound brothers and sisters raced joyfully at our side, clearly in their element. The youngest four of our children would not join in the actual hunt, but my heart danced on that bright day as we trotted merrily all together through the sun-dappled forest, (all but three-year-old Jane, who remained in the nursery with her nanny), safely in my sight. Four-year-old Ralph bounced merrily in the saddle in front of his father, who clutched him tightly.

The day after our fateful meeting with Corfe Castle's ancient vicar, I sent a message to Mair-Mair and Father telling them of our crazy new acquisition and pleading with them to look through the closets of all in their household— men, women, and children—in search of any soon to be cast off clothing that might reappear as "new" garments on the backs of Corfe's threadbare villagers. Earlier in 1635, to raise money in the face of dwindling income, King Charles I allowed members of the public to pay his messengers to carry letters. This beginning of the Royal Mail greatly expedited communication throughout the kingdom.

On that lovely afternoon, when we returned to the castle from our day of exploration and hunting instruction in the enchanting forest, a grand surprise awaited. Mair-Mair and Father had arrived. Along with several carriages of supplies and sacks of castoff (but eminently reusable) clothing. Mair-Mair had even brought her favorite seamstress.

"My Darlings!" Mair-Mair exclaimed. "We decided to surprise you. Your own Castle! How could we possibly stay away? I want to see everything. I am sure you must have plenty of bedrooms. However, we brought our own pillows and sheets and blankets in case there are not yet enough."

"Oh, Mair-Mair and Father—how I have needed you. How did you know to come?" I melted into the embraces of my parents.

All too soon the day of the hunt arrived. Early in the morning the villagers, decked in their "new" clothes, arrived to set up the tables in the flower-graced garden for our post-hunt dining. Mair-Mair and Father declined to join in the hunt and stayed behind to entertain their youngest grandchildren, Elizabeth, eight, Joanne, six, Ralph, four, and Baby Jane. It was a bit questionable, as to whether son, John, then nine, was old enough for the "hunt," but no way would he have been left behind. We conceded to his demands. Oldest daughters, Alice, fourteen, and Mary, twelve, held their own when we eventually galloped into the lovely Corfe Castle Forest.

Our beaming, diminutive vicar bobbed welcomingly about prior to the hunt as guests arrived and as initial introductions were made. He nonchalantly ignored the openly hostile glances by several of the "Gentry" who were our guests. The weather was beyond perfect, and as we had practiced, the hunt proceeded without incident. A stag was duly brought down and with all required ceremonies everyone eventually returned to the castle and the festive garden repast Clodagh had inspired.

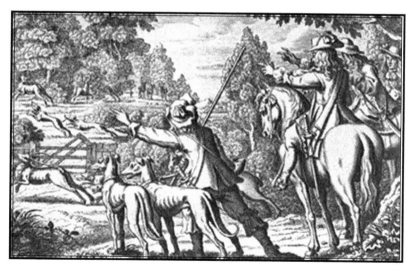

old print, Stag Hunt in Forest with Greyhounds print,
source unknown

Knowing there was no one on earth who could withstand Mair-Mair's magic, I deliberately seated her and Father across from the famously crotchety Sir Walter Erle and his wife. The meal seemed to go on forever. I kept a bright smile on my face as I attempted to converse with my dour neighbors. The wives did not seem to have much to say, deferring to their husbands. I prattled inanely about my children, the lovely weather, the breezes from the nearby sea. John looked utterly at ease. He sat several chairs away from me. I could not make out all his conversation. He seemed to be intently discussing…sheep? I could not help glancing at the end of the table where my parents were seated. Mair-Mair looked to be her usual lovely self, completely self-possessed, smiling and nodding and chattering. At last, the meal ended. John and I toured our stony guests through the main rooms of the castle before they departed.

"What an impossible, miserable, cantankerous old coot!" Mair-Mair collapsed on a couch in the library. "Your thoroughly obnoxious Sir Walter Erle never smiled once! He was positively rude to his own wife! How dare he call our worship idolatrous and popish—sorry darling, Clodagh—you know I would absolutely not belittle your faith for anything in this world. That is so not my intent. But this sorry excuse for 'Gentry' makes me want to—well—just shout! My wonderful son-in-law, I definitely need a glass of wine!" Indeed, she looked to be on the verge of weeping.

Sir John, of course, jumped to, bringing goblets for all. Father could only gaze at his famously sweet-tempered wife in astonishment.

Mair-Mair continued to sputter. "He actually *boasted* that his Puritan friends stole surplices worn by our revered church leaders and thrust them into a privy dung pit. He claimed surplices are "too popish" and have no place in church. And—and—he *bragged* that they threw buckets of pitch at altar hangings in our sacred cathedrals to destroy them. And he called Archbishop Laud the 'Antichrist.'"

Father responded placatingly, "Well, now, none of us is overly fond of Archbishop Laud, that's for sure. Especially since he was one of the few voices who argued so vehemently against King Charles's decision to appoint our John as Attorney General. And Laud does delight in unnecessarily stirring up of trouble, instead of working to make peace among the various factions of our Church family. His idea of confronting discord is to levy cruel punishments against any Calvinist-leaning Puritans who dare to oppose him. But I must say, my darling wife, you were truly beyond amazing in your performance this afternoon. No one could have detected how hostile you were feeling."

I hugged my always astounding mother and turned to John. "Did I overhear you talking about sheep? What was that all about?"

"That was your Father's idea," he said. "He mentioned that the outlying fields to the castle looked like excellent sheep pasture. Indeed, our neighbors confirm that all the lands that surround the castle were once inhabited by sheep when the castle belonged to the Crown. And shepherds from the village here were paid to look after them. The sheep were then bought by the surrounding villages for food and clothing, with the wages paid to them to raise the sheep. And then they traded sheep or wages for other food and goods they needed from nearby villages. However, the more recent owners of Corfe Castle have shown little interest in maintaining this investment and that industry has faded away—much to the detriment of the villagers of Corfe Castle."

The accountant in me was not sure there was any profit

for the current "Lord of the Manor" in this roundabout commercial endeavor, but I was already hooked. It seemed we were now not only the owners of a grand royal castle, but the patrons of a most needy village that was surrounded by hostile neighbors and a soon-to-be sheep farm!

For the next several years we lived peacefully, if not intimately, with our ideologically fanatical Dorset neighbors. After some trial and error on the part of the novice castle owners, mutton and wool and other goods from Corfe lands, bit by bit, wended their way into markets of the nearer villages. The by then well-fed Corfe Castle villagers blossomed and were no longer threadbare. And every year on the first day in May the neighboring (ever annoyingly condescending) Puritan "Gentry" jumped at the chance to join in the annual hunt we hosted in Corfe Castle's bountiful forest.

AUTHOR ENDNOTES, CHAPTER FIFTEEN: *Available records show that the then religious leader for the St. Edward King and Martyr Parish Church of Corfe Castle was a rector. I have chosen to portray him as a fictionalized, feisty vicar.*

CHAPTER SIXTEEN

"When sorrows come, they come not single spies,
but in battalions"
Shakespeare, Hamlet
1635 to 1638

Shortly after we arrived At Corfe Castle in late April 1635, it became apparent I was yet again with child. Our wonderful Jerome was on his way. There was now no way my John would ever consent to my returning, even briefly, to the poisonous air of London for many months to come.

Soon to be fifteen-year-old Alice was not happy in Corfe Castle. She missed the fun and excitement of London life. She missed her London friends. And if our oldest daughter was not happy, her eighteen months younger "almost twin" Mary was also, of course, not happy. Clodagh set about teaching them both all the skills I had never embraced—those of effectively managing an "upper Gentry" household. Naturally, they both readily breathed in the intricate skills of embroidery.

Clodagh, of course, had long ago committed the favorite family recipes to memory. My ever opinionated, outspoken oldest daughter (clearly blessed—or perhaps cursed—with her great-grandmother's brusque spunk) rebelled at having to remember so many recipes. "Why aren't they already all written down?" was her imperious demand. "It is not as if writing has not been invented."

"Well, indeed they should be all written down," I said. "And you should do it." And so, she did over the years.

The months sped by as we settled into our luxurious Castle. Oldest son, John, was ten, Elizabeth was nine, Joanne was seven, Ralph was five, and baby sister Jane was three. For the moment, all these younger ones, except Ralph and Baby Jane, shared one tutor in our Corfe Castle home. Our now dear vicar often stopped by, inserting always provocative, seemingly innocent questions into the thought processes of our budding scholars. Soon, he was inviting children from the village to sit in now and then. I became ever more immersed with the families that surrounded Corfe Castle.

True to his word, my John was with us frequently (although never as often or for as long as I wished). Not content with the lavish furnishings handed down by the infamous Sir Hatton during his tenure, my increasingly extravagant husband delighted in arriving with ever more luxuriant adornments, including big-ticket inlaid and upholstered furniture, Persian and Turkish carpets, velvet and damask cushions, a sizable library of rare and costly books, and important paintings by such leading artists as Van Dyck, Lely and more. He was determined in these refurbishings that his family should live from that time forward at the absolute height of fashion and comfort. At one point he arrived laden with cases of Plate—costly utensils and dining ware made of solid silver. I stamped my foot down. "But my darling John, we live in the country. We seldom entertain. And when we do, it is picnics, not banquets. We will soon be forced to hire armed guards just to watch over a bunch of things we will never actually use and don't even really care about."

I kept reminding myself this excessive extravagance was simply a delayed reaction to the long years of privation and indeed deep loneliness he endured for such a dreadfully long time. When he lived so far from those who loved him while he subjected himself to the isolation and rigors of the study of law.

And then my world again turned upside down. We reveled at having "The Lord of the Manor" with us at Corfe Castle even if only for just a few days. But the discussions since his arrival were breaking my heart. Possibly, the fact that our new baby was about to make an appearance did not enhance my emotional stability. It was time to set out a long-term plan for the proper continuing education for our precocious oldest son and heir. His perfectionist father, of course, demanded the ultimate best. He had found an amazing Tutor. An eminently successful and learned member of the Peerage had agreed to be our John's mentor in guiding his preparatory studies for the next few years. The catch was—our son would now necessarily spend most of his days in London. And then Alice and Mary pounced. They, too, wanted to return to London. They missed all their friends. There was nothing to do in the country. They could encourage their younger brother in his studies and watch over him. They could look after their adored father. They would all be back often to see me. Even Clodagh abandoned me, assuring me her two proteges had already mastered the art of managing a household.

"They will surely be of much comfort to their father and younger brother in London," she promised.

My husband looked at me with pleading eyes. And so, in a torrent of tears, I acquiesced. Middle daughter, Elizabeth's, heartbreak at losing the adored big brother she had idolized and tagged after all the years since she could barely toddle matched my own. She was indeed a lost soul for many days after his departure and we hovered together trying to comfort each other.

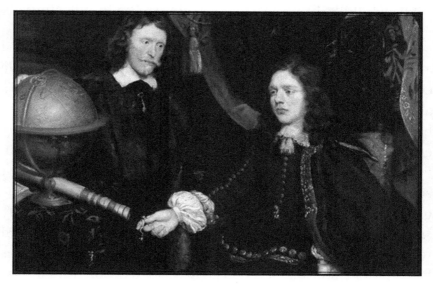

*John Bankes (1626-1656) and Sir Maurice Williams
(1599/1601), His Tutor
by Franz Cleyn (1582-1658)*

I did rejoice that Christmas of 1635 to have my entire family again gathered around. Son John seemed as cheered to reunite with his "tagalong" younger sister, Elizabeth, as she was to see her much loved big brother. Mair-Mair and Father also came, as did Aunt Joane and all her children, who were almost as dear to me as my own. There were many tears for our missing Uncle Edward, along with many smiles as we recalled his now legendary amusing antics.

Our new baby, Jerome, of course, captured the hearts of all. We did not invite any of our Christmas-hating Puritan 'Gentry' neighbors to join in our festivities. Nor did any bawdy Mummers grace our door. Our delightful vicar did appear on Christmas Eve with a group of Corfe Castle villagers, who filled the air with the joyous carols of Christmas as they gathered outside the entrance to the castle. We shared our Wassail bowl with these now so dear to us carolers. They marched with us as we merrily blessed a nearby gnarled old apple tree with good wishes for the New Year. After the villagers had departed, we pulled out the gambling dice and small sacks of coins and merrily concluded our Christmas Eve, engaging in lively (also soon to be forbidden as "evil") games of chance. Our Puritan neighbors in the nearby villages would have been horrified. They claimed they had no specific dogmatic objection to sports or games in general. They were scandalized, however, should there be any hint of "gambling." And their idea of what amounted to gambling was broad. Billiards, shuffleboard, horse racing, bowling, cards, and just about anything that could be deemed "fun" seemed to be on their gambling "taboo" list.

The fragrance of tomorrow's (soon to be outlawed) plum pudding spiced the air as we drifted into sleep.

Our large extended family engulfed the St. Edward King and Martyr Church the next morning when we all marched in to celebrate together. On Boxing Day, we all gaily, with much laughter, delivered overflowing boxes to the villagers who had supported us so loyally in making our Castle our home and who had also become our extended family. My life was beyond privileged. I was so deeply blessed. The memory of that warm and wonderful family gathering was to warm my heart many times in the cold years that lay ahead.

In 1637, we received more devastating news. Uncle Emmanuel Altham had died the year before in a faraway land. Mair-Mair was especially bereft. Emmanuel was always more son than brother in her tender heart. They were incredibly close during his growing-up years, many of which were spent in our home.

1637 was the year Archbishop Laud and his cronies cruelly revived statutes passed during the reign of Elizabeth I. Laws about church attendance and fines for objecting Puritans for not attending the increasingly (according to the Puritans) Roman Catholic leaning Anglican services they despised. Religion, of course, was not a matter of personal choice, but commanded and enforced by the "divine right" of the ruling king.

1637 was also the year King Charles mandatorily, at Archbishop Laud's urging, imposed the Scottish Episcopal Book of Common Prayer on the Puritan-leaning Scottish people to align them more with the Anglican Church in England. Here is how it all went down.

Jenny Geddes was a street-seller. On Sundays she augmented her meager income as one of a number of "waiting women" who were paid to get to the church early and sit on their folding stools to save favored places for their benefactors. On 23 July 1637, when the Dean of Edinburgh began to read from the first use of the new King Charles mandated prayer book, Jenny threw her stool at his head, shouting, *"De'il gie you colic, the wame o' ye, fause thief; daur ye say Mass in my lug?'* meaning "Devil cause you colic in your stomach, false thief: dare you say the Mass in my ear?" In the ensuing tumult Bibles, stools, sticks and stones filled the air as the rioting spread to the streets and throughout Scotland.

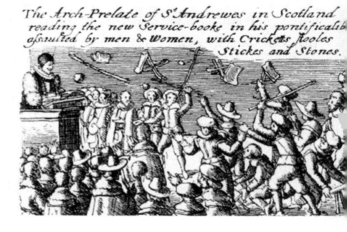

Riot sparked by Jenny Geddes over the imposition of Charles I's Book of Common Prayer in Presbyterian Scotland. Civil disobedience soon turned into armed defiance. Wikipedia

Despite my John's expressed leanings toward a more conciliatory approach for those with Puritan sympathies, in 1637 his boss, King Charles I, ordered him to initiate the second prosecution of the pamphleteer William Prynne. Two other writers of mutinous pamphlets were included in this trial—the clergyman Henry Burton (a popular, vocal minister from the pulpit and prolific pamphleteer and another inflammatory religious zealot, the physician John Bastwick, who blasted the Laudian bishops as being the enemies of God and "the tail of the beast." The specific charge against the three of them was of publishing "...libelous books with intent to move the people to discontent against the King's ecclesiastical government." Of course, the royalist-leaning judges appointed to hear the trial convicted them all. Prynne was sentenced to stand in the pillory, to cruelly have what was left of his ears cut off, his nose slit and the letters SL, for "Seditious Libeller" branded into his cheeks. Prynne defiantly proclaimed them as signifying "Stigmata Laudes"—Stigma of Laud—another jab at his prominent tormenter.

Prynne, Burton and Bastwick were mutinously supported by large crowds who gathered to witness the punishments and voice their disapproval of this brutal retribution. Many say this trial—a preliminary skirmish in the quest for freedom of the press—was among the chief agitating factors for the Civil War that soon followed.

John returned to Corfe Castle for a quick respite following the intensity of the Prynne trial. The oldest children remained in London for this hurried break. My haggard and worried husband brought bad news. King Charles now demanded that he prosecute yet another exceedingly controversial trial. It might be weeks or even months before he could get away again.

"Tell me about this new case."

Linda Sindt

Dinner was over. Our children safely tucked away. Our shoes were off. We relaxed on a sofa near the fire in our private quarters. I poured my love a glass of wine. Expertly prepared by the servants of Corfe Castle, I might add. Under Clodagh's adept supervision, of course.

"It is an old case, really. You remember several years ago when the king assigned me to handle the "Ship Money Case?"

"I believe it was another money-making scheme by our esteemed king?"

John sighed. "The so-called 'Ship Money' goes back to medieval times. It has never needed the approval of Parliament. It was initially levied only on cities and counties on the coast and then only for naval defense in time of war. It required those taxed to provide a specific number of warships or pay a commensurate amount in cash. Even though we are not currently at war, King Charles has arbitrarily revived this technical taxation "loophole." It is his way of expressing disdain for the will of Parliament. And now the king wants to make this devious "Ship Money" tax permanent, and to extend the burden of who pays to all landowners throughout England—not just those along our coastal waters. More worrying—he continues to increase the amount of money he demands, year by year. The king contends 'Ship Money' is a type of tax that by custom does not need the approval of Parliament. Technically, he may "legally" be right, but it increasingly does not sit well with many up and down the social scale."

"And so, what will be your role in all this controversy?" I asked.

"John Hampden, who is a prominent Parliamentarian, has refused to pay this Ship Money and challenges the authority of the king to demand it. The king will not back down and has ordered me to convene the Court of Exchequer to hear the case. I will act on behalf of the king as the prosecuting attorney. Twelve judges must be appointed. The trial is expected to be lengthy and arouse much public sentiment. It promises to be a difficult trial."

"Hampden is to be represented by two co-counsels, one of whom I understand is a former relative of yours." I looked at him questioningly. "It is Oliver St. John, former husband of your late Uncle James's daughter, Johanna."

"Oh," I said. My sweet Puritan-raised niece died in childbirth recently. St. John had already re-married—a marriage that brought him, ever so conveniently, to a closer connection with Oliver Cromwell, as well as John Hampden himself. I had pitied my sweet niece for her difficult marriage to this cold and forbidding man, who was known for his lack of patience with those he deemed less clever than himself.

I sighed, "Poor dear. Notwithstanding your long-time dislike of St. John, I can tell your heart that always sees every possible side to every question is possibly balancing with the Parliamentarians on this? I suppose there is no way anyone else could present the case?"

I slipped my husband's stockinged feet into my lap and began massaging them.

He sighed. "You are so good for me. I miss you all the time."

He looked at me hesitantly and then closed his eyes, wiggling his feet into my fond massage.

"All right, why are you really here?"

John's eyes flew open. "How do you always see right through me?" he asked. He hesitated, looking somewhere between worried and contrite. "Do you think you can avoid getting pregnant again until after Christmas?"

I stopped my tender ministrations to his feet and stared at him. "You need to be in London in December," he continued, looking at me with trepidation. "Our Alice has received a most advantageous offer of marriage from a prominent family."

I dumped my husband's feet on the floor.

"NO!" I shouted. "She's far too young! She is only sixteen."

"She has known the young man in question for several years. She is personally very much in favor of this union."

Tears burned behind my eyes. "Who is it?"

"Sir John Borlase, the eldest son of Sir William Borlase, who died several years ago. You have met his family over the years. His father attended Gray's Inn. John is only eighteen years old and an exceptional student. He has already been called to the bar by the Inner Temple."

"So—another lawyer! A very young and inexperienced lawyer."

"Ah, but an absolutely brilliant scholar. And you can be assured he will be ably mentored by "the top legal mind in this land." Plus, his estate is substantial. More than adequate to also comfortably accommodate our entire family, which he and his mother most generously wish to happen. We could live comfortably in our oldest daughter's home when we are in London. We could give up our London house, which would simplify life for everyone."

Let's just say this particular argument ended with the fact that I indeed did not become pregnant and was there, along with the entire Hawtrey and Altham clans, trying not to sob, when my oldest baby was married on 4 December 1637, at St. Giles in the Fields Church in London.

AUTHOR ENDNOTES, CHAPTER SIXTEEN: A *collection Alice Bankes Borlase eventually compiled of recipes and other observations—was published centuries after her death—by the University of Iowa Press and edited by David Schoonover in "Ladie Borlase's Receiptes Booke." Here's one of her recipes: The Queen's ordinary Bouillon de santa in a morning was thus. A hen,* *a handful of parsley, a sprig of thyme, three of spearmint, a little balm, half a great onion, a little pepper and salt, and a clove, as much water as would cover the hen; and this boiled to less than a pint, for one good porrenger full. Put all ingredients in a pot with water to cover, bring to a boil, and simmer until the liquid is reduced to 3/4 pint. Strain and serve.*

CHAPTER SEVENTEEN

"The raven himself is hoarse That croaks
the fatal entrance ... under my battlements."
Shakespeare, Macbeth
Late 1638

Nine months later, our first granddaughter, Mary, was born. Our delight was much muted by the fact that my wonderful father did not get to meet his first great-grandchild. We lost him on 31 March 1638. His monument at St. Martin's Church, Ruislip reads in part, *"Raphe Hawtrey, d.1638... He was a Justice of the Peace and Deputy Lieutenant for the County of Middlesex.* The inscription notes his children— oldest twin, John Hawtrey, married to Susanna James, a co-heir of her father Jacob James of London, younger twin, Edward Hawtrey, married to Margaret Wright of Burnham, Buckinghamshire, Mary Hawtrey, married to Sir John Bankes of Keswick, Cumbria, a knight and Lord Chief Justice of the Court of Common Pleas and a Privy Counsellor, and Raphe Hawtrey, married to Mary Beadle, daughter of Mathew Beadle of London. The monument is signed by the sculptors: Johannes and Matthias Christmas Fratres fecerunt. John and Matthew Christmas, brothers, made it."

My John, of course, was still mired in the ongoing Hampden trial about the "Ship Money" the king was demanding from his unwilling citizens without the consent of Parliament and was much overwrought that he could not attend the services of his longtime friend.

The rest of our family gathered at Eastcote Manor to mourn their beloved husband/father/grandfather/uncle and so wise and loving mentor to all. All departed shortly after his service, to return to their various studies and occupations. I stayed on for a fortnight to comfort Mair-Mair as best I could, as well as make certain our family's financial affairs were in order for her and the oldest twin as stipulated by my father's will. I, of course, informally represented my husband, who was the official arbiter of my father's will.

En route back to Corfe Castle, I stopped for a few days in London to visit my husband and London children and spend a few precious days with my then three months pregnant daughter. Apparently, her body did not share my hypersensitivity to London's foul air. She bloomed with excellent maternal health. I wore a light mourning veil in deference to my dear father.

Our daughter, Alice, was in high spirits. She and her husband had recently had their portraits painted by the leading, ever-fashionable court painter, Anthony Van Dyck and she was perishing to show them to me. When I saw hers, I bit my tongue to keep from crying out in dismay! Had my sweet daughter learned nothing about modesty from Mair-Mair and me? To say there was an exaggerated display of "cleavage" would be an understatement. With effort I managed to confine myself to simply stating the artist had "masterfully captured" my daughter's lovely face.

I could not help asking, "Has your father seen this?"

"Of course."

"And what was his response?"

"I believe it was something to the effect of, 'Wait until your mother sees this.' Do you *really* like it?"

I rose to the occasion. Who was I to question the fashion sense of London's 'high society,' including our current queen and her late mother-in-law, our former Queen? I put my best smile on my face and assured our daughter her portrait was the ultimate in "modern fashion and sophistication."

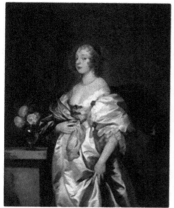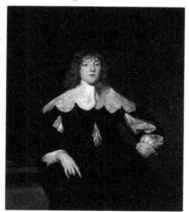

Alice Banks, Lady Borlase
(1621-1683)

Sir John Borlase, ST BT, MP
(1619-1672)

Both portraits painted by Sir Anthony Van Dyck
Both portraits on display at Lingston Lacy Estate at National Trust

But my dear Alice was not yet done. "Mother—you must have your portrait done, also."

"What?" I could not help clasping my arms defensively across the top of my high-necked dress.

"Father gets so lonely when he has to be away from you. It would be wonderful for him to have maybe just a small picture of you—I know—a miniature—they are all the rage. He could keep it in his pocket and have you with him always."

"But darling, I must get back to Corfe Castle and have no time to pose. Plus, I did not bring an appropriate wardrobe."

"That's not how it works. The best artists are in such demand, they don't have much time, either. You can select from a large array of wardrobe samples they have already painted as models. You actually only have to pose for a very short time as the master artist does a preliminary sketch of your face and coloring. They eventually paint your face atop the wardrobe you have selected. It shouldn't take more than an hour or two of your time. Oh, and I know just the miniaturist. He often duplicates the large Van Dyck portraits into charming miniatures that are easily transportable and can be shared with other family members. He is said to be extraordinarily talented. His name is John Hoskins. I will send a messenger to set it up."

"Wait!" I cried, but I was too late. My oldest daughter's forceful personality prevailed again. When I went for my "sitting," which was indeed brief, I selected the least "low cut" neckline I could find, that was further adorned with a discreet "cleavage concealing" ruffle at the top. I insisted that the light mourning veil I then wore be included in the portrait as a permanently recorded tribute to my much-loved father.

Shortly after I returned to Corfe Castle in April 1638, the ever-present, raucous, but somehow endearing ravens ominously disappeared, suddenly and entirely, from Corfe Castle. The abrupt silence unnerved—adding to my growing melancholy. Nobody knows why they left. The Corfe Castle villagers superstitiously called it an omen of doom—that the castle would soon crumble.

Ancient Seal of Corfe Castle
featuring ravens.
Image at bing.com

My melancholy continued. I returned to London later in 1638 to cuddle my newly arrived granddaughter, Mary, my namesake, and also Mair-Mair's. Well, of course, Alice would choose to also honor her lifelong "partner in crime," her eighteen-months younger sister, Mary. I was there to not only greet my oldest grandchild, but also for another wedding. Yes, my second oldest daughter, Mary, was also getting married. To another up-and-coming young peer of the realm, soon to be—naturally—another lawyer and eventually to become 1st Baronet, Sir Robert Jenkinson, of Walcot, Oxfordshire and Hawkesbury, Gloucestershire.

Oil painting on canvas, Mary Bankes, Lady Jenkinson (1623-1691), after Sir Peter Lely (Soest 1618 – London 1680), circa 1660/65.
Kingston Lacy Estate, Dorset, South West, National Trust

Both daughters, always so close in spirit, greeted me in the Borlase Manor when I arrived from Corfe Castle to attend the wedding. Looking very pretty and very merry, as if they had a wonderful surprise. I had not been there since my portrait was painted by John Hoskins. And had not seen the painting itself.

My daughters tagged after me as I headed to the rooms I (all too seldom) shared with my husband in the Borlase mansion. He, of course, was still intensely immersed in the ever-ongoing Hampden Ship Money trial and would not join us until dinnertime. They chattered away as they followed. I assured them I could find my way and only needed to freshen up a bit, but they kept prattling and tagging along. The chitchat was typical, but I sensed an underlying edge of anticipation. I wondered what was going on. And then I opened the door to my room. An immense portrait of *me* gazed down from above the fireplace. Featuring an indecorous display of cleavage. Wearing an extravagant gown and in an artificially dramatic and ridiculous pose.

"Isn't it wonderful?" cried Mary.

"Father absolutely adores it," said Alice. "It's a knock-off of the one Van Dyck did of my dear friend, Lady Dorothy Spencer. Van Dyck painted her at the same time he did my John and me. You know she is considered one of the most beautiful and fascinating women in all of England," Alice gushed. "And she has such a romantic and tragic history."

Mary continued, "Father says it makes him smile every night before he goes to sleep. And isn't it fun that it is in the pose of one of the most admired women in all of England? When Alice and I heard of this talented, unknown young artist who could quickly copy a Van Dyck for practically nothing, we could not resist and went in together on it as a special gift. The artist used the Hoskins miniature, which is also delightful, as a model. Father has been so melancholy to have to spend so much time apart from you."

"And my friend, Lady Dorothy, was so generous to lend us her portrait for a short time if it would help cheer our famous Father up," Alice concluded.

I later commanded my husband, on pain of being chained and tortured forever in the dungeons of Corfe Castle, that he *never* display this portrait to anyone other than the two daughters and the few servants who had already seen it.

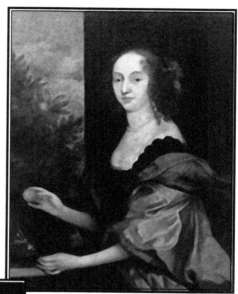

Oil painting on canvas, An Unknown Lady, formally known as Mary Hawtrey. Lady Banks (1598-1661), in the Pose of Dorothy, Countess of Suderland after Sir Anthony Van Dyck (Antwerp 1599-London 1641) Circa 1640. On show at Sudbury Hall and the National Trust Museum of Childhood, Derbyshire, Midlands, National Trust

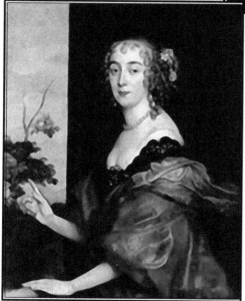

Portrait of Dorothy Spencer, Countess of Sunderland (Anthony Van Dyck) [Note: tragic, cleaver, elegant, and famously virtuous beauty of 17th Century London society, her life story is fascinating in its own right. Even more significantly, the writings of her brother, Algernon Sydney, are considered by some to be the "cornerstone of western thought" ...the idea that "individuals have the right to choose their own form of government and that, if that government became corrupt, the people retained the power to abolish it and form another." Algernon Sydney was beheaded on 7 December 1683 for expressing these thoughts.

Linda Sindt

AUTHOR ENDNOTES, CHAPTER SEVENTEEN: The years that soon followed did not dispel the superstition about the ravens that if the ravens disappeared the castle would crumble. Eight years later, the Castle was destroyed, much of it reduced to (crumbly) gravel by the massive loads of gunpowder Cromwell's forces used to blow it up in the Civil War. It is well documented that the ravens did not return to Corfe Castle until 2003, well after the Bankes family generously granted its estate to the National Trust in 1981, assuring that it would be preserved and retained as a national treasure.

Lady Mary Jenkinson and her husband were the great-great-grandparents of Robert Banks Jenkinson, who entered Parliament in 1790 as 2nd Earl of Liverpool and was Prime Minister of the United Kingdom from 1812 to 1827.

A 400-Year-Old Art Mystery

Think about this scenario: Sir John and Lady Mary Bankes were incredibly wealthy. Sir Anthony Van Dyck was a then favorite and prolific artist for the incredibly wealthy. It was not uncommon for lesser artists to copy the original works of Sir Anthony Van Dyck. (Possibly to create duplicate mages that could be shared with other family members?)

Accomplished miniaturist artists notably copied the larger-than-life original portraits by Van Dyck and other Masters, transforming them into tiny, perfect art treasures that were easily transportable in the pockets or travel cases of loved ones. The best of these masterful miniaturists, who famously mimicked the style of Van Dyck, was Anthony Hoskins. He created a miniature—an art treasure in its own right—of Lady Mary. Henry Pierce Bone, who copied the Hoskins portrait in 1837, states on the reverse of his portrait that the Hoskins miniature was painted in 1656. Fifteen years after the estimated 1641 dates of the two "Unknown Ladies." It seems doubtful that the Hoskins miniature would have been an original portrait. Most typically it would have been copied from an oversized original portrait. The 1656 Hoskins miniature remained with the Bankes family at Kingston Lacy until 1920 when it was given to a nearby great (many greats) granddaughter of Lady Mary, a Norah Letitia Bankes, who married a John Edward Acland. The Peerage shows Norah and John Acland had four sons and four daughters. The Hoskins miniature has been "missing" since 1920 and no one knows its current whereabouts. Is it possible the missing tiny art treasure yet exists, unrecognized, in the private art collections of one of the Acland descendants? Could it one day be "re-discovered," and its image shared as a gift to the world?

Two hundred years after the (now missing) Hoskins miniature was created, the accomplished 19th Century artist, Henry Pierce Bone, copied the Hoskins miniature, creating the now most widely known portrait of Lady Mary. Here's what a later relative of Lady Mary has to say about that: Florence Molesworth Hawtrey in her 1903 book, "The History of the Hawtrey Family," quoted a letter from her brother, who visited the Bankes later family home, Kingston Lacy, on the 28th day of June 1864. He stated, "This day we set out by invitation… Mrs. Bankes received us with every attention…there were two miniatures of Lady [Mary] Bankes, both copied by Bone, a famous enamel painter, from an old miniature by Hoskyns. But where was the old miniature itself? Mrs. Bankes was at fault for a moment, but recollecting, said, I know—it is in a case in the room where you are to sleep—afterwards I looked at the miniatures in the case, and then I saw how the miniature of Lady Bankes had been altered from its simple look of bonhomie, to the stern and proud countenance which it assumes in Bone's enamel, and the other ideal representations of her."

Van Dyck painted a portrait of Lady Mary's then sixteen-year-old oldest daughter, Alice on the occasion of her marriage in 1637 to John Borlase, a soon-to-be Baronet. Is it possible a Van Dyck original of Lady Mary was also painted in that same time frame? Could Lady Mary have commissioned a lesser artist to copy this original as a wedding gift to her much loved daughter, the new Lady Alice Borlase? Could Lady Mary have also commissioned a second copy to gift to another daughter, Joan (Joanna), who also married into the Borlase family? It is recorded that Lady Mary's sons, Ralph and Jerome, bought the manor of Eastcourt on Lady Mary's behalf following the destruction of Corfe Castle. Upon her death, the manor passed to her daughter, Joan (Joanna) Borlase who in turn passed it on to her daughters and co-heirs. It is significant that both portraits came to the National Trust from the Vernon Collection in 1967 which originated with the Borlase family.

THREE (Possible?) VERSIONS OF LADY MARY BANKES?
Perhaps all copied from a yet missing original?
What do YOU see?

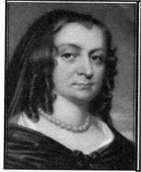 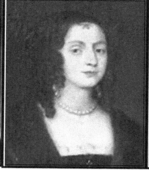 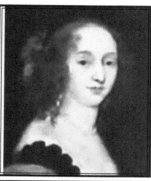

by Henry Pierce Bone, 1837. Copied from miniature by Century Miniature by John Hoskins. Bone certifies on reverse that Hoskins miniature was painted in 1656.	*Both of the above portraits that so closely resemble the 1837 Bone Portrait are estimated to have been painted in 1641. Both are on display by the National Trust at Sudbury Hall in the UK. Both are currently identified as "Unknown Ladies thought to be Lady Mary Bankes." Both came to the National Trust from the Vernon Collection which originated with the Borlase family.*

Could these images and the missing Hoskins miniature all perhaps be copies of the same original? Possibly an authentic Van Dyck(?) that has disappeared in the mists of 400 years?

CHAPTER EIGHTEEN

"In War events of importance are the result of trivial causes."
Shakespeare, Julius Caesar
1637-1642

The Hampden Ship Money trial, which had begun in November 1637, wore excruciatingly on and on. It finally concluded on 12 June 1638. When it was clear that the end was near, I returned to London to hold my dear husband's hand during those final, nerve-wracking days. The pain in his intense blue eyes hurt my heart. At long last the judges decided seven to five in favor of the Crown. Which meant my darling Sir John technically "won" as prosecuting attorney. But he was not celebrating. The judges profoundly disagreed in their opinions. The narrowness of the decision encouraged further Parliamentary resistance. Public opinion loudly stood by Hampden. King Charles's opponents deemed the close vote as a victory against tyranny. My Mair-Mair would have stood both sides with their noses in opposite corners of the room and told them they would have to stand there until they could play nicely together. But neither she nor I got to be in charge. In the continuing escalation of fiercely opposing forces, the "Long" Parliament that soon followed indicted the deciding Royalist judges who voted against Hampden for treason.

In truth, I did not much care for the antics of either side of this increasingly combative political spectrum. And I could tell my John was also painfully torn.

"It will all be all right if you resign from the king's service," I assured him.

"Don't think I haven't considered it. But honestly, the Parliamentarians can be equally dangerous and bull-headed. No, I think I will still be the most effective in protecting this land that we love if I stand by the king and hope to be a countering influence against the rash thinking of some of the idiots he has surrounded himself with. And work behind the scenes with the few remaining friends I have in Parliament in possibly hammering out reasonable solutions to some of the urgent issues facing our country."

"Why can't there be a way to put the best thinkers from the very *middle* of both political spectrums together and ask them to come up with compromising, creative solutions that will let everyone mostly, but just a little bit not quite win? Why are we eternally divided by the extreme minority ends of the far reaches of both sides that won't give up one inch on their unreasonable and even dangerous demands?" I lamented. "How do we allow such a minority of extremists to have so much undue influence over the vast majority of all of us?"

My brilliant husband had no answer for my lament.

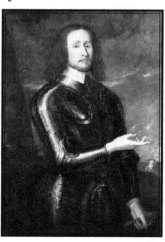

John Hampden by the circle of Godfrey Knellar, image from Wikipedia

Oliver Cromwell, who was Hampden's cousin and an ardent Puritan, also loudly argued against the Ship Tax, calling it "...a prejudice to the liberties of the kingdom," and declaring that there should be no taxation without consent of Parliament. During this interim period, he became one of the most vital voices opposing the government of King Charles.

A little less than a year after the Hampden Trial, our adorable baby Charles (our ninth child) was born. My husband insisted on the name.

"I am not sure I want to saddle our new sweet child with the name of that ridiculous man," I argued.

"I need all the influence with our king I can get," was his response. "I am hoping our Charlie will be my little good luck charm." And so, "Charlie the charmer" came into our busy lives.

By this time the Presbyterian (Puritan/Calvinist) leaning religious leaders in Scotland faced accusations of treason by King Charles for their ongoing protests against the bishops and the unwanted Book of Common Prayer imposed by the king. The protestors gathered together and signed the National Covenant of Scotland as a way of uniting in defying these attacks on their fervent religious beliefs. The Scottish protestors voted to expel all bishops from their spiritual hierarchy. These protestors became known as "the Covenanters." The unrest continued for a year and in February 1639 the Covenanters seized control of the city of Aberdeen. In May 1639, King Charles scrabbled together an army and moved to the border of Scotland to forcibly bring the dissenters into line. His bungling army was no match for the Covenanters. In June 1639, he signed the Treaty of Berwick. The ever-devious King Charles, of course, never meant to honor the treaty and used this pretense of concessions to gain time to plan his next move.

King Charles continued to flail about ineffectively, attempting to fund his activities without going through Parliament. His game was to try to quash the overall influence of Parliament in setting the economic agenda, while he also pressed on with his floundering efforts to reform the church without the meddling of Parliament. My John grew ever more troubled about the ongoing, increasing general turmoil throughout our land. Well, and so did I, of course.

On 29 Jan 1640, my John received yet another honor. Despite—or possibly because of—my darling's careful and "middle of the road" relationships with members of Parliament and the Royal Court, the king selected him as the Chief Justice of the Common Pleas.

One of the most challenging figures from well before the onset of these increasingly troubling times was "Black Tom Tyrant", also known as Sir Thomas Wentworth, also known as the Earl of Strafford. Much to our dear Clodagh's dismay, he is credited with thoroughly tyrannizing the unlucky Irish from 1632 to 1639, when he instituted a harsh rule as Lord Deputy of Ireland. He evicted Irish landowners from lands held for generations by their ancestors and granted ownership to new English settlers. In fairness, he also assured the poor were no longer at the mercy of the rich and did not go hungry. Many Irish merchants prospered when he established measures that increased trade, industry, and agriculture. He instituted more effective law and order and he rid the land of troubling pirates who preyed upon commercial enterprises. He put together an intimidating, well-trained Irish militia.

It was in that early time that he became a frequent correspondent with my husband, seeking his advice on the recurring legal issues in which he became embroiled. In the privacy of our bedchambers, England's Chief Justice of the Common Pleas sometimes confided his worry to me about his confidante's often rash behavior. Still, he maintained their correspondence, hoping to wield a positive influence.

"Black Tom Tyrant" was surely a double-dealing contradiction in terms. He wore the plain black clothing of a stern-hearted Puritan but was a close confidante of Puritan-hating Archbishop Laud. Ambitious, ruthless, and a little bit dishonest, he played a double game. He pretended to support measures to put brakes on the powers of our pompous and— let's be brutally honest— not too brilliant king, while at the same time begging favors from him. He, in time, became one of the most trusted advisors to King Charles I. Sir Thomas Wentworth, the Earl of Strafford, is another from those ever-darkening days my heart struggles to forgive for his double-dealing ways.

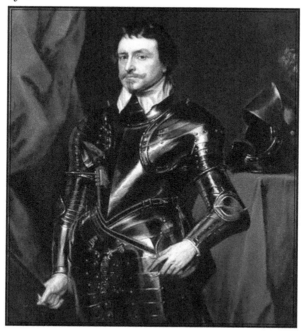

Thomas Wentworth, 1st Earl of Strafford about 1639, portrait by Van Dyck, source of image, Wikipedia

Meanwhile, King Charles was determined to continue the war against Scotland. Sir Thomas Wentworth coerced the Irish Parliament into raising a new Irish Army to do battle with the Scots on the king's behalf. "Black Tom Tyrant" further persuaded the king that he had no choice but to reconvene Parliament to fund an additional English army.

On 20 February 1640, King Charles reluctantly, at Wentworth's urging, recalled Parliament after ruling eleven years without it. Although willing to grant some of the subsidies the king solicited, Parliament would only do so if the king addressed their numerous grievances about State and Church policy. The king was outraged.

Sir Wentworth then reversed his previous advice and convinced the king to raise a less robust army in England from other resources, which, when reinforced by Irish troops, he promised, should be enough to bring the Scots to their knees. The king then abruptly dissolved the Parliament, since it was no longer theoretically needed as a source of funds. It actually "sat" from 13 April to 5 May 1640. It was forever after known as the "Short Parliament" because of its short life of only three weeks.

It would have been laughable were it not so sad. The king did not even wait for the well-trained troops from Ireland to arrive. The militia raised in the north of England was let go. By August, he put together another army in the south of England, which sparked much unrest. Most of the troops were poorly armed, unpaid, and underfed, not to mention untrained and badly disciplined. Many deserted on the march to the north. The Scots forces far outnumbered this motley assortment of English troops and easily defeated them in the Battle of Newburn on 28 August 1640. The Scots went on to hold down the town of Newcastle, which granted them strategic control of the critical coal supply for London.

King Charles was now desperate. He had no choice but to agree to a treaty on 26 October 1640, under which the Scottish army in northern England would be paid daily expenses, pending a final treaty of peace.

The king reluctantly again convened Parliament, which was forever after known as "The Long Parliament." This Parliament did not delay taking action on a long agenda of grievances against the king in exchange for providing the funds he needed to pay his army and buy off the Scots. An emboldened Parliament pounced with dizzying speed. Infamous pamphleteer, Sir William Prynne, was immediately released from imprisonment. The House of Commons declared the two sentences against him illegal, restored to him his degree and to his membership of Lincoln's Inn as a lawyer. He was even soon able to have the gruesome satisfaction of personally overseeing the trial and beheading of his chief tormenter, the Archbishop, William Laud.

As a first order of business, Parliament impeached Sir Thomas Wentworth, The Earl of Strafford for treason. They accused Sir Wentworth primarily of advocating that the king use the Irish Army not only against the Scots, but possibly against the king's own citizens in England.

The House of Commons jumped into the fray and declared "ship money" to be an illegal tax.

The much-reviled Archbishop Laud did not escape Parliament's wrath. He was officially impeached for high treason.

The only really bright spot in this entire devastating year was the birth of our second darling granddaughter, Katherine, to our oldest daughter, Alice Borlase.

As promised, my John proved an inspiring mentor in furthering the political career of the husband of our oldest daughter, "His Alice." Her husband, Sir John Borlase was selected as a Member of Parliament for Great Marlow in the brief Short Parliament. He was subsequently named a Member of Parliament for Corfe Castle in 1641.

Time seemed to compress. The momentous events that happened in the next few months crowd together in my mind. Here is what I wrote in my diary.

> *In February 1641 the* **Triennial Act** *was passed, requiring that Parliament be summoned every three years. John is not displeased. He has long believed the king should not be a despot, but that the people he governs should have a say in their destiny. He also confessed to me that he could not fault Parliament for demanding that it could not be ended without its own consent."*

In early March, I wrote.

> *As if he already is not overtaxed, my John has been appointed as acting Speaker of the Lords, due to the illness of the regular Speaker of the Lords, Sir Edward Littleton. But that is not the worst part. The king now demands that John personally preside over the opening days of the trial for the impeachment of my husband's former colleague and sometime client, the now infamous Earl of Strafford (Sir Thomas Wentworth).*

"Our prior relationship taints the whole proceedings," my husband complained to me in the privacy of our bedchambers. "Black Tom Tyrant has become a fall guy for all of England's ills."

Thankfully for John and indeed for all my family, Lord

Littleton's ailment was only temporary, and my husband was soon relieved of the painful responsibility for overseeing the proceedings of the anguishing days that followed.

I came to London to again hold my dear husband's hand during the harrowing trial of "Black Tom Tyrant." It officially ended on 13 April, but not, of course, without great controversy. To the surprise of all, Sir Wentworth personally defended himself against his charges so skillfully that it soon seemed possible that the charges of treason against him could not be legally proved. So, his accusers in the House of Commons adopted a different ploy. They passed a "Bill of Attainder," declaring him to be guilty of treason without benefit of trial. This legally suspect act had to be also signed by the House of Lords and the king. The mandated punishment was that he be beheaded. The House of Lords members cravenly gave in to the demands of the angry London mobs that stood watch on this trial. They mistakenly hoped that with the death of Sir Wentworth the unrest would be quelled.

The Parliamentarians stooped to threatening the queen's safety if the king did not sign. Sir Wentworth himself encouraged the king in writing to sign the Bill of Attainder that ordered his death. King Charles reportedly wept but was overcome by the need to make his troubles with the Scots go away. He famously signed the Bill of Attainder on 10 May 1641. The next day, Parliament agreed to draft a treaty with the Scots.

Two days later the Earl of Strafford was beheaded to the cheers of London's mobs. Our younger children were safely tucked away back at Corfe Castle under the watchful eye of Clodagh. I was in London to hold my husband's hand during this terrible time. Even late into the evening on the day of the execution, we could hear the noise of the mobs from our private rooms in our daughter Alice's London estate.

My John had not been especially fond of the double-dealing Sir Wentworth in his later years, but he had been a former client of sorts. The death of the complicated man he had once advised gnawed at his heart. Mostly, his heart was breaking at the increasing disregard for the rule of law by all in his beloved England.

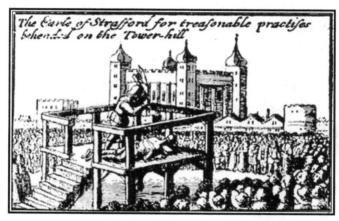

Execution of the Earle of Strafford, 12 May 1641. Image source bing.com

Scottish forces marched out of Newcastle in August 1641. While the House of Commons continued relentlessly checking off its "to do" list of complaints against King Charles with dizzying speed.

More excerpts from my diary—early May 1641.

> *...the House of Commons drew up the "Protestation Oath" against "popery" in its continuing, cruel crusade to rid England of Roman Catholicism.*

A few days later, Parliament demanded it could not be dismissed without its own consent.

Shortly after, the House of Commons passed a resolution

mandating the destruction of altar rails, crucifixes and other 'innovations' introduced under the reforms of now former Archbishop Laud.

Just before Christmas in 1641 Archbishop Laud was formally accused of high treason and was taken to the Tower of London. His trial did not actually occur until several years later in the midst of the Civil War. It was managed by his vindictive former foe, the newly released Sir William Prynne. As with the Earl of Strafford, the House of Commons abandoned legal proof of wrongdoing and resorted to yet another ordinance of attainder. Which the House of Lords again, cravenly, approved. The archbishop was ultimately beheaded. Few mourned him. He was never truly liked, even by those who doctrinally supported his extremist religious views. As the top legal advisor to King Charles, my John was necessarily privy to almost everything that happened. Notwithstanding the fact that his best advice was often not heeded.

The English Parliament concluded 1641 by presenting a list of grievances to King Charles. Known as "The Grand Remonstrance," it had been passed by the House of Commons less than a week earlier. It noted Parliament's defiant opposition to the king's foreign, financial, legal, and religious policies. It listed more than two hundred objections, including expelling all bishops from Parliament, granting Parliament the right to veto royal appointments, and ending the sale of land confiscated from Irish dissenters. Oliver Cromwell famously commented that if the Grand Remonstrance had been defeated, "I would have sold all I had the next morning and never seen England more; and I know there are many other honest men of the same resolution."

I had by then returned to Corfe Castle. My love, however, did not return to his Corfe Castle family during that sad

Christmas season that ended 1641. He remained in London with our older children to hold the king's hand and try to reason with him. I was (very) pregnant again, and John would not hear of my bringing the younger children to be with him. I think he was also concerned about the mobs of protestors that continued to gather in London's streets.

I did not relish the discomforts of pregnancy and always vowed, "never again," but every time each beautiful new child appeared, I was overwhelmed with delight and could not imagine our family without it.

Two days before Christmas, in 1641, the king finally replied to Parliament's latest demand and refused to remove the bishops from the Church hierarchy. He was unyielding in declaring he could not reconcile Parliament's view of the state of England with his own. But then cravenly proclaimed his opposition to Roman Catholicism (notwithstanding his own wife's staunchly avowed faith). His reply attempted at moderation hoping (but failing) to win back the support of more moderate members of Parliament. The quickly ensuing developments made any further hopes for reconciliation impossible. I sensed John's increasing desolation in the frequent letters that he sent.

The ever-growing chaos continued into 1642 as the days sped by from alarming crisis to even more alarming crisis. My husband, of course, was privy to the everlasting chaos, but his caring heart and brilliant mind were not enough to bring about moderation and common sense as the king continued to flounder ineptly.

The only bright spot in that grey January dawning of a new year, was the arrival of our precious Arabella. Our very special Christmas present. The Bankes children now numbered ten. It was the first time my John had not been by my side to joyfully welcome the miracle of a new baby into our family. It was by then not clear whether we were looking out for our villagers, or they were taking care of us. One by one the village women stopped by to lovingly drop off small offerings of carefully hand-crafted new baby clothing and soft toys at the Castle door.

The drama continued into the new year. I continued to receive frequent updates from my absent husband. He reported that on 4 January 1642, in a ridiculously inept ploy, the king sent his soldiers to arrest five top leaders in the House of Commons that he considered to be his strongest foes in Parliament. Alerted to the plot, they escaped before the soldiers arrived. Members of Parliament, of course, now no longer felt safe from their own king. They decided to put together their own army.

Six days later, facing overwhelming popular support for Parliament following his failed escapade, the king and royal family began plans to flee from London.

In mid-February, the increasingly infuriated king refused Parliament's new demand that he surrender control of the militia to Parliament.

In late March word arrived at our village that a fearful King Charles had officially escaped from London and set up his court at York.

There was no immediate word from my John. The only thing that registered at that point in my then panic-stricken heart was that anyone who remained in London with even the slightest royalist leanings was no longer safe. I was frantic to hear personally from my husband and my three oldest children. The king's mail was by then sporadic. But rumors of pending violence abounded in our tiny Corfe Village and the nearby Parliamentarian leaning (king hating) villages that surrounded us. And so I waited. And worried. And showered our darling new Arabella with my tears. I don't know how I could have managed without Clodagh there to hold my hand and comfort our children. The younger ones, especially, could not understand why their father stayed away so long.

AUTHOR ENDNOTES, CHAPTER EIGHTEEN: *A statue of Hampden, to this day, stands at the entrance to the Central Lobby in the Palace of Westminster. In a quirky ceremony, he is even today remembered at the State Opening of every session of Parliament by the reigning British monarch each year. The doors of the Commons Chamber are ceremonially slammed in the face of the reigning monarch's pretended "messenger," symbolizing the right of Parliament to be independent from the monarch.*

Here is an extract from "The Story of Corfe Castle and Many Who Have Lived There," by the Right Honorable George Bankes, providing added insights regarding Strafford's execution: "He proceeded on foot dressed in deep mourning, wearing a long cloak, many nobles and other friends attending him; large bodies of (the militia) preceded him, and he looked more like a general commanding an army than like a condemned traitor going to execution…"

CHAPTER NINETEEN

"He is come to open the purple testament of bleeding war."
Shakespeare, Macbeth
1642

By Spring in 1642, letters from John had grown even more sparse. He remained at his post in London for two endless weeks after the king and his family fled from London to York in March. My darling husband optimistically held futilely to the hope a peaceful conclusion might yet be brokered with Parliament. He perilously, if doggedly, supported King Charles' cause. His close friends and I worried that such an open display of loyalty to the king could be downright dangerous in the growing antagonism. Yet John also drew the king's rancor for staying in London, perceiving it as a lack of loyalty.

Parliament knew my John to be unflinching in his loyalty to the king. But they were aware, also, that this loyal feeling involved no subordination of his character to the king, or anyone else, and absolutely no sacrifice of principle in any way. Through him, rather than through any other of the king's advisors, they hoped to make an accommodation between Parliament and the Crown. Letters to my John from the Earl of Northumberland, Denzill Holles, the Earl of Essex, Lords Say and Sele, and others, who stood highest in the Parliamentary party show how highly they valued my dear husband's character in a station of highest trust and power.

In a letter, dated May 1642, addressed to one of the Members of Parliament for Corfe Castle (Mr. Giles Green), my John wrote:

> *The King is extremely offended with me touching the militia; saith that I should have performed the part of an honest man in protesting against the illegality of the ordinance; commands me upon my allegiance yet to do it. I have told him it is not safe for me to deliver anie opinion in things which are voted in the housses." In this and other private letters to the leaders of Parliament he continued to urge the necessity of honesty and compromise on both sides with a view to an 'accommodation,' foreseeing that "if we should have civile wars it would make us a miserable people.*

Meanwhile, at our castle, a semblance of life went on. Elizabeth, then fifteen, doted on her new baby sister, Arabella, proprietarily seeing to her every need, and spending hours entertaining her with lullabies and cuddles. With Elizabeth, I had firmly stamped my foot down. I demanded that my John not even *think* of negotiating with anyone for this daughter's hand until she was a *t least eighteen.* As I had been. She had been tucked away safely in Corfe Castle since before she arrived at adolescence. The glamour and sophistication of the London scene had not yet tempted her. Indeed, she seemed to revel in her quiet country home. Both she and her brother, John, inherited my Uncle Edward's striking Altham looks. With the generous Bride's Portion her adoring father was sure to provide, I did not doubt she would eventually attract a suitable mate.

Both Elizabeth and Joanne (then thirteen) were willing shadows of their ultimate role model— Clodagh. She was intent on passing along to the next wave of growing Bankes daughters the skills every highborn lady of that era was expected to master in properly managing an aristocratic household.

Son Ralph, then eleven, entertained himself by engaging Jane, nine, and Jerome, seven, in various, wildly imagined outdoor games and competitions. He even taught both Jane and Jerome how to use a bow and arrow. I wasn't sure how "proper" that was for an aristocratic young lady, but it seemed a harmless enough pastime during this anxious time of endless waiting.

"Charlie the charmer" at almost four remained mostly under the guidance of his devoted nanny in the castle nursery. In the absence of his father, I relaxed the dining room protocol. Young Charlie was allowed to join us at the dinner table each evening, where he entertained us with his amusing prattle.

We often invited our ancient vicar to join us for our meals. He regaled us with any gossip he had picked up of the ongoing turmoil in London. It was the vicar who gingerly broached the unthinkable subject of how best to take care of Corfe Castle and especially the villagers if our Parliament-loving neighbors became more hostile than they already were.

For a time, I considered abandoning everything and running "home" with my children to the comparative safety of Eastcote Manor and into Mair-Mair's always sheltering arms. There were two things that deterred me. By then I had become utterly, intricately involved in the lives and welfare of the loyal villagers, who depended so much on the support and income from the castle for their wellbeing. In the seven years since Corfe Castle had become our home, the families that lived in the Village of Corfe Castle had become our extended family. I could not bring myself to abandon them. Perhaps at least as compelling was my stubborn heart, which rebelled at the thought of marauding strangers pillaging our home and rummaging through the handsome furnishings my doting John and those that had lived there before had so lovingly accumulated. As was sure to happen if we abandoned our now treasured home and left it unguarded for an extended time. Unless we hired a small army to permanently defend it, which did not seem to be a practical solution. And would surely have invited more hostility from our Parliamentarian neighbors.

Cautiously and quietly, as Spring crept in, Clodagh and our Corfe village neighbors began to plan for an expanded garden inside the Castle gates. Just in case our antagonistic Parliamentarian neighbors became openly hostile, we needed to be prepared to feed ourselves (and our village) for an extended time.

On her daily excursions into the village just below the castle, Clodagh unobtrusively gathered extra containers in which she would oversee sealing extra backup stores of her lovely fruit preserves, "just in case," as the various crops came into season in the next few months. Thank Heaven she had paid attention to the homemaking skills that had bored me so much. We expanded the flocks of chickens and geese and tame ducks we sheltered inside the inner gates in preparation for possible coming want should we become prisoners in our own home.

One bright Spring morning, my, by now, very dear vicar advisor and the ever-doughty Captain Bond and I walked the ramparts of the perimeter walls, trying, but failing, to imagine how exactly an enemy military force might hammer their way into the naturally fortified Castle. Son Ralph tagged along. He idolized both men—currently the dominant male figures in his female-governed life. He was, of course, followed by his ever-present shadows, younger siblings Jerome and Jane.

The castle stood on a natural hill. It was separated from

the village by a deep ditch that cut across a narrow tongue of land. The thick walls, built of sturdy Purbeck stone, were ten to thirteen feet high. The outer Bailey had a defensive system of walls and towers that were surely impregnable?

I deferred to Captain Bond.

"Surely, if the gates are closed and locked, it would be all but impossible to batter them down?" I said.

His response was not encouraging, but he looked at me with new respect.

"Ay, mistress, you have hit upon the current great weakness. Everyone knows you leave the gates open day and night."

"B-but we cannot just bar out our dear villagers," I sputtered. "What if we are not under attack and there is an emergency in the middle of the night? We have to be ready to help! And if we are attacked, we must hurry our dear villagers all inside the gates for their own safety. We have to protect them."

"Keep in mind, there are only five not so young men in your little Guard," my snowy-haired protector worried. "And should trouble suddenly come to us, we will undoubtedly be manning our weapons. We will not be available to shutter the gate.

"Well, then, we should plan for someone else to do it," I said. "Let's go see how it works."

We trooped down to the gate. It turned out that one person, properly trained, could manage all the bars and winches in alternately raising and lowering the dual portcullis gates. At the entry just beyond the moat that surrounded the castle. The idea was that the outer gate would be opened first, permitting entry of a limited number of visitors. The outer gate would then be closed, essentially temporarily imprisoning the visitors in the small space between the two gates. The inner gate could then be opened, with guards prepared to search, or otherwise take charge of the visitors, if necessary. Captain Bond instructed me in the drill. I could sense my Ralph's rapt attention as we worked through the complexities of raising and lowering the inner and outer gates.

"I've got it, Mother," exclaimed Ralph. "I'll show you." And then he proceeded to flawlessly, albeit with some effort, open and close the gate pulleys and slides.

"It is so easy. Even a girl could do it," declared my son— our already ever so masculine, budding mini-hero.

"Well, then I am putting you in charge of teaching your sisters. And a few of the village children, also."

Along the way back to our upper-level quarters we passed several ancient arrowslits—where long-ago archers had stood in protective concealment as they aimed their arrows at invading forces.

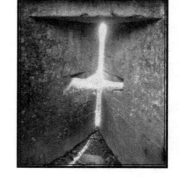

*Arrowslit at Corfe Castle,
photo by author*

My militarily inclined Ralph could not help but soberly note, "This will be a perfect place for me to defend you with my arrows, Mother," he promised. "And I would be completely safe from any return fire."

How had my dear second son come by this ardent, soldierly bravado? Surely, not from his now far away, bookish father who fought his battles not with arrows or musket fire, but with eloquent words?

Okay, it was my sweet babies and me against the world. We would do the best we could with the resources available to us.

One of our first tasks was to set up an alarm drum in one of the towers facing the village. If the drum sounded, the vicar and village elders would see that the villagers quickly ran for the castle gates before they were closed.

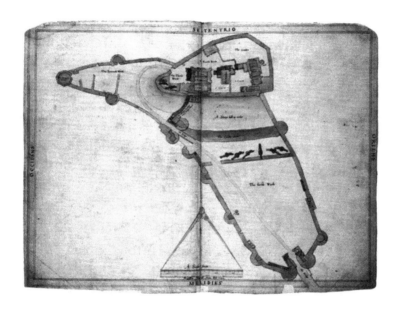

Old diagram of Corfe Castle. Note the placement of cannons on the inner wall.
Source of image, ntpl.org.uk

It was the end of April. The day was bright and beautiful. At mid-afternoon I took a break from my chores and ever-present worries and carried Arabella to the garden to nurse her, breathing in the warm sunshine and the fresh smells of new life stirring in the earth. Nearby woodlarks filled the air with happy songs. The latest Canute dozed at my feet. He raised his head by way of welcome when Elizabeth wandered out to join us and lifted her no longer hungry baby sister from my arms.

"You look tired. Did you sleep at all last night?" she asked.

"A little," I replied.

"You worry too much. Father is so resourceful. He'll find a way to let us know if anything terrible happens." She thumped Arabella's tiny back expertly.

"There has just been so little news since the king and many of his court left for York two months ago. It seems as if we should have had some message from London by now."

A most unladylike belch erupted from my tiny daughter. Her big sister laughed. She lifted Arabella above her head into the dazzling sunlight. Their eyes connected in perfect communication. Arabella gurgled down in delight at her big sister.

That exquisite image became indelibly imprinted in my heart. I called it out often to comfort my sorrowing soul on the bleak days that were so soon to close in.

Elizabeth gently rocked Arabella into a nap.

"You are so good with her," I said.

"I would destroy anyone who tried to do her harm," she said, fiercely.

"I am sure we will be quite safe here. Especially since the whole area is currently a Parliamentarian stronghold except for Corfe Castle. It makes no strategic sense for the Royalists to even think of bringing any fighting to this area. As long as we live quietly and don't involve ourselves in any way in the ongoing difficulties, I don't see how our Parliamentarian neighbors would gain anything by doing us harm."

"Well, it just breaks my heart that everyone is intent on killing each other because of their religion," my daughter complained.

"Why do you say that?" I asked.

"Well, I guess I heard my brother John and Clodagh discussing it one day."

"Ah, two of our greatest theologians," I said.

"Don't laugh at me, Mother. I'm serious. If the war that is coming is not about religion, why is everyone right now so dead set on killing each other?"

"Pure greed, selfishness, a lack of principles, and the inability to compromise." I paused. "Okay, maybe more than a little bit about religions, also," I confessed.

"Spoken like a true mother—or perhaps I should say, a politician?" My daughter mocked me back. "But seriously. Why are there such different religions in the world, all bent on spewing hatred and ill will at each other?"

"I don't think it has to be that way," I said. "And I don't think your interpretation is necessarily universal. Since you mentioned Clodagh, just look at her. She is devoted to a religion that is expressed very differently than ours and yet we all absolutely adore her and she us." I paused to try to collect my thoughts. "Our very wise vicar once told me he believes that each of us has a little piece of God's grace and spirit born into us. Individually, every human being has a special, but necessarily limited, power for doing good in the world. But what if collectively, if each of us added our special power from that always mysterious God to that of our neighbors, in, say, a church or other community, or even government setting? Wouldn't our capacity to do good for this world be vastly multiplied?"

Elizabeth considered this. "I think I can feel that spirit in our St. Edward, King and Martyr, Parish Church in Corfe Castle, and in the lovely church that Mair-Mair attends at Eastcote Manor. But all the fake pomp and ceremony at the church you make us go to in London makes my heart hurt."

"Your Mair-Mair would have plenty to say about that.

There is no one on earth more devoted to her church than your grandmother, yet she confesses she did a little dance of celebration when the Parliamentarians locked up the former Archbishop Laud with all his pretentious reforms in the Tower of London."

"Well then, why did you and Father make us all go to that ridiculous church in London?" Elizabeth complained.

"It was not us—it was the king. He demanded that all the citizens of the kingdom attend the nearest Anglican church every Sunday. And it is ultimately the king who yet decides what will be said and how the services will be conducted. Although, as you have noted, the further one gets from London, the more latitude there seems to be in how the Anglican services are led. I am sure our surrounding Puritan-leaning neighbors would also share your disdain for the London services. Just as I am certain your open and caring heart would not be comforted by the messages set forth from their judgmental pulpits."

"Well, I am certainly not going to give up all the fun and magic of Christmas!" she vowed.

Arabella erupted with another colossal burp, spitting up all over her sister's blouse. Elizabeth laughed and wrinkled her nose. "Our little darling needs cleaning up on both ends. Don't get up. Just sit here for a bit longer and enjoy this glorious sunshine while you can."

Somehow, even though my "to-do" list for this day was still very long, I relaxed in the sunshine and drifted into a nap. I was startled awake by the excited shouts of my fearsome trio, Ralph. Jane, and Jerome. They dashed breathlessly into the garden.

"Mother—Come see—"

"Is it Father?"

"There are so many carriages."

My heart set up a little flutter. "Well, let's go have a look.

Be careful on the stairs." We raced down to the first tower by the Outer Gatehouse and pounded up the winding stairs. Thankfully, it did, indeed, appear to be—not a hostile army, praise Heaven—but a parade of carriages. And the horses were being hurried. Indeed, from the distance, there appeared to be more carriages than would be needed for just my husband and the retinue that normally accompanied him.

I sent my children scurrying. "Jerome—run tell Clodagh we have company coming. Jane—fly and alert Cook that we will have many more for dinner tonight. Ralph—hurry down and tell the village elder we will need much extra help at the castle for the next few days. Especially tell him we need boys right now who can help feed and groom those exhausted horses."

At last, the parade of carriages rumbled through the Outer Bailey, passed through the inner gate to the West Bailey, and drew to a stop at the entry to the Castle Keep, which was our main residence. My children's father barely waited for the carriage to draw to a stop before he burst through its door and grabbed me into his embrace. I sobbed incoherently into his shoulder. "I thought you would never come. I thought you might be dead. What took you so long?"

Elizabeth interrupted us, tapping her father impatiently on the shoulder. When he turned to add her to his embrace, she thrust his newest daughter into his arms. He gave a little whoop and, in a gesture reminiscent of Elizabeth's earlier that day, he swung his tiny daughter over his head in the lovely afternoon sun. Their matching bright blue gazes locked as they took stock of each other. Another treasured image etched indelibly in my heart.

And then there were more surprises. The doors to the following carriages flew open. My three oldest children tumbled out. There were cries of "Grandmother—Grandmother—" as my sweet granddaughters scampered to me and hugged my knees. I had worried they would have forgotten me by now.

At last, we made our way upstairs and settled into the library. Everyone seemed to be a bit teary-eyed and, of course, we all talked at once. I could not let go of my John's hand. Our thighs seemed glued together as we cozied up on a couch.

Clodagh had stood at a discreet distance as we worked through the initial emotion of our little family reunion. Then she swooped in with goblets of wine and savory tidbits as we settled in. Gradually, I sorted through all the news. My son-in-law, John Borlase, it seemed, had not accompanied his wife because he was about to be made a Baronet by King Charles three days hence.

"But why are you not with him?" I asked Alice. "Shouldn't you be standing by your husband's side for this honor?"

"It is a dubious distinction at best and really, just another of King Charles's blatant money-making schemes. In exchange for the privilege of being a Baronet, we must pay the King £1095—which is the estimated cost of keeping thirty soldiers for three years. Trust me, my new Baronet would much rather be here visiting with his dear mother-in-law. But since we have thrown our lot in with the king, it was an offer we could not refuse. At any rate, since, with Father's help, my husband has also been selected a Member of Parliament from Corfe Castle, we should both be able to check in here at the Castle more often."

I turned to my husband. "I am so glad you have finally come away from London. I have been so frightened for you with all the raising of armies by both sides and talk of war. Can you now stay with us in Corfe Castle for a while?"

John sighed and tousled the head of our almost-four-year-old "Charlie the charmer," who sat at our feet, cuddled into his father's knees. Of all our children, I worried he was the most affected by his father's prolonged absences. "I fear that my longer stay in London after the king and his entourage departed might be construed by some as showing approval of the Parliamentary cause. It is time for me to join the king in York." His eyes held mine pleadingly. "I understand the Oxford air is much cleaner than the London air."

"Oxford—didn't you just say you were going to York?"

"York is where the king currently has his headquarters and now assembles his support staff and army. But that base will undoubtedly change if the war commences. Both Alice and Mary's extended families are already in the process of settling in at their estates near Oxford—a safer distance from all the London turmoil. It is time for our oldest son to begin his formal higher education. My hope is that he can soon be enrolled at Oxford. Our oldest daughters came here with me because they hope to persuade you to join them at Oxford."

Tears blurred my eyes. I wanted so much to just say yes. But I could not bring myself to do it. "It sounds like you won't even be in Oxford much of the time?" I ventured.

"Well, no—but York is not too much further from Oxford than London is from Corfe Castle."

That was hardly comforting. "And where would I live?"

"That is the best part. Both Alice and Mary's families have already established estates nearby. Their homes have excellent nurseries and servants. Both have plenty of spare rooms for the older children. We could alternate between the two large estates of our dear daughters as we wished."

"Please say yes," both daughters chimed in. "We miss you so. We want you to be part of the lives of your grandchildren as they grow up."

I buried my face in my hands and sobbed. Son Ralph pulled a reasonably fresh handkerchief from his pocket and solemnly handed it to me.

Son Charlie patted my knee from his seat by my feet. "Don't cry, Mother."

"I just can't bear to leave Corfe Castle behind," I sobbed. "It would be such a blow to the villagers, who have come so far in the past seven years since we made the castle our home. We would surely lose our castle and all our belongings if we abandoned it and left it unguarded. No one could possibly find reason to attack a middle-aged woman, a mother of ten, living quietly alone with her youngest children!"

"Ah, about our children—" my lawyer husband threw out his final, most painful argument. "You know it would be tempting fate to leave a potential male heir unprotected and in residence. It would be far too dangerous to leave any of our young sons without defense at Corfe Castle for an extended time."

I drew Charlie the charmer from the floor and into my lap and sobbed into his mop of curls.

"C-could you all at least come to Corfe Castle for Christmas if the current difficulties last that long?" They all promised they would, but I did not believe them.

And so we spent the next few days basking in our blissful interval of treasured family togetherness, dreading the days of loneliness and worry that we knew lay just ahead. We endlessly planned as best we could for the unknown perils that would soon befall us and forever change our entire way of life. John managed to single out each child and grandchild for a special private time of bonding, storing up golden moments to help him (and them) in the face of the devastating trials to come. On Sunday, we marched together into the St. Edward King and Martyr Parish Church of Corfe Castle. To the delight of the Corfe Castle villagers who greeted us with heartfelt smiles and words of welcome.

All too soon it was May Day—our last day together. We

pretended it was not, laughing and teasing over a leisurely breakfast. We were interrupted by the sounds of horses outside the door of the Keep. We looked at each other in alarm. Were we already under attack by hostile forces? Clodagh slipped over to the window and turned in relief. "It is your Dorset neighbors. We forgot about the annual May Day hunt that has become our tradition. Shall I send them away?"

I said, "Yes." But I was overruled by John. "You cannot afford to offend these neighbors, as unpleasant as they may be. We shall all go as a family, even the littlest ones. All but the tiny granddaughters and Baby Arabella. You will all smile and laugh and look as if you are completely free from worries and having the time of your life," he commanded his offspring. Cook hastily rounded up some breakfast beer and assorted breads to tide our guests over as we dashed to our rooms to don our riding trousers. The servants scrambled to saddle our horses.

And so we trotted into the sun-dappled forest. Charlie the Charmer bounced merrily in his perch in front of his father, who held to him tightly. Jane and Ralph and Jerome insisted on bringing their bows and arrows. Some of the wives directed disapproving glares at my little tomboy, Jane, with her bow strapped so proudly to her back. I simply waved merrily at the unfriendly busybodies and sent twinkling smiles into their dour faces. It was one of our final adventures ever in this world as a family all together. One most treasured among all the cherished family memories I stored up.

Early the next morning, the parade of carriages bound for Oxford rumbled away just as another bright dawn bloomed into the May sky above Corfe Castle. John arranged for five men from the village to live in the castle with us for the time being and serve as our "security force." They were all getting on in years. Only one, the oldest, the courtly Captain Bond, could boast any formal military training, but they could all aim and load a musket if need be. John worried that he should have also arranged for a trained military garrison for our added protection, but I argued that would only attract attention and add to our image as a potentially hostile force.

A handful of female servants—women from the village—served as our household staff—cooking, cleaning, and washing up. And so, Clodagh, Elizabeth, Joanne, Jane, Baby Arabella, and I settled into our little universe and new daily routines at Corfe Castle. Mostly we waited and watched anxiously for any tidbit of news that would let us know what was happening in the rest of the world.

And news slowly got through, bit by bit. John ultimately journeyed North to York to join the king and his Royalist Army. He was quickly appointed to King Charles's Privy Council. On 16 June 1642, my John was among those who signed the declaration made by the Lords at York, asserting to all that the king had no intention of making war on the Parliament.

Of course, a bare two months later, on 22 August 1642, that promise was broken. King Charles and his Royalist Cavaliers and the Parliamentarian Roundheads officially went to war against each other.

A few days before Christmas in 1642 we celebrated with a crying spree of relief and joy when we got the news that John had safely accompanied King Charles to Oxford to settle in for the winter. We considered that to be our greatest Christmas blessing. Knowing that for a few winter months he was blessedly safe from hostile bullets and spears. Amid all this turmoil, yet another accolade was bestowed on him on 20 December 1642 when he received an honorary doctorate from the University of Oxford. And, of course, King Charles's displeasure against my husband was further eased when my

John gave ample proofs of his devotion to the king by his liberal contributions to the royal treasury. Despite his loyal support for the king at the outbreak of the Civil War, my darling was initially well-regarded by the London Parliament, which in February 1643 recommended that he be retained as Lord Chief Justice of the realm. But they soon turned on him.

AUTHOR ENDNOTES, CHAPTER NINETEEN:
Key English Civil War Battles Prior to the First Siege on Corfe Castle This synopsis provides only the barest overview of the ensuing conflicts, both political and on the battlefield, from 1642-1643, leading up to the point where the Civil War arrived at Corfe Castle's door and Lady Mary was herself forced into the battle.

On 22 August 1642 Charles the First erected his Standard in Nottingham. This officially marked the start of the English Civil War.

On 13 September, the main campaign opened. King Charles moved westward from Nottingham through Cheshire to Shrewsbury. He wanted to reach the armories of Derbyshire and Staffordshire and sought recruits from sympathizers along the way. The Parliamentarian Earl of Essex, with an army of about 20,000 had his eye on the same armories. He marched his troops from Northampton to Worcester.

23 September 1642 The Battle of Powick Bridge was the first important cavalry clash of the English Civil War. It was more a scuffle than an outright battle. The leaders were Prince Rupert (nephew of King Charles I) and The Earl of Essex for the Parliamentarians. The Royalists won. According to Hugh Peters (an outspoken Parliamentary/Puritan supporting preacher), it was "where England's sorrows began."

17 October 1642, The Battle of Kings Norton happened when elements of the <u>Royalists</u> under the command of <u>Prince Rupert</u> (German nephew of King Charles) and <u>Parliamentarians</u> under the command of <u>Lord Willoughby</u> accidentally crossed paths. Both forces had been on their way to join their larger respective armies and continued on after their intense clash.

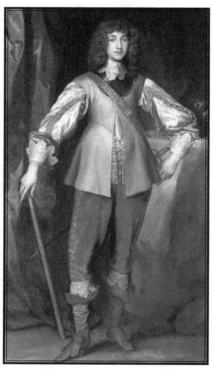

Prince Rupert
by Sir Anthony Van Dyck
Nephew of King Charles I. Fierce
Royalist military leader in the
English Civil War.

23 October 1642, The Battle of Edgehill. Both larger armies unexpectedly found themselves near each other and the battle was on. The opposing forces similarly consisted mostly of inexperienced, badly outfitted troops. Soldiers from each side routinely abandoned their posts to loot enemy supplies. Neither enemy conclusively "won" the battle. This lack of a conclusive, quick victory led to a devastating conflict that lasted four years.

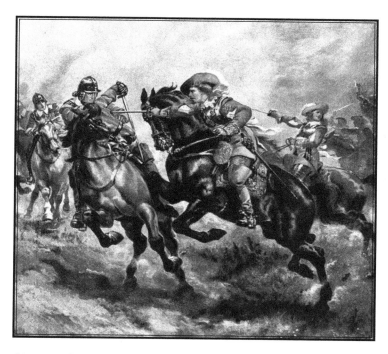

Royalist cavalry attacking at the Battle of Edgehill on 23 October 1642. Painting by Harry Payne. Image from britishbattles.com

On 29 October 1642, King Charles was greeted by cheering crowds as he arrived in Oxford. Prince Rupert and his troops had galloped down the Thames Valley, adding to the Royalist wins. Many Royalist officers now wanted to open peace negotiations. Prince Rupert argued to carry on to London. The king sided with the officers and against his nephew. The arguing gave the Earl of Essex time to overtake the Royalists. Essex reached London with his Parliamentary army on 8 November.

13 November 1642, The Battle of Turnham Green was fought at the end of the first English Civil War campaign. It ended in a stalemate between the Royalists and the much larger Parliamentarian army under the Earl of Essex. By barring the Royalists' entry to London, the Parliamentarians won a huge advantage. King Charles and his army were forced to withdraw to Oxford for safe winter quarters.

19 January 1643, The Battle of Braddock Down was fought in Cornwall. An easy victory for the Royalists, who won Cornwall for King Charles. 1,500 Parliamentarians were taken prisoner during and after the battle, but their lives were spared.

19 March 1643, The Battle of Hopton Heath (in Stafford). Fierce fighting by both sides. Both claimed victory.

30 March 1643, The Battle of Seacroft Moor was a huge loss for the Parliamentary forces. Legends say the fierce fighting turned the Cock Beck, a stream running through the battlefield, red with the casualties' blood for several days.

April 1643, the Battle of Birmingham. 300 Parliamentarians tried to keep 1,400 Royalists from passing through the unshielded Parliamentary town of Birmingham. The vastly outnumbered Parliamentarians hid in the private homes and fired on the Royalists, who in revenge torched the houses and pillaged the town. This gave the Parliamentary side a propaganda boost in condemning the Royalists for viciously attacking unarmed citizens.

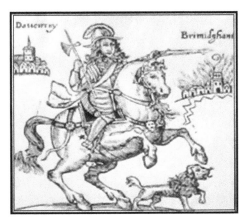 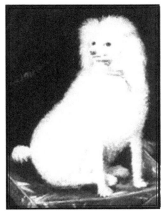

Prince Rupert shown attacking Brimidgham (Birmingham). Parliamentarian pamphlet states, "A True Relation of Prince Rupert's Barbarous Cruelty Against Brimidgham."

Author's Note: *Prince Rupert's (female) hunting poodle was given to him as a puppy. No one knows why she was called Boye. She accompanied him into battle. Boye was killed at the battle of Marston Moor on 2 July 1644. The image of Boye is attributed to Prince Rupert's siste, Louise, the "Princess Palatine." Their moher was the oldest sister of (Elizabeth) of King Charles I. Their father was the German Prince Frederick V of the Palatinate.*

Prince Rupert's adventures later included overseeing the infancy of modern Canada, where he was a colorful founder of the Hudson's Bay Company.

8-21 April 1643, The Siege of Lichfield. Another Royalist victory led by Prince Rupert. This opened access to a top supply of ammunition in the northern counties.

25 April 1643, Battle of Sourton Down. A successful Parliamentarian surprise attack. As the Royalists advanced in an attempt to gain control of southwest England, the Parliamentarians sent a small force to meet them at Sourton Down. The armies battled through the night. The Parliamentarians overcame the much larger Royalist army, forcing them to withdraw back into Cornwall.

KEY CIVIL WAR BATTLES DURING THE SIEGE OF CORFE CASTLE

16 May 1643, The Battle of Stratton. Against the odds, the Royalists defeated a Parliamentarian force fighting to block Cornish Royalists from joining up with Prince Maurice's larger army in Somerset.

18 June 1643, The Battle of Chalgrove. A fight that happened when the Royalist cavalry commanded by Prince Rupert met a similar-sized Parliamentary cavalry. It was a Royalist victory of such enormity the Parliamentarian army fled from Oxfordshire. Among the many senior officers killed at Chalgrove was the enormously popular Parliamentarian, Colonel John Hampden.

18 June 1643, Battle of Adwalton Moor was also "won" by the Royalists. It consolidated their control of Yorkshire, leaving the Parliamentarians with only one stronghold in the north. Sadly, as John later pointed out to me, this was the victory that led to the Royalists' ultimate defeat. It forced the Parliamentarians into a religious and political alliance with Scotland. This, in turn, led to a huge Parliamentary victory at the Battle of Marston Moor a year later in 1644.

4 July 1643, Battle of Burton Bridge. Control of this strategic town seesawed between both sides. On this date Queen Henrietta Maria herself headed from Yorkshire to Oxford with a convoy of supplies for King Charles. The Royalists defeated the Parliamentarians who were blocking the bridge, allowing the queen's convoy to continue on its way. Burton Bridge changed hands several more times during the war before finally coming under Parliamentary control in 1646.

5 July 1643, Battle of Lansdowne Hill, fought near Bath. The Parliamentarians retreated from the Royalists. The Royalists, however suffered so many casualties themselves and were in such disarray and so short of ammunition, they also fell back.

13 July 1643, Battle of Roundway Down was fought near Devizes. A Royalist cavalry force won a crushing victory over the Parliamentarians. Many historians consider this the most successful Royalist battle of the English Civil War.

20 July 1643, Battle of Gainsborough. Gainsborough was an important Royalist base, used to intimidate the Parliamentarians who generally controlled in Lincolnshire eighteen miles away. In a brief attempt to capture Gainsborough for Parliament, Colonel Oliver Cromwell lost, but gained fame as a cavalry leader. After the town was back in

Royalist control, Parliamentarians sent small groups in now and then to torment the Royalists.

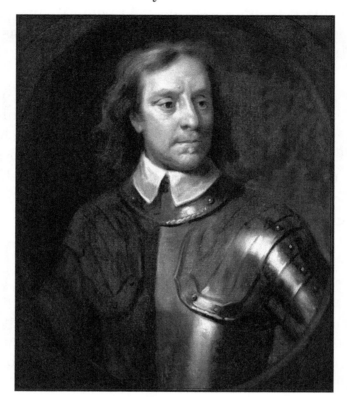

Oliver Cromwell by Samuel Cooper, image in public domain

26 July 1643, The Storming of the Port of Bristol. Prince Rupert took Bristol for the Royalists. They gained a massive stockpile of munitions. Their spoils of war included eight, armed merchant ships that later formed the nucleus of a Royalist fleet. The Bristol munitions makers eventually armed the entire Royalist army with muskets.

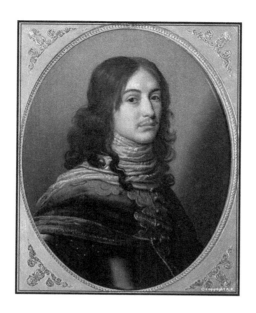

Prince Maurice was a younger brother of Prince Rupert. He commanded the 'Cornish' Army. Both Princes were sons of King Charles's sister, Elizabeth, who was Electress of the Palatinate and briefly Queen of Bohemia as the wife of Frederick V of the Palatinate. In August 1642 both princes arrived in England accompanied by a staff of mostly English and Scottish professional soldiers to fight for their uncle in the Civil War. (Creator of portrait unknown).

CHAPTER TWENTY

"The Cannons have their bowels full of wrath
and ready mounted are they to spit forth
Their iron indignation 'gainst your walls."
Shakespeare, King John
30 April 1643

It was the last day of April. An endless year since I had last seen my husband. And my oldest daughters. And all my sons. Not to mention my darling granddaughters. Indeed, enough time had passed that I might even have had more grandchildren already. And not even known of it.

Clodagh and I sat in the garden, enjoying the fresh spring air and going over our "to do" list for the day. A lonely falcon soared overhead. Male redstarts flashed their crimson feathers as they trilled their sweet song in nearby trees that burst with new green leaves of Spring. Meadow pipits, yellowhammers, linnets, and song thrush added to the birdsong chorus. In my long untended garden, early spider orchids, gentians, milkwort, and eyebrights added their springtime essence, if a bit randomly. Baby Arabella babbled at our feet. She was not only walking but scurrying everywhere on her toddler legs—darting into danger and reaching for every forbidden thing she could get her eager little hands on, if we so much as glanced away. With her incessant curiosity and merry antics, she was indeed our chief source of entertainment during that time of endless waiting.

Daughters Elizabeth and Joanna were already busy with their little classroom. In the absence of an official tutor, the older girls had conspired to be sure their little sister, Jane's, education was not neglected. Jane—lost without her brothers, who had also been her chief playmates, blossomed with the encouragement and attention of the big sisters she idolized. Our cagey vicar offered to help with some of the lessons and soon several of the younger village children, who could be spared from endless work, became her eager classmates. Normally, women who were not Gentry were not taught to read and write, but that little detail did not deter my daughters. And Jane blossomed with playmates closer to her in age than her older sisters.

"The gossip in the Village yesterday about this never-ending war was not good," Clodagh said.

"It is so hard to tell what is true and what is exaggeration," I said. "I cannot even get my head to comprehend reports of 'streams running red with blood.' Twelve hundred reportedly slaughtered one day—even more the next. In such unimaginably violent head-on encounters of muskets and pikes."

"It is indeed too grisly to think about," Clodagh agreed. Her face shuttered and one of the sorrowing silences that periodically closed in on her since her return from Ireland enshrouded her.

The ensuing silence was interrupted by the sound of a horse galloping in through the Corfe Castle's open, welcoming gate. My heart set up a little pitter-patter. Was it at last one of the king's mail couriers? They came through so sporadically now. It had been months since I had last heard from John, or any of my children. We all knew the few bare snippets of news about our Oxford family by heart. Their brief notes were long tattered from frequent reading and blurred by our tears.

Since we never knew when a courier might arrive, we kept loving letters written and ready to thrust quickly into a pouch should an available postal rider happen our way.

I left Arabella in Clodagh's care and ran to fetch our waiting letters.

It was not the mail courier, after all. It was our steadfast advisor, the vicar, who had arrived at the castle in such haste. His face crumpled into a map of worry, and he kept muttering, "Oh my, oh my." He did not pause for his usual chitter-chatter.

"We need to have a word with your little security force right away. And you'd better ask Clodagh and your two older girls to join us."

"Oh, dear Heaven, no." For a moment I could not still the quaver that shook my voice. And then I squared my shoulders and resolutely called together my "troops."

The news was not yet dire, but it was not good. All of Dorset at that time was generally understood to be a Parliamentarian stronghold. Standing firm against King Charles's forces. But now, my long-time, ill-natured and pompously disagreeable neighbor, Sir Walter Erle, had just been named by the Parliamentarians as "military governor of Dorchester for Parliament and Lieutenant of Ordnance." His equally ridiculous ally, Sir Thomas Trenchard, now enjoyed the title of "High Sheriff of Dorset." I am certain these were intended by the Parliamentarians to be "honorary appointments"—to recognize their loyalty (and especially, financial contributions) to the Parliamentary cause. Now I learned that those ridiculous men were taking their "appointments" seriously.

"Dear Lady Bankes, I am so sorry to bring you this alarming news!" Our always cheerful vicar now looked as if he might weep. "I have received most anxious reports from several sources!"

The news was indeed concerning. Sir Erle and Sir

Trenchard had been prancing all over the neighboring towns and villages of Dorchester, Lyme, Melcombe, Weymouth, Wareham, and Poole. They had been enlisting military forces off the streets and boasting of their intent to make the entire seacoast a "stronghold" for Parliamentary forces."

Since at that time there was only one tiny outpost in all of Dorset that could be accused of favoring the Royalist cause, those grandiloquent boasts could not be ignored, as ridiculous as they sounded. They were blatantly, and publicly, threatening Corfe Castle. And, by inference, my children.

To their credit, my little security force did not flinch at this news. I suppose we had all anticipated in our deepest heart that it would come to this. We gathered around to review our "battle plans," such as they were. The natural leader of our group was Captain Bond. Grizzled, and a bit unsteady on his feet with age, he was the only one with any military experience and that was very long ago. He still had the bearing of a military leader. Never a hair out of place. Ramrod straight back. Not prone to many words. But we all listened up when he spoke. And now, he told us we needed to send for help.

"My sources," he said, "have whispered that Royalist forces led by Prince Maurice, King Charles's younger nephew, and the Marquis of Hertford are heading toward Blandford."

I knew this to be a market town north of Poole in Dorset. I looked at our aging captain in surprise. How had this savage Civil War already arrived so close to the gates of Corfe Castle?

Captain Bond urged, "We must send a messenger from the Corfe Castle to Prince Maurice requesting help under cover of darkness this very night."

I fought back hot tears at the thought of what this might mean for the dear villagers that had so captured our hearts.

The castle walls seemed unassailable. Our ultimate undoing would be the vulnerable village that lay just beyond the safety of the outer gates. Our village neighbors were completely unprotected. There couldn't be more perfect hostages in undermining the ultimate safety of all of us.

The Vicar sighed. "I fear there is more worrisome news to relate. I know that you and your family have always honored the long-time tradition on the Isle of Purbeck of allowing the local Gentry to enter your forest surrounding Corfe Castle with their hunting hounds to course a stag every May Day."

"Of course!" I said. "I would much prefer that my husband be here to host this tradition, but we have made plans for the annual May Day hunt to proceed as usual tomorrow morning."

"My dear Lady Mary—It pains me so much to say this, but the current whispers are that Sir Walter Erle is conspiring with some of your neighbors to disrupt this festive event. He intends to use it as an opportunity to invade the castle grounds and take control of it."

Why did this not surprise me? We all looked in unison toward our top military advisor with the same question in our eyes. Captain Bond, despite his many years, still exuded authority. He inspired our confidence and gave us courage.

He nodded sharply. "Let's get on with it. We trooped behind our stalwart leader down to the heretofore always open, welcoming, gates at the Outer Bailey. With solemn ceremony we closed and set in place the hefty locking bars. The vicar led us through a brief prayer urging that we be granted "the will to forgive those who were seeking to harm us." I confess—my unwilling heart was not quite yet ready to go there.

Early on May Day, some of our "gentlemen" neighbors and their "ladies" did indeed arrive for the annual May Day hunt. I presumed these to be friendly souls and not party to the treachery we had been warned about. My five-man security force, led by the intrepid Captain Bond, stood by but chose not to make their presence known. Eventually, the erstwhile hunting party departed from the closed portcullis, obviously in some puzzlement. I wondered (hopefully) if we had been falsely alarmed. An hour or so later, however, an armed Parliamentary troop arrived on horseback and dispelled that hope. The officers in charge seemed to be educated gentlemen. The unruly forces with them were of a more common sort. Openly rude and rowdy, they did not display normal military discipline. Had they just been rounded up from outside a pub? There was much taunting and shouting.

"Better open them gates 'afore anyone gets hurt."

"It won't take long to bash in them walls."

There was more, which I will not repeat. We were hugely outnumbered. I could not bear the thought of my minuscule, five-man security guard even thinking of raising their muskets against this unruly mob. Before Captain Bond could veto the idea, I leaned out from my perch in the window of the tower at the entry gates to the Outer Bailey and shouted down.

"I wish to speak to your Commander."

The crowd, surprised, quieted a bit. I repeated my demand. Two men, by their uniforms, seeming to be Parliamentary officers, rode to the window. They looked up at me a bit sheepishly but spoke respectfully.

"We are sorry to disturb you," said one.

"We mean you no harm," assured another.

"This Castle is not open to the public. You must leave. Now! Before any harm comes to you and your troops."

I wanted to laugh. They looked so startled and a bit shamefaced. As if they were back in the Nursery and had been caught in a forbidden act by their Nanny.

"Now!" I again shouted, even more sternly.

Much to my surprise (and relief) the two nonplused fledgling officers gained a modicum of control over their undisciplined soldiers, and they all galloped away. I had no doubt that once they gathered their composure, they, or others like them, would be ordered back. And would not in the future be scared away by a crazy, shouting lady.

It became rumored about by many who were watching us, including my neighboring Parliamentarians, that I was in fact in the process of reinforcing the castle's defenses. I then came under the most watchful surveillance. Everything we did was exaggerated out of all proportion. If we sent out for fresh vegetables in the local marketplace for our evening dinner rumors circulated that I must be stockpiling enough supplies to singlehandedly take on the entire Parliamentary forces.

And then, for some unfathomable reason, the Parliamentary Committee at Poole fixated on the ancient cannons that stood at Corfe Castle since the days of Lord Hatton under Queen Elizabeth, when the Spanish Armada threatened England. They now served essentially as ornamental garden statuary. I received an official letter from this esteemed Poole committee demanding that I hand over the castle's cannons. They claimed many of my neighbors were worried about their safety should the cannons be turned on them.

I responded to this outrageous complaint (quite politely, and most reasonably, I thought) by messenger that I would prefer to leave the cannons in place. That as a woman living peacefully and quietly alone with four young daughters, I felt most defenseless—that the cannons would seem to provide a visible deterrent against unwarranted aggression from passing criminals who might seek to take advantage of my vulnerability. As a compromise I most generously promised that if the cannons could remain in my possession, I would remove them from their carriages on the high wall to make them immediately less accessible, and, most importantly, not as prominently visible to any neighbors in the vicinity. To my surprise, I received a most courteous response to my request.

The commissioners agreed that the cannons could remain in my possession.

Only a few days had passed, however, when I was awakened early by Captain Bond's insistent rapping on my bedroom door. Did the dear man never sleep?

"I am sorry to awaken you. There is trouble at the front gate. A large group of seamen—forty at least—have arrived from Poole. They are waiting outside the gate and are demanding to take possession of the cannons."

Grandmother Altham would definitely not have approved of the epithet that slipped unbidden from my lips. "Run and wake Clodagh. Tell her to quickly gather the maidservants and meet us at the wall where the cannons were mounted. You gather your men, also. I will be there in three minutes! We need to quickly remount the cannons!"

The good captain turned to carry out my demands, but I said, "Wait. I know we have powder and cannonballs somewhere—bring that out also. Does anyone on our security team know how to load a cannon?"

My security chief did not flinch. "We will figure it out." However, as he sped off to carry out my urgent demands, I caught an expression of purest alarm on his face.

I took only seconds to slip into my clothes and also rushed down to the garden wall where my hastily called team was already gathering in various stages of bedragglement in the early dawn. I put them to work setting the cannons back up in their carriages and securing them in their mounts. Clodagh and my daughters raced up. Elizabeth was carrying Baby Arabella.

Elizabeth said, "There was no one left to watch over her. She is safer with us."

"OK, here I go," I said. Patting futilely at my uncombed hair, I asked Captain Bond to accompany me to the castle entry.

Captain Bond looked worried. "I'm not sure it is a good idea to raise the gates," he ventured.

"I need to be certain they have an actual warrant to take possession of the cannons."

"And if they don't?"

"I won't open the gates at all and will just tell them to go away."

"And if they do?"

"Then I will know my worst fears have been realized. We will officially be at war with our neighbors. Are you up for that?"

My stalwart protector looked sad. "I wish there were another choice. I hope I am worthy of the trust you have placed in me."

Together we hurried up the stairs of the tower that overlooked the gate.

I leaned out of the window in the tower above the gate and shouted down with my most authoritative voice. "Why are you here?"

"We have been ordered to confiscate your cannons!" The leader of the sailors identified himself.

"Who issued the order?"

"The Commissioner of the Parliamentary Committee in Poole."

"May I see that order?"

The assigned leader of this motley crew swaggered up to the gate The seamen with him followed closely. "You will have to open the gates."

"Here is what you are going to do. You must all move back from the gates at least thirty feet. At my signal, you alone will approach the gate. When you reach the gate, you can thrust it through the bars. Then you yourself will quickly move back with the rest of your men, until further notice."

"No need to be so suspicious. We are just following orders. We don't mean you any harm."

His words were conciliatory enough, but there was something about his tone that set my hackles on alert. "Do as I say, or be on your way," I said in my most commanding tone. As a then mother of ten I was certainly well accustomed to using my voice to demand obedience.

"There are security guards posted at the top of the wall with muskets pointed at each of you," I lied, to further urge compliance with my demands.

At this they quickly backed away and the leader sauntered forward, putting on a show of bravado for his companions. He thrust the summons through the grille of the outer portcullis. When he returned to his troops, Captain Bond opened the inner portcullis slightly and reached in for the document. It was true. The Parliamentary Committee at Poole had already broken its promise to allow Corfe Castle to keep its cannons. Leaving Captain Bond to guard the gate, I hurried back to the cannons.

My loyal team had just anchored the last cannon back in its carriage. Now they were puzzling as to what to do with the powder and fuses and cannonballs that Captain Bond had left there.

"Hurry—run tell Captain Bond I need him," I ordered one of my stalwart guards. "And you stand guard in his place." In the interim, I hopped up on the wall where the cannons stood and joined the guards who were attempting to load one of them. All my daughters and all the maidservants looked up at me, alarmed. (Except for Baby Arabella, who was still clutched tightly in Elizabeth's arms and delightedly hollering "Ma Ma" at me).

"Be careful, Mother," Joanna cried out.

"Wait for Captain Bond. Please." Elizabeth panicked.

"How hard can it be?" I responded. "Look, here is a little hole in the top of the cannon where you probably stick the fuse down to light it. And Captain Bond has left this container with slender pieces of wood that seem to just fit, so let's just jam one down this hole. So, then we need to put some of this black powder way back in the cannon under the match hole." I looked about for anything that might logically be used to load black powder.

"Lady Mary, please let us help," urged one of the guards who had been standing by. "I've never fired a cannon before, but it can't be all that different than the matchlocks we have been using. And I have a "slow match" already burning in my musket that we can use to light the fuse."

I stood aside and watched as they poured a small bucket full of black powder pellets into the front of the cannon and then used a round pole that had been cut to just the right size to push the powder back under the fuse. They were getting ready to roll in a few of the small cannonballs that were also standing ready when I stopped them.

"The whole point of this is to create shock and fear. We need a really big bang."

So, they shoveled another bucket of the black powder down the nose of the cannon and tamped it in. And then added several of the three-pound cannonballs.

"All right. Now, how do we light it?" One of the guards pulled out a "slow match" that had been attached to his matchlock musket. I knew from growing up with my three sports fanatic brothers that a "slow match" was usually a length of hemp or flax cord that had been chemically treated to make it burn exceedingly slowly and consistently for a prolonged time. It enabled soldiers to quickly fire their muskets in the heat of battle.

I had already lit the fuse when Captain Bond came rushing

up. When he saw what we were up to, he shouted, "Wait—"

Too late. The fuse was already lit. In a flash it burned down below the top of the hole in which it was stuck.

"Jump away." The guards beside me scrambled off the wall on which the cannons stood. I had not yet made it off the wall when the cannon fired. Or rather exploded. I fell on my backside but saw the huge charge of flame that burst from the mouth of the cannon, followed by an imposing plume of black smoke. The acrid smell of the black powder filled the air.

There was a moment of stunned silence. And then Arabella erupted in peals of laughter, interrupting her giggles with shouts of "Ma-Ma, Ma-Ma." Apparently, she found my pratfall too funny. Arabella's amusement became contagious. Soon we were all gasping in hilarity (which was only slightly tinged with hysteria). "Maybe we didn't need that last load of black powder," I said to more shouts of laughter.

And then the guard who had remained on duty at the front gate came racing up. The forty seamen who had been sent to the castle to cause us fright had been so terrified by the cannonballs flying over their heads they had all run away.

CHAPTER TWENTY-ONE
"Fight valiantly today;
and yet I do thee wrong to mind thee of it.
For thou art framed of the firm truth of valor,"
Shakespeare, Henry V
May 1643

We did not delude ourselves. Trouble was inevitable for Corfe Castle. And especially for the villagers just outside our gates. We had no choice but to sound the alarm. We dashed from the cannons back to the greater safety of the Castle Keep. Clodagh and Elizabeth hurried to the tower. Our signal drum already sat in its place—for just this emergency. Their frantic pounding signaled imminent danger to the villagers. Tenants and neighbors rushed to the castle to form a considerable garrison. They brought whatever they could quickly grab—needed weapons, ammunition, gunpowder, and other war accessories. What they did not bring was a lot of food.

Our every move was now suspect and closely watched by those who wished us harm. Armed troops guarded the outer entry to the castle and intercepted any supplies we attempted to carry inside the gates. In Wareham, a nearby market town, the Parliamentarians ordered that there be no commerce with anyone on behalf of Corfe Castle. Shopkeepers could sell no beef, beer, mutton, or other provisions to me or anyone else representing Corfe Castle. They blocked any outside means of feeding the volunteers who now defended us. Even though we had made some preparations, we were ill-prepared to provide for a lengthy siege for the stouthearted volunteers who not only sought refuge but stood ready to defend us.

Any messengers sent from the castle, potentially seeking outside assistance, were also intercepted. During the next week, increasingly threatening letters were delivered to the castle gate from the Parliamentary Committee at Poole. They threatened to send a large army to forcibly bash down the gates if I would not voluntarily give up the cannons. They warned that they would set fire to the houses of any villagers who aided us. And then the tearful wives of my volunteer defensive force stepped in. They implored their husbands to return to their homes and not expose them to ruin.

How could I have deluded myself so foolishly? I should have been preparing for the worst. I had wasted the entire past year absurdly hoping the Parliamentarians would never have anything to gain by attacking a woman living essentially unguarded with her four young daughters. How could I recover some of this lost time? My sweet daughters and my wonderful villagers now faced urgent peril.

And so, at last I humbled myself. In a letter I abjectly begged the pardon of the Parliamentary Commission at Poole. I pleaded with them to understand my previous caution as a helpless woman living unprotected with her young daughters. I sweetly beseeched them to please, please take the offending cannons off my hands so that all could be convinced of my innocent intent to only live peacefully with my neighbors. And so they did. In a show of contemptuous braggadocio, an armed force of Parliamentary forces carried my offending cannons away.

The ridiculous dunderheads actually bought it. After they confiscated my cannons, they smugly gloated to anyone who would listen how they had "forced me into submission." I most humbly withstood their patronizing taunts. My ploy seemed so ridiculously easy. Our anti-Royalist foes, with arrogantly dismissive ease, soon grew remiss in their observation of the comings and goings at the castle. They seemed to think possession of the castle cannons was tantamount to possessing the castle itself, as surely as if they now lived within its walls.

In fact, of course, I used this interlude to stealthily and sometimes not so stealthily set about seriously supplying the castle for a long-term siege. Something I should have taken more to heart a year ago. More quickly than I had ever anticipated, the Parliamentarian observers grew negligent in their watches—no longer heeding what we brought in—or seizing supplies that might fortify the castle. We even sneaked in a hundred and half weight of powder for muskets and a commensurate quantity of match. And, of course, food. We even somehow openly herded cattle and sheep through the gates without attracting undue notice. The Villagers, during this temporary lull, returned for the moment to their homes.

The greater Civil War marched on. During this interim period at Corfe Castle, news of the ensuing battles trickled into the village, adding to growing confidence in the Royalist cause. My heart cheered at the news of each victory. I dared to hope my John at last might return soon to me.

The Royalists decisively won the Battle of Stratton in mid-May 1643. They not only controlled Cornwall but crushed the Parliamentary field army in Devon.

The following week, in the "Siege of Worcester," a Parliamentary army of about 3,000 failed to capture the city, which only about 1,700 Royalists defended. The Royalists could not help gloating. My girls and I cried happy tears at the news of this hopeful victory.

And yet, the local grapevine was not good. Whispers grew louder that local Parliamentary forces intended to take down Corfe Castle. Captain Bond and I sent another update to Prince Maurice and the Marquis of Hertford. We knew they continued their advance in our direction with a large Royalist army. I reminded them of the strategic and psychological value of Corfe Castle as a Royalist stronghold and warned them of the current peril we faced.

To my huge relief, this time the prince and the marquis responded immediately, but from an unexpected source. Those that heeded our call arrived wearing no "official" Royalist insignia. It seems that when the English Civil War hostilities were just beginning, King Charles revived another ancient Royal prerogative that had long been dormant. He issued a summons to members of aristocracy and gentry who might be presumed to have some influence over the local population to raise their own defensive forces. These reserves would stand ready should the king need them. Not all who received this order responded, but Sir Edward Lawrence of nearby Creech Grange appointed his son, Robert, as a local captain to quietly recruit and train a cadre of Royal supporters. Creech Grange is only four miles from Corfe Castle. (Although Sir Edward Lawrence, himself, did not play a significant role in the greater hostilities, he was later knighted at Oxford for his loyalty in this effort.)

Sir Edward Lawrence's son, Captain Robert Lawrence, and a garrison of eighty men arrived quietly, under cover of darkness. He came without a royal commission. Which meant he could not "command moneys or provisions from the king" to feed and arm his troops. I mentally just shrugged. Lucky for all of us the master of the castle had deep pockets. I was enormously relieved to have even this comparatively small force onboard. Of course, the arrival of our "guard" could not remain concealed for long. We quickly and quietly gathered as many of the villagers as would agree to come inside the safety of the castle gates.

Clodagh deftly organized the women and older children into crews with specific duties in cooking and tending to the needs of all. We could not all dine at once, but initially ate in shifts. Thank goodness it was June. We set up impromptu tables outside in the garden. Our beaming vicar bobbed about, blessing the meals and providing words of encouragement and cheer to all. The "party" atmosphere too soon shattered.

The early daybreak of 23 June 1643 was misty for a summer day. It had sprinkled the night before. Hazy cloud tendrils swirled around the castle windows, blurring the dawn. Dense white fog blanketed the village just below us. It was not concealment enough to mask the sounds of six hundred men arriving to attack my home. I slipped into my clothes and alerted Clodagh that the fireplaces in the Upper Ward rooms should be quickly lit and made ready. Just in case. I then hurried to the Middle Ward, which Captain Lawrence and I had agreed his troops would defend if necessary. High, sturdy walls and tall towers also protected this ward. My stalwart friend was already there. He grimly, but coolly, shouted orders to his small garrison. They pointed their eighty muskets down at the hundreds of mightily armed men that now surrounded Corfe Castle.

"I hoped it would not come to this! These are people from nearby communities. Neighbors. My family has shopped in their markets and supported their businesses for generations. No matter which side wins this terrible war, how will we ever get over it? How can we ever face each other again after we have shot bullets at each other?"

He was so young, only a few years older than my oldest son. I did not know how to comfort him. The same unanswerable questions were breaking my heart. "Are you married?"

His smile was wan. "My first son is six months old."

"I think he will be proud one day to know his father risked his life to defend a woman and her young daughters from harm. Not to mention a small, unprotected village of very dear people."

A smile briefly illuminated his face. "Your esteemed vicar has already commended the protection of his little flock to me." He sighed and dipped his head in a brief salute. "We will do what we can." By then, the dense mist was dissipating. We began to discern the heavy armaments now assembled outside the castle walls. The mass of forces that met our eyes dismayed us. There were indeed at least six hundred men. Against a protective force of eighty military troops, a ragtag security guard of five, a few housemaids, assorted terrified and mostly unarmed villagers, and a foolhardy, middle-aged woman with her four young daughters. How could we possibly hold out against such ludicrously excessive numbers? According to later reporting in the *Mercurius Rusticus,* a popular daily Royalist newsletter, Sir Erle brought three captains with him (Captains Sydenham, Scott, and Jarvis) to help command his large force. The Mercurius also reported the Parliamentarians offered tempting bribes to the servants and villagers supporting me to help bring me down. There are no reports anyone ever responded to that offer. The soldiers participating in the attacks against me reportedly were made to swear to an oath that they would "give no quarter," mercilessly taking the lives of all—even any women and children—they might find inside the castle walls.

From our tower perch we could hear shouting below us. I recognized the arrogant voice of Sir Walter Erle, bellowing out orders. "I once chastised my children for privately calling him "Old Watt," I commented to Captain Lawrence. "I can't say he was a close friend, but he pretended to be. He accepted the hospitality of our home, and rode in every May Day hunt we hosted on our land since we acquired the castle eight years ago."

While we watched from the tower at the gate the preparations of those bent on demolishing my world, Captain Lawrence briefed me on the various types of weapons he observed below. No shots had been fired—yet. Our attackers remained at a safe distance—out of reach of the matchlocks now aimed at them by Captain Lawrences' men. 'Demy cannons,' culverins and sakers (all basically cannons of different sizes) now aimed straight at the castle towers. My young defender grimly assured me of the varying degrees of firepower the Parliamentarians might employ to batter down walls (or gates). Armaments that now stood at strategic intervals—aimed straight at both the castle's Upper and Lower Wards.

Captain Lawrence, observing my terrified demeanor, reassured me. "Do not fear. Corfe Castle sits on such a high hill, the walls are mostly out of range. The need to aim the cannonballs upward dampens the speed of the ordnance. Any ammunition that might reach a wall, won't have much destructive power. I think these weapons are meant to strike fear but will generally be ineffective against your high castle."

He continued, "They also have petards, which are explosives in small containers that could help them break down a door, gate, or breach a wall. I am also not too alarmed about those, as they must get close to the gates to set them off, and we are well-positioned to keep that from happening. They are probably more dangerous to the ones who carry them than to anyone else."

"How do those two large triangular things on wheels that are framed with wood and lined so thickly with wool fleeces work? Are they some kind of battering rams?" I asked.

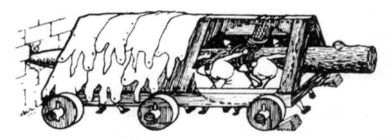

The Roundheads (Parliamentarians) used a huge battering ram called a "sow" to attack the castle. They hid behind a huge triangular wooden, shield, but as soon as they were within range their foes fired muskets at the Roundheads' enemy's legs.

"That they essentially are. They are called 'siege engines.' They are very effective at breaking down castle walls and heavily fortified gates."

I caught my breath in alarm.

"Never fear. The catch is the siege engines are exceedingly heavy and must be propelled forward up a steep hill by many men on foot if they are to get close enough to batter any part of the castle. The legs and feet of those tasked with propelling them are necessarily dangerously exposed and easy targets. My men are excellent marksmen. Even if they try to ram us under cover of darkness, they will be lit enough by the stars and the light from the campfires of the attackers that we will see them coming and we know where to aim our fire."

Even as he spoke, eleven men took their places inside one of the "siege engines" and laboriously began slowly rolling the heavy machine toward the main castle gate. Just below the tower where we stood. My instinct was to flee, but Captain Lawrence put a steadying hand on my arm. The heavy siege engine inched ever closer. I could scarcely breathe. My heart hammered. When they were about one hundred yards away my companion told me to cover my ears. A simultaneous barrage of musket fire erupted from the castle walls. Anguished screams burst from the men who were propelling the siege engine as their legs shattered. Nine of the men ran screaming away as well as their broken ankles would allow. One desperately wounded man lay screaming. One had immediately died of his wounds. Our assailants made no further attempt to use either "siege engine" during the six endless weeks that followed.

A momentary silence ensued as our attackers considered what next move they would take.

"Why are the Parliamentarians so intent on adding Corfe Castle to their conquests? Do you have unusual riches stored away here?" Captain Lawrence wondered.

"Very little, in terms of such things as actual gold or jewels. The furnishings, most of which came from previous owners, must have been originally costly, but would have little value in terms of arming and feeding an army, or paying the costs of a government. No, I fear, it is simply revenge by the Parliamentarians at the very top levels of leadership in the House of Commons. My husband fights with his words—not bullets. Top Parliamentarians are outraged that my husband, who has long sought to broker a peaceful settlement with both sides, finally chose to support the king. They are furious that earlier this year while on the Court Circuit, he declared from the bench that the top Parliamentary Army leaders, the Earl of Essex, Sir William Waller, and Lord Manchester, had committed treason by leading an armed militia aimed at destroying King Charles. The House of Commons retaliated by declaring my John and the rest of the judges who concurred in that judgment to be 'traitors.'"

"So now these 'brave' Parliamentarians who would govern England want to kill a woman and her four young daughters? Where is the honor in that?"

I found myself becoming increasingly fond of this caring

young man. "It probably doesn't help that King Charles himself is so difficult to like," was the only response I could come up with.

Our assailants soon began a simultaneous assault with their muskets upon both the Upper and Middle Wards. At Captain Lawrence's insistence, we did not return fire. He shrugged at my questioning eyes. "It will be extremely difficult for us to replenish our ammunition if we run out. Let them amuse themselves by firing away. Distant muskets can do no real harm."

I left the young captain to tend to his troops and returned to the Upper Ward to check on mine. Captain Bond and Clodagh, of course, had everything well in hand. Although they now complained of the heat from the fires that stood ready. With musket fire so distant and no scaling ladders in sight to reach up to the high walls, it did not seem that we were yet in danger of being invaded in the Upper Ward any time soon, so we let the fires die back. Constant bursts of gunfire from too far away to matter assaulted our ears for the next several days. We were essentially prisoners, but we seemed to be safe, for the moment.

And then our attackers, frustrated that they could wreak no physical harm, assaulted our hearts. They profaned the St. Edward King and Martyr Parish Church of Corfe Castle by converting it into a battery from which they played musket fire upon the castle. They used it as a shelter for their meetings to plot against us. They broke down our lovely organ and converted the pipes to serve as cases for their gunpowder and shot. To augment their ever-dwindling supply of musket ammunition they cut off the lead from the church roof and rolled it up into primitive bullets. They even desecrated a surplice by making it into shirts for two soldiers. As a final sacrilege, they housed horses inside the church and allowed them to drink from the baptismal font.

We were all distraught—except for our still beaming vicar. "Our Church is not a building made of wood and stones," he assured us. "It is *us*. And here we still all are. So let us celebrate our community of people—even as we mourn the devastating loss of life throughout our land that is happening at the hands of those we once called neighbors."

The worst part was being locked in without any word of how the larger world was faring. Where were my husband and oldest children? What was happening to my Mair-Mair? One morning my heart was all at odds and ends. I could not concentrate on the chores I had set out to do. People I cared deeply about surrounded me, but I had never felt so alone. Irrationally, I blamed my absent husband—the one who had pleaded with me to go with him. How could he have gone off with the king and left me so abandoned and alone? My lovely garden provided no solace. I needed to find a quiet place to just, well, cry… I did not notice the little shadow that tagged behind me.

I made my way to the tiny chapel inside the castle walls we now all crowded into on Sundays in small shifts. Where our vicar ministered to all now confined within the Corfe Castle gates with such passion. According to his version of the Anglican faith. I stood quietly and bowed my head as my eyes adjusted to the unlit consecrated sanctuary. No candles lightened the gloom within. Yet, my attention was drawn to the front of the chapel where I sensed quiet movement in the shadows. Suddenly, the silence was shattered with an explosion of sound, coming from the small harpsichord that stood in the front of the chapel. And then I recognized Clodagh's unmistakable voice. She was not singing one of the merry madrigals of our youth. I did not recognize the language. Was it Latin, or maybe Italian? Her voice both soared and throbbed with a fierce passion. Something inexplicably powerful about the music released a torrent of tears down my cheeks. A small hand slipped into my own. My darling ten-year-old Jane stood by my side. She turned her head and dampened the side of my frock with her tears. Teardrops from my own eyes were lost in her curls when I bent down to hug her.

"I just know it will all turn out all right," my sweet daughter sobbed into my ear.

We crept in the darkened chapel down to Clodagh and wrapped our arms around her as she sat, weeping, on the harpsichord bench.

"You learned that amazing music from the nuns in Ireland, didn't you?" I asked my 'almost sister.' In all the time since she had returned to me and to my family she had never spoken of her stay in Ireland or the convent she had committed to join. Now, she said, "One of them was sent from a convent in Italy to help with our mission in feeding the poor. She became a dear friend to me. We shared a passion for music, and I learned much from her. It is still so hard to know they were all slaughtered on that dreadful day while I had slipped away to search for food."

The three of us remained in the comforting peace and darkness of the chapel for some time, hanging tightly to each other's hands, until we could steel ourselves for another day in the world that faced us outside.

The days wore on. We were all grew weary. We were, in fact, bored. And all getting on one another's nerves. The enemy also seemed to be growing lax in their vigilance of our activities. They awakened us every morning to a few halfhearted too far away to reach us musket shots, but otherwise entertained themselves with their own devised activities and other non-military pursuits throughout the long July days.

The outrageous behavior of our foe's leader, Sir Walter

Erle, incited much hilarity among us as he sought to avoid exposing himself to any possible danger. From our towers we could often see him creeping around on the hillsides on his hands and knees, covered in a bearskin, apparently using it as a kind of armor, lest he be hit by a bullet from us.

We were not yet in need of extra food supplies, but we were also bored. One afternoon, several older teenagers from the village, who now lodged at the castle, got up to their own brand of mischief. Observing that a bull and eight cows wandered near the entry to the castle, they conspired with several of Captain Lawrence's garrison to set up distracting gunfire from a distant tower. With the enemy preoccupied, our skylarking teenagers sallied out and herded the cattle mockingly through the gate to the castle to the cheers of those who stood watching. Neither Captain Lawrence nor I had been in on this little escapade. He promised to discipline his troops who participated in this misbegotten adventure, but I deterred him. We all welcomed the laughter their outrageous antics brought.

Several days later there was a similar escapade. This time five high-spirited younger boys from the castle, not wanting to be outdone by their older brothers, took their turn at their own devilment, venturing out to fetch in four more cows from a further hill. Distant Parliamentary forces, who were, thankfully, out of firing range, spotted them. Then, to our alarm, we heard them hollering, "Shoot, Anthony! Shoot, Anthony!" As they herded the cows toward the castle, the boys passed by a villager's hut, which we erroneously presumed to be empty. We soon learned, however, an armed enemy named Anthony was now on duty inside and supposed to be standing watch. To my horror a face appeared in the window of the hut. Just as quickly, the face disappeared. It did not appear again. My heart raced as I watched the now panicked boys hightail it past the window of the hut, still prodding their ill-gotten trophies in front of them. Apparently, Anthony did not care to take a chance that the boys might also be armed and better shots than he. Anthony did not shoot. "Shoot, Anthony!" became our mocking rallying cry after that. However, Captain Lawrence and I both firmly put our feet down. There were to be no further such rash incidents. On pain of possible imprisonment in the Corfe Castle dungeon.

CHAPTER TWENTY-TWO

"The fire eyed maid of smoky war
All hot and bleeding we will offer them."
Shakespeare, Henry IV
early August 1643

At Corfe Castle, the Parliamentary "siege" to remove me and my children and my small group of defenders took on a new urgency in late July/early August 1643. Word seeped in that there had been a calamitous loss of the Port of Bristol. Parliamentary leaders, frustrated with this huge loss, grew increasingly impatient with the excessive length of time it was taking to conclude the assault on Corfe Castle. After nearly six weeks the Parliamentarians were no nearer to taking my castle than they had been on day one.

We later learned that the hapless Sir Walter Erle received clear orders. Bring the siege to an end. Now! "Old Sir Watt" fortified the Parliamentary forces with 150 seamen (many of whom, we later discovered, were recruited from local gaoles and released early to the Parliamentary navy. Some bore recent burn marks on their faces, marking them as felons— the burns being part of the punishment for the crimes for which they were imprisoned. Rumors that reached the castle had it that some were even convicted murderers, sentenced to death. These "recruits" brought with them several cartloads of petards, grenades, and—most worrying of all—very tall scaling ladders. According to the venerable "Mercurius

Rusticus" the promises of enormous financial rewards to the first to scale the walls into the castle were huge—£20 to the first man over the wall and £1 to the 20th man over the walls—a virtual fortune in those days.

On the morning of the 4th of August 1643, I saw the new reinforcements arrive and grasped the intent of the tall scaling ladders. I rushed to find Captain Lawrence, carrying Arabella in my arms. She reached out to him, and he swung her up on his shoulders so she, too, could peer over the parapets with us. They were by now bosom buddies.

My companion was grim. "If they get many ladders up and can motivate enough of them to climb the ladders simultaneously, a few might get through. But it is still going to be ridiculously easy to pick them off with pikes and musket shots before they even get near the tops of the ladders." We could hear the lily-livered Sir Walter Erle and Captain Sydenham, who were standing safely back, out of range of any potential musket fire from the castle, barking out orders.

"It appears they are preparing to attack both the Upper and Middle Wards at the same time," I pointed out.

"You should be all right with your Captain Bond and his four men armed with muskets. And, as we have planned, if you and your daughters and maidservants keep a steady supply of embers from the fireplaces raining down on them, that will probably be as much of a deterrent as any musket fire."

I sighed. "I would gladly and with no regret at all slay anyone with my bare hands who intended harm to my daughters—or my dear villagers! It nevertheless seems so beyond unfair that I must now ask my sweet daughters to bear the weight on their young hearts of possibly causing another human being deadly harm."

I caught the wry expression on my companion's face, who was young enough to be my son. Who commanded a guard composed of mostly younger men than he—barely beyond late-teen-hood themselves. "Well of course my sentiment applies to young men as well as young women." I amended defensively. I continued my lament.

"What kind of future England are we building with this dreadful war? What are we doing to the very souls of our young people who will one day be tasked to lead England themselves?"

Captain Lawrence reached inside his shirt and drew out a folded sheet of paper. His expression was sardonic. "You need to read our enemy's orders which were earlier this morning thrust in through the gate."

Our enemy's orders were clear. "If you find the defendants obstinate not to yield, you will maintain the siege to victory, and then deny quarter unto all, killing without mercy men, women, and children."

He handed my cheerfully babbling baby back to me. The crowd below us was growing noisy. The captain's expression was grim. "Look. The so-called leaders have no honor. It seems they have not yet found willing volunteers to scale the ladders. Now they are plying them with spirits to give them courage. Only the basest military so-called leader would ascribe to the idea that drunkenness makes some men fight like lions, that if sober, would flee like rabbits. How can I ask my honorable soldiers to take the lives of drunken men?"

He sighed deeply. "It looks like the real fun is about to begin. You'd best hurry to the Upper Ward and get everyone ready for the worst. If you see your wonderful vicar along the way, send him to me. His are the only kind of spirits I'll be giving to my brave marksmen."

I sped up the stairs, hugging a now protesting Arabella

to me. I heard behind me the firing of muskets from the Middle Ward I had just left. The sounds of the muskets were occasionally punctuated by a scream as a rum-fueled assailant was knocked off a scaling ladder. I knew some of Colonel Lawrence's men were also now armed with pikes— as effective as musket fire at knocking drunken men off perilously high ladders.

My heart hammered by the time I arrived at the Upper Ward. And not just from my mad dash up the long flight of stairs. Captain Bond and Clodagh, of course, had everything well in hand. He and his four aging men were evenly spaced along the wall. They may have seen a few years, but they aimed their muskets with deadly accuracy. My three daughters and assorted loyal maidservants stood beside the musketeers, ready to toss down burning coals on any liquor-fueled assailant who might poke up his head. Even ten-year-old Jane, her ever-present bow attached to her straight little back, stood poised with a bucket of glowing cinders at her feet.

We hardened our ears to the ululant screams coming from the Middle Ward, as tipsy, would-be assailants continued to topple from precarious scaling ladders.

I had no choice. I imprisoned my darling Arabella behind the rails of her crib, which I had long ago moved to my bedroom, for my peace of mind as well as hers. Her wails assaulted us as we hurried about on our grim errands. I returned to my bedroom often to check on her and resupply my bucket with embers from the fireplace. I gave her another quick hug and returned to the outer wall with a new supply of glowing coals. An alarming sight met my eyes. A drunken sailor had made it over the high parapet. His arms circled my terrified Elizabeth's neck.

He laughed but was so full of spirits he could scarcely

stand. A brief second, which seemed an endless eternity, passed. And then he let out a strangled cry and grabbed his backside from which an arrow now protruded. My grim-faced ten-year-old Jane stood behind him and was already loading another arrow into her bow. Before she could act, a bombshell erupted from the sidelines. Fourteen-year-old Joanna hurled her compact body at the legs of the towering, unfortunate wretch who had chosen to assault her big sister. By now Elizabeth had fallen to the floor. The ferocity of Joanna's attack caused the assailant to stumble backward against the parapet. For an agonizing moment he teetered, and then, in his rummy stupor, lost his balance and disappeared. I wanted so much to grab my darling daughters into my embrace and just escape somewhere from all the madness. But there was nowhere to flee. We grimly returned to our posts. And tossed our coals. Arabella's angry wails from her crib in my room serenaded us.

The drunken shouting below us gradually slowed. Those daring to scale the ladders dwindled. It seemed like hours longer, but in reality, it must have been mere moments. The sounds of musket fire from our assailants all but stopped. Our demoralized enemy below tended to their dead and wounded. Captain Bond came and stood by my side as we assessed what was happening.

Linda Sindt

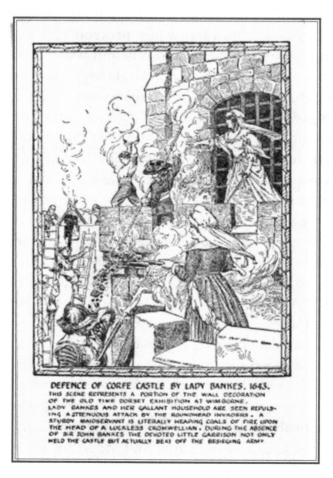

*Inscription reads, "DEFENCE OF CORFE CASTLE
BY LADY BANKES 1635. The scene represents a portion
of the wall decoration of the old time Dorsey exhibition at
Wimborne. Lady Bankes and her gallant household are seen
repulsing a strenuous attack by the Roundhead invaders. A
sturdy maidservant is literally heaping coals of fire upon the
head of a luckless Cromwellian. During the absence of
Sir John Bankes the devoted little garrison not only held
the castle, but actually beat off the besieging army.*

"My aging eyes may deceive me but is that the dust of horses approaching in the distance?" he asked.

And then we heard loud cheering from the Middle Ward. They also spied what was indeed a Royalist banner. And many horses. Great panic now appeared among our attackers below. We watched them flee, leaving behind their cannons, ammunition, tents, and stores. And, sadly, their dead and wounded. More than one hundred were dead when we counted and mopped up later. Men we had once called friends. And neighbors.

I ran to the Middle Ward to find our most wonderful Captain Lawrence. Our solemn-faced vicar was already with him. I caught my breath in dismay. The men who not so long ago arrived so courageously to stand with me against my enemy now stood in a reverent circle. Their heads bowed. Several of these now battle-hardened heroes dabbed at their eyes. Two prone figures lay in the middle of the circle. We did not escape unscathed after all. At the end of this six-week ordeal, on this last frantic day, we lost two of the stouthearted men who defended us so gallantly.

The Royalist newspaper, *"Mercurius Rusticus,"* later reported it this way:

> *"Old Sir Wat,"* the hapless Sir *Walter Erle, was seen fleeing, with terrified tears running down his cheeks, as the Royalist forces neared the castle, led by the Royalist hero, the most gallant Earl of Caernarvon.*

"Old Sir Wat" left the unfortunate Captain Sydenham in charge of carrying away the weapons, ammunition, and the remainder of the army. The craven Sydenham, however, hid in the relative safety of the mostly destroyed St. Edward King and Martyr Parish Church of Corfe Castle. He ordered his few remaining attendants to prepare dinner for him. He planned to remain hidden in the church until night, eat supper, and run away by starlight. However, he lost his appetite for supper when news of the imminent arrival of the king's forces arrived. It was still on the table when he scurried away by boat for the town of Poole.

Parliamentary propaganda at that time blamed their own men. Such was the baseness and cowardice of the seamen and landsmen, they said, that scarce one man in five came on... (they) "...advanced thirty or forty paces, the bullets coming thick about their ears, they shamefully ran away and left him (Erle) alone and to make a single retreat."

We mopped up, collecting artillery, ammunition, tents, and abandoned horses. And buried the dead. While we congratulated ourselves on only losing two men, we deeply mourned those two incredibly courageous lives. The castle was battered, the town was ravaged and burned, our lovely church was violated, stripped of its lead roof and gutters, and the church tower was set up as an irreverent artillery platform that had been aimed straight at us. Many of the former village residents found their homes and shops plundered and remained within the safe refuge of the castle gates until rebuilding could begin.

The Earl of Caernarvon arrived with a spirited Royalist force, sweeping any lingering Parliamentary troops from his path. Our hearts cheered at the news that the Royalists now held all of Dorset except Lyme Regis and Poole.

As an added sad footnote, *the Mercurius Aurelius* reported:

> *Sir Walter Erle, having thus failed in his attempt to take the castle, was so enraged at the valorous conduct of his adversary that, in revenge, he sent a party to Creech Grange, the residence of Sir Edward*

Lawrence, Captain Robert Lawrence's father, situated about four miles from Corfe Castle, which they plundered and destroyed, leaving nothing but bare walls. His mother, Lady Lawrence, was found taking refuge in the wood to save her life."

My heart ached at this vicious outrage against the innocent family of one who had so valiantly protected my home and children and my precious villagers.

Memory is a funny thing. Every second of the six-week siege remains indelibly burnt eternally into my recollection. The immediate weeks that ensued after our "liberation" are a complete blur. I remember spending my darling husband's lifetime savings liberally as we set about repairing our precious church and rebuilding the shops and homes in our ravaged village. I hovered over my dear daughters, clutching them and hugging them to me at every possible moment. Finally, even Baby Arabella rebelled against my clinginess.

The always amazing Captain Bond remained at alert. Ever fearful that the fickle winds of war could yet again turn against us. He again staggered the duties of our five-man "security team" so someone was always on watch around the clock. We continued to keep the main gates closed and barred. One bright sunny September afternoon, he found me in the garden strategizing our lengthy to do list with Clodagh and several maidservants. Arabella played babblingly with her toys at my feet. Elisabeth and Joanna were in the library leading Jane with her lessons—determined their sister should "grow up a lady" even in the face of her mother's now perpetual distractedness.

"I am sorry to interrupt you," the good Captain Bond apologized. "Several carriages are approaching. They are accompanied by what appears to be a cadre of armed men on horseback. They carry the king's flag."

I screamed. "John!" Hot tears washed my cheeks. I scooped Arabella into my arms.

"Get the girls!" I shouted at Clodagh. I flew out to open the gates and welcome home My John.

CHAPTER TWENTY-THREE

"Give sorrow words;
the grief that does not speak
knits up the o'er wrought heart and bids it break."
Shakespeare, Macbeth
1643-1644

I will spare you the details of my joyous, incoherent, tear-gushing reunion with my husband and the three children he brought with him. The oldest daughters, Alice and Mary, remained in Oxford with their families. Oldest son, John (under the watchful eyes of his two bossy big sisters), continued in his intense studies at Oxford, which carried on as if there had been no ongoing, raging war.

And so, my "grave and learned judge" returned to me after an endless absence. To his home with battered, but still standing walls. One day we wandered together through the destroyed homes in the Village. We paused in front of the much-loved church, roofless and desecrated, just outside the castle gates.

John frowned as we paused by the church. "To think that all this wanton destruction and all the danger you faced happened while I was so far from any fighting and real danger," He lamented.

We continued our sad tour through the ravaged shops in the little town that surrounded Corfe Castle. Everything that would burn in the stone-built cottages surrounding our castle had gone up in flames. Yet, in the face of this destruction and despair, we rejoiced. We were together again.

My brave young daughters rightfully delighted in boasting about their military prowess. Best of all, it seemed as if the king's Royalist forces were trouncing the Parliamentarians everywhere and that peace would soon prevail in our land.

"Brave Dame Mary!" my darling kept teasing me. "Everyone in the Kingdom is talking about the valor of *my* personal 'Brave Dame Mary!'"

I could not keep my hands off my three youngest sons, who had grown so much taller in their nearly year and a half of absence from me. Five-year-old "Charlie the charmer" was my chatty little shadow, tagging after me as if fearing I might again soon disappear. He was already learning to read. Ralph must have gained at least twelve inches and was now a self-contained, independent teenager. Ten-year-old Jerome, quiet and studious, who most resembled his father physically, showed signs he had also inherited sparks of his father's academic prowess.

John was equally closely followed by "his girls," especially the exuberant, blond curled, bright-eyed toddler-sprite, Arabella, who was finally learning to say "Father," and who had quickly made her adoring father her slave.

The days flew by. We continued overseeing repairs to the castle's battle damage and our Village. We basked in the delight of having most of our family together at long last. The war carried on. The news that dribbled in was beginning to be not so good, but we were not yet alarmed.

News of the following clashes in the fall of 1643 arrived at Corfe Castle. The Parliamentarians were beginning to reverse the fortunes of the Royalists.

2 September 1643, The Second Siege of Hull. A Royalist loss in Lincolnshire; re-established Parliamentary control in Yorkshire.

18 September 1643, Battle of Aldbourne Chase. Prince

Rupert's fast-moving Royalist force attacked Parliamentarian troops. No clear winner, but the skirmish allowed the Royalists to arrive at Newbury ahead of the Parliamentarians, where there was another not so fortunate fight.

20 September 1643, First Battle of Newbury. After a year of Royalist victories, the Parliamentarians had no real army deployed. They began a retreat to London under the command of General Essex. The Royalist Army, personally commanded by King Charles, met them at Newbury. The vicious attacks and counterattacks led to huge losses to both sides. Both weary armies stopped fighting at dusk. The next morning, there was no more ammunition. The Royalists had to stand back as the Parliamentarians under General Essex passed by and continued its hasty retreat to London. Not good news for either side, but especially demoralizing for the Royalists.

11 October 1643, Battle of Winceby. A relatively small conflict fought mostly on horseback. Royalist forces opposed Parliamentarians led by Oliver Cromwell. He prevailed in less than an hour. Oliver Cromwell was quickly gaining in "name recognition."

The sparkling, laughter and family bejeweled days flashed by. I was giddy with joy and release from the previous, fear-choked months. Suddenly, we were making plans for Christmas. Naturally, I was three months pregnant again. Many villagers yet lived with us in the safety of the castle as the rebuilding of their homes continued. Repairs to the church were far from finished. Our vicar nevertheless held joyful weekly services, with everyone crowding, elbow to elbow, into the tiny castle chapel to celebrate and give fervent thanks for our recent escape from those who sought to destroy us. Clodagh and her kitchen crew planned a gala Christmas feast for the whole village.

Linda Sindt

On Christmas Eve, the ever-vigilant Captain Bond, who was still on duty around the clock with his loyal band of four was suddenly at my elbow.

His eyes twinkled. "There is a group of several carriages in the distance, my lady. They appear to be carrying the king's banner."

My eyes caught my husband's. He beamed, clearly in on the big surprise. I shrieked and ran to greet the new arrivals. Our two oldest daughters tumbled from the carriages, along with their husbands and our grandchildren. I alternated between joyful laughing and sobbing. A pang of sharpest sorrow yet stabbed at my heart. Where was my oldest son? My (now not so little) John?

"He is heartbroken he couldn't come with us," said Alice.

"He is immersed in his studies and is such a dedicated scholar," said daughter Mary, comforting me.

Throughout their brief stay they pestered me to abandon Corfe Castle and come to stay with them in Oxford. Yet my heart was not ready. "Surely this dreadful war will soon be decided." I daydreamed. "I am praying your father will be able to serve the king from the comfort of Corfe Castle when this war dies down," I fantasized. "I can't possibly leave until the villagers who sacrificed so much are safely settled in new homes and have new shops in which to sell their wares."

The next day—the "First Day of Christmas"—we celebrated with joyful hearts and much merriment. Following a celebratory Christmas service in our overflowing chapel inside Corfe Castle, we feasted. An old-fashioned Christmas dinner, fragrant with plum pudding, was consumed in the grand Corfe Castle dining room with the entire village as our guests. (With the help of ample extra tables in the library to accommodate the overflow.) Our constant Christmas prayer was that peace would finally return to all in our land. An abundance of wassail was quaffed. A gaily decorated kissing bush was well used by many loving couples. Especially by my ardent husband, who lurked about hoping to catch me unaware. (Did he guess I planned my many errands to coincide with moments in which he might be lurking about?) I piled up precious family memories and stowed them away in my heart. Memories I didn't then know would sustain me in the dark years to come.

New Year's Day—the 8th Day of Christmas—was a lazy one. My family and I observed it in the sitting room in our private quarters. It was necessarily and wonderfully a very large gathering. We exchanged small gifts and were generally idling about, chattering, and laughing with our treasured children and grandchildren. For the first time in forever, we were all together as a family—all except one.

Clodagh had discreetly left us to this private family time. Now she rapped on the door and cracked it open a bit. Enough so I could see the delight sparkling in her bright, green-blue eyes. "I hate to disturb you," she apologized, "but a very handsome, dark-haired young man has asked for entrance. He seems to be bearing strange gifts. He tells me he has brought a silver coin, a loaf of bread, a packet of salt, a lump of coal, an evergreen sprig, and a bottle of whisky, which are guaranteed to bring you all 'prosperity, food, flavor, warmth, long-life, and good cheer.' I believe he is what you English call a 'first footer?'" She flung the door open, and I burst out crying. My now tall seventeen-year-old son John, the very image of my beloved Uncle Edward, embraced me. The current Canute, who had been peacefully dozing at my feet, danced and barked and whimpered in delight to be reunited with his long-lost buddy. I dragged Clodagh into our fold. She also needed to be with my children, to whom she had always been a bonus "fairy godmother" throughout most of their lives.

Two days later, amid copious tears, my oldest daughters and their families left to return to Oxford to celebrate Twelfth Night with their prominent husbands' families. My oldest son accompanied them to return again to the rigors of his demanding Oxford studies. I privately rejoiced that through a combination of privilege and age he could still be for the moment a student and not a soldier.

As it turned out, I was also denied the joy of having my so dear husband with me on Twelfth Night. King Charles decided to convene his own version of "Parliament." He publicly asserted the Westminster Parliament in London no longer had governing power. The day after my oldest children left, a messenger from the king arrived demanding my John's immediate return to Oxford to oversee the legalities of establishing this new alternate "Parliament," which he ordered to convene on 22 January 1644. With this hopeful outlook for a new beginning for our embattled country, it no longer seemed so urgent that my sons be hidden away from potential execution. But, after much discussion, I had to agree with my annoyingly always "right" husband that older sons, Ralph and Jerome, under their father's watchful eye, would have access to much superior educational opportunities in Oxford. I would keep my darling "Charlie the charmer" with me, and together with his older sisters and our always resourceful vicar, we would see to his early education, while I administered some much-needed "mothering."

One hundred eighteen members of the former House of Commons responded to King Charles's order, including our son-in-law, Sir John Borlase. The traitorous London Parliament immediately declared our son-in-law to have lost his seat in "their Parliament" for Corfe Castle.

The next few months flew by. Despite the confidence of King Charles that he had all but won, the old Parliament in London did not concede. They continued to convene with their remaining members. Their military assaults on Royalist strongholds and their victories piled up alarmingly.

Soon it was June and my final, precious child, William, safely made his entry into a desperately troubled world. As with Arabella, his father was not present to welcome him. Also, like Arabella, he was showered with affectionate, handmade gifts from loyal Corfe Castle Villagers. We hired a local nanny, but, of course, his devoted older sisters also hovered over him protectively, catering to his every whimper. Meanwhile, every day brought news of another Royalist loss.

A few weeks following the arrival of William, frightening news came of two more decisive battlefield confrontations—

The Battle of Marston Moor was the largest single battle of the English Civil War, pitting 45,000 men against each other. The Royalists, under Prince Rupert, knew they were outnumbered, but fought fiercely anyway. For the first time, Prince Rupert suffered a crippling, bloody, undeniably clear defeat.

The Parliamentarians took advantage of the Royalists' weakened condition in mid-September. They attacked Prince Rupert at Montgomery in Wales, winning complete control of Wales. Five hundred Royalists fled from the battle. Fifteen hundred died. Our hearts mourned this massive loss of life. My anxiety for my husband and my children colored those dark and joyless days. No messengers brought news of my husband and my dear ones.

All too soon, a gloomy Christmas of 1644 loomed ahead of us. With sad news all about. I could not bring myself to celebrate or decorate or enter into any frivolity. Fear and gloom once more overwhelmed our days as news of Parliamentary victories grew ever nearer. The neighboring towns renewed their hostility as support for the king waned. Corfe Castle was once more the only Royalist stronghold between Exeter and London. Nearby Weymouth and Wareham were again our open enemies. On Captain Bond's advice, we sent for another garrison of Royalist forces to deter a possible new attack against Corfe Castle. I did not take these brave soldiers into my heart, as I had the stalwart Captain Lawrence's courageous men.

The gloomy winter had just begun and already seemed

endless. Christmas drearily passed. To our everlastingly hopeful vicar's dismay, we barely acknowledged this traditionally uplifting holiday, so deep was our melancholy.

Shortly after Twelfth Night in the New Year of 1645, a messenger arrived from Oxford bearing news that forever shattered my heart. On the 28th of December 1644 in the Oxford home of our son-in-law, Sir Robert Jenkinson, attended by both our oldest daughters, Alice and Mary, after a sudden and very brief illness, my darling John had died. It was believed he succumbed to the Plague that then sporadically afflicted our land, trumping even violent war.

The depths of my grief and outrage savaged the essence of my soul. I was beyond reasonable thought. The suspicion of Plague demanded interment of my dearest one's remains be hasty. He had already been entombed without me there.

My John had in recent months updated his will in writing and personally reinforced with me his unequivocal wish that the words (in plain King's English) "Not unto us, O Lord, not unto us, but unto Thy name be glory," should be the only inscription placed upon his monument in the eventual event of his death.

My heart raged when I learned something more had been added. At the instigation of those in King Charles's entourage who had insisted on overseeing my darling, high-ranking husband's hasty funeral. Pretentiously—in Latin. John would have hated it. This is the inscription as it now eternally stands in Christ Church Cathedral at Oxford.

> *"P. M. S. Hoc loco in Spem, Futuri loci depositum*
> *Jacet Johannes Bankes, Qui Reginalis CoUegii in*
> *hac Academia Alumnus, Eques Auratus ornatissimus*
> *Attornatus generalis De communi Banco Capitalis*
> *Justiciaris a secretioribus Consilii Regis Caroli*
> *Peritiam, Integritatem, Fidem, Egregie Prasstitit:*
> *Ex aede Christi in asdes Christi Transiit mense*

*Decembris die 28, Anno Domini 1644. ^Etatis suae
55. Non nobis Domine non nobis: Sed nomini Tuo
sit Gloria"*

"Translation: To pious memory sacred. Laid in this place, in
hope of another place hereafter, lies the body of John Bankes,
student of Queen's College in this University. A most distinguished
Knight, Attorney General, Chief Justice of Common Pleas, Privy
Councillor to King Charles; a rare example of ability, integrity,
fidelity. He passed from Christ Church to the Mansions of Christ,
December 28, a.d. 1644. Aged 55 "Not unto us, O Lord, not unto
us, but unto Thy name be glory."

More than a year earlier, in a publication called the
Moderator, an article had appeared that stirred up much
discussion. We found a copy among my John's belongings.
There were many markings on it in his handwriting. It seemed
he must surely have been the author. The sentiments echo his
often-expressed personal convictions. Here is an extract:

"Amongst the many complaints which posterity
may justly take up against us, it shall never be said
that we all did willfully blind the eyes of our reason
and would not see the evils which with unveiled face,
showed themselves in their full horror, before they
came upon us.

"We have arrived almost at the extremities of ill;
and yet some believe there is a way to grow better, by
growing worse; I pray Heaven this paradox may not
undo us.

A set battle hath been fought, with almost equal
loss and success, as if Heaven had told us we are both
in fault; both worthy of overthrow, but neither of us
of victory.

The true character of a moderate man I conceive
to be this. He is one that could never be so well satisfied

of the necessity why this war began as he is now why it should see an end, and who knows not how to pray for a victory; one that in earnest loves the King, and thinks him essential to the well-being of a Parliament, one that honours, not adores the Parliament because he sees that they also are but men, and rather wishes them what they should be than omnipotent. One who would have his religion not gaudy, nor stripped stark naked. One that would have peace, not as an effect of war but of accommodation."

If only both sides had listened to him.

As an additional eulogy, Edward Hyde, the first Earl of Clarendon and an English Statesman, who served as a close advisor to King Charles, described my husband as "a grave and learned man. He lived in times when no man of any eminence was treated with moderation by either party, and Bankes was no exception to the general rule."

CHAPTER TWENTY- FOUR

"O grief hath changed me since you saw me last..."
Shakespeare, Comedy of Errors
1644—1645

Upon learning of the death of my husband, the London Parliamentarians were quick to pounce. They formally declared all our children and me to be "malignants." And ordered all our properties be forfeited to the same London Parliament that once demanded that King Charles continue my darling John in his position as top legal advisor in the land. Now they changed their opinion. In the year following his death, they formally impeached him before the House of Lords in London for adhering to his King.

Throughout the endless, bleak winter of 1644 and 1645, my bereft Bankes family and the Corfe Villagers remained in a state of semi-barricade inside the castle in a stunned state of mourning. We survived halfhearted onslaughts from the Parliamentarians, but, of course, continued to be essentially unassailable. New Royalist forces arrived to defend us. They came and went.

I took little notice of much that went on. I was numb with grief and despair. I longed to flee to the caring arms and comfort of Mair-Mair, but I dared not risk going home to her. She was still at Eastcote Manor and, so far, safe and well cared for by the Twins and their own growing families. In this interim lull in the fierce fighting, a few cherished letters from her managed to get through to Corfe Castle.

Spring arrived, but my depression persisted. I drifted about in a dreary fog. Even the merry antics of our rapidly growing Arabella could not lift my gloom. On a particularly lovely day, my daughters urged me outside to sit in the garden to nurse baby William. Maintaining the formal gardens was not a priority during these endless wartime years. Yet the overgrown and now randomly shaped garden still soothed. The lovely wildflowers of the Isle of Purbeck encroached. Spider orchids with their velvety teardrop shape. The delicate, white, spiked blooms of wild garlic. Yellow patches of horseshoe vetch. Sunny cowslip clusters. Blue chalk milkweed.

Sweet baby William dozed by my side. I also slumbered. The fragrant flowers and the gentle touch of the sun lulled my soul. I dreamed. Something tickled my cheek. Light, feathery touches. I sleepily batted at it. The teasing flutters persisted. My eyes flew open. No, it was not a feather from the New World. A white butterfly danced against my face. A few more flits and a light breeze carried it away. I could never explain why, but the moment brought an odd comfort, as if my John had whispered down to me from Heaven. The black hole of loss was forever embedded in my heart—a now permanent part of who I was. And yet the sharp, debilitating stab of grief at last numbed a bit. I felt I could begin again to carry on. I squared my shoulders and changed my son's diaper.

A Colonel Anketell came from Somerset to command the Royalist forces in possible defense should there be another attack on Corfe Castle. As an outsider, he was unencumbered by personal relationships, friendships, and loyalties among the local people. I could see his advantage in making difficult decisions and issuing necessary orders to defend the castle.

His first decrees again broke my already shattered heart. He demolished the newly restored homes and buildings in the village around the castle to deny cover and shelter to any besieging forces. He even ordered the rubble to be removed and brought inside the Castle to prevent it from being of possible use to the enemy.

My wonderful Captain Lawrence was now a Colonel. He had gone on other Royalist missions after the initial siege of Corfe Castle. Now he was back and several of his original garrison were again assigned to defend Corfe Castle, along with various Royalist reinforcements from other pockets of the King's defenders who yet survived.

After long months of doing battle and suffering loss on the battlefield, as well as the destruction of his own home, now Colonel Lawrence was no longer the idealistic visionary who had previously inspired in me such bright hope and promise for the future. Even his former faithful, and adoring friend, my now three-year-old Arabella, could not lift his ongoing melancholy.

The endless months of tedium and anxiety kept everyone jittery. News of the devastating fighting trickled in. The enormous casualties were beyond comprehension, adding to our gloom and ever-growing dread. The indomitable Prince Rupert, once hailed by both Royalists and Parliamentarians as a "military genius," was losing ground.

Less than two months after my John died, news came to us on 17 February 1645 that "The New Model Army of England" had been formed by now leading Parliamentary military leader, Oliver Cromwell. It differed from previous Civil War era armies in that it was meant to serve anywhere in the country (including in Scotland and Ireland), instead of being tied to a single area or garrison. Its soldiers were full-time professionals, rather than part-time militia. A huge difference was that the army leaders were banned from serving in either the Parliamentary dominated House of Lords or House of

Commons. Cromwell also stacked the deck by only accepting as leaders experienced veterans who were committed to Puritan religious beliefs. These differing viewpoints and their new independence from Parliament ultimately led to the army's willingness to support overthrowing both the Crown and Parliament's authority, and to establish a Commonwealth of England from 1649 to 1660, which included a period of direct (dictatorial) military rule. Oliver Cromwell and his "New Modern Army" fundamentally about-faced the English Civil War.

The ultimately decisive battle was led by King Charles against the New Modern Army, with Oliver Cromwell as one of the opposing leaders. Word came that the Royalist Army was demolished on 14 June 1645 (its back broken), suffering 7,000 casualties out of 7,400 on the battlefield.

After the Battle of Naseby all was essentially lost, except for pockets of Royalist resistance throughout the country—including Corfe Castle. We remained in a state of semi-blockade, vulnerable to new attacks at any time.

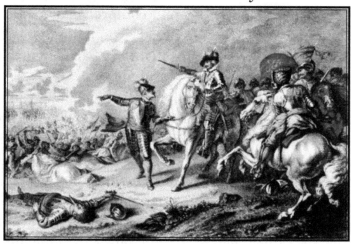

Battle of Naseby, hand-colored copper engraving by Dupuis after Parrocel, 1727 (from Rapins History)

For reasons I cannot fully explain, the Royalist forces protecting Corfe Castle still held firm. For the moment, we continued to be unassailable, so sturdy were Corfe Castle's natural defenses. We wanted to see what would happen to our king. We wanted to see what kind of rule would be established. We held out. Semi-blockaded, but not yet under full siege, we carried on.

In June, four days after the Battle of Naseby, we did suffer a minor setback. The clever and conniving (Parliamentary) military governor of nearby Wareham, a Colonel Butler, who was soon to become very well known to the Corfe Castle Royalist forces, mockingly carried off a small coup when he sent a garrison to harass us. More embarrassing than truly damaging. With only a semi-blockade in effect, we were in the habit of grazing our cows and horses outside the castle walls during the day and bringing them in at night. A company of Parliamentarian foot soldiers entered our village intent on pillage and succeeded in rounding up 140 head of cattle and 20 horses and driving them away to Wareham. It was a blow to our ego but did not destitute us. We still had ample food supplies stored away and horses in the stables.

On 28 October 1645, Parliament issued orders for more effective operations against Corfe Castle. Colonel John Bingham, military governor of the nearby port town of Poole, was assigned to finally oust us from our impenetrable fortress. Another dreary Christmas drew near. It was still 1645—nearly a year since my husband's death forever shattered my heart. Baby William was nearly a year and a half old. Not only walking, but, like his older siblings had done before him, forever scampering into perpetual mischief. The word "father" was not one we were trying to teach him.

By the 16th of December, our enemy was again at the castle gates and fully blockading us. We heard that more would soon be on their way from Sir Thomas Fairfax, the then overall Parliamentary Commander-in-Chief. Even then we did not overly worry. Our besiegers did again attempt several times to ascend the castle walls via scaling ladders, but as before, we easily knocked them away with musket fire, pikes, and hot embers from our fireplaces.

One dreary morning, our foes distracted us with a new weapon. I had just finished a cozy breakfast with my children in my chambers. A noxious smell assaulted us. We gagged. Our eyes burned. We could scarcely breathe. One of the enemy had managed to lob a "stink bomb" over the parapet. It was a weapon that had never been employed against us before. Captain Bond and his loyal team, holding their noses, courageously managed to gather up the broken pieces of the clay pot and throw them back over the parapet. Observing this, our pint-sized, outraged Arabella followed suit. Before her sisters could stop her, she grabbed her un-emptied chamber pot from beneath her crib, scampered out, and tossed the contents over the side of the parapet onto the unsuspecting head of a Parliamentary soldier who lurked below. We heard his outraged shout. Arabella hollered back at him with an equally outraged, "Pooh!"

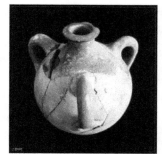

400-year-old stink pot from the Civil War recovered by archeologists at Corfe Castle.

We carried on. With the Royalist war effort in such disarray, we understood there could be no organized attempt by any of King Charles's forces to relieve us anytime soon.

And then, uninvited and out of nowhere, a completely audacious, foolhardy, very young Royalist officer captured my heart, He bore a hated name—Cromwell. I believe they were actually distant relatives. But I adored him anyway. How could I not? Madcap adventurer that he was. Hearing of my plight as a widowed lady confined with my children in a surrounded castle, he decided all on his own and against all rationality to rescue us. His high-spirited troop of one hundred twenty men set out from Oxford. (Had my two oldest, strong-willed Oxford daughters influenced him on this daring escapade? If so, they never confessed.) My audacious young Colonel Cromwell and his troops marched rapidly through Parliamentary strongholds without discovery until they arrived at nearby Wareham.

His eyes sparkled with mischief as he later recounted his exploits from the comfort of my sofa before a crackling blaze in my private rooms. Several of his young officers also lounged about. All sipped goblets of Clodagh's special wine appreciatively. They looked to be not much beyond merry teenagers. How did these "children" get involved in this dreadful war? I could not help noticing them noticing my lovely teenage daughters Elizabeth, then fifteen, and Joanne, fourteen. Or the merry glances my brazen daughters sent them right back.

I, myself, was swept away by the daring Colonel Cromwell's youthful charm.

"It was not that hard to disguise our troops," he boasted. "All we had to do was wrap the tawny-colored scarves of the Parliamentarians about our necks and we were completely disguised. The guards at the Wareham military governor's house did not even question who we were and waved us right on by them."

I interrupted his tale. "Surely you do not mean Colonel

Butler?" I asked. "Not the cheeky fellow who stole the castle's cattle and horses, not so long ago?"

"If he has a clever and cunning tongue in him, that's him, all right," said one of Colonel Cromwell's deputies.

"Colonel Butler himself, however, was not fooled by our disguise. He immediately barricaded himself in his house and began firing back at us. We knew speed was essential to our plan. We did not have time to spare. We spied a powder keg not far from Colonel Butler's house. So by way of encouragement, we quickly set it on fire. The house would soon explode violently. This motivated the governor/colonel and the two men with him that were firing back at us to hastily surrender. We took them, as planned, as hostages to your castle."

"I watched from one of our towers when you came to our gate," I said. "You did not seem a bit daunted by the huge Parliamentary force that barricades the entry to our Castle. We were most impressed by your threatening and feisty demeanor as well as the pleas of your prominent Parliamentary hostages for safe entry."

"We also welcomed your shouted threats from within the castle to sally forth if a contest should begin," laughed Colonel Cromwell. "That is what ultimately convinced the Parliamentary forces to give way and allow you to so jubilantly welcome us inside the castle gates."

The noble, chivalrous intent of this daring, if foolhardy, young officer and his devil-may-care men was to "rescue" my children and me, and safely evacuate the castle before it ultimately fell to the cruel, vengeful Parliamentary forces. A final act of derring-do before ultimately conceding defeat of the Royalist cause.

Charming as my new hero was, I was not sure I wanted rescuing. I felt invincible, even safe, inside my fortress. The horrifying tales I had heard of many thousands of brave men so cruelly slaughtered on the battlefields did not inspire confidence. How could this spunky band of only one hundred twenty men possibly hold out in defending us against such massive foes? Even if fortified by the seasoned Royalist soldiers currently on duty inside the Corfe compound, that did not seem like sufficient firepower. Where could we quickly and safely flee and how could we survive as refugees with warrants on our heads, without resources to feed and shelter ourselves? How could I subject my children and my dear villagers to such prolonged terror? No, I reasoned, if we were going to be brutally massacred, anyway, it would be mercifully, and quickly, in the comfort of our own beds, thank you. And so, I ultimately said, "No, thank you," to our gallant would-be rescuers.

The ever-beguiling Colonel Cromwell and his men understandably did not want to linger long with us, so we sent them on their way. Sadly, my premonition that their "escape plan" was "too optimistic to be true," came true. We sneaked them out through a secret sally gate, to safely exit the castle walls, but all did not go well. They were unfamiliar with the terrain. The Parliamentary forces waited for them on strategic roads leading away from Corfe Castle. They were ambushed as they marched northward. Those who stood guard outside our gates later taunted us with the fact that they had captured Colonel Cromwell and some of his high-spirited men and held them as prisoners. Not all of Colonel Cromwell's troops were captured. Many took flight, bolting in various directions. Some stealthily returned, eventually finding refuge back inside the Castle walls. I never learned of the ultimate fate of my dashing, would-be rescuer. I like to think he eventually charmed himself away from his captors.

The ensuing days, barricaded inside the castle, wore wearyingly long. There was not much actual exchange of gunfire, other than to show off on either side now and then. Mostly, both combatting sides seemed to be waiting each other (and the ultimate course of the endless war) out.

I was forewarned by my wonderfully loyal Captain Bond, but I did not take him seriously at first. Our most distinguished prisoner, the eloquent military governor of Wareham, also known, officially, as Colonel Butler, who had been brought to us by the dashing Colonel Cromwell, was preying on the hearts and minds of his captors. The boredom and uncertainty of the Royalist soldiers defending Corfe Castle grew daily more toxic. They feared for the welfare of their families, from whom they had been separated for long months and even years. They were easy marks. I thought my old friend was overly nervous, but together we brought his concern to the current Royalist garrison commander, Colonel Anketell, who promised to review those assigned as guards—to assign only the most trusted soldiers to perform guard duties. And so, he did. Among his reinforcements, he assigned my absolutely most trusted soldier as a guard—my longtime friend that I loved as if he were my own son—the now weary and heartsick Colonel Lawrence.

I cannot exactly explain why. I don't know if it was a mother's instinct or some other internal warning system. I needed to personally check out our now infamous captive, the Governor of Wareham, also known as the Parliamentarian Captain Butler, myself. Colonel Anketell and Captain Bond, and even my most trusted mentor, the vicar, strenuously objected to this meeting. I overruled them. I knew our prisoners dined on the same simple fare as the rest of the castle—porridge from giant pots that simmered and were added to throughout the day. Crusty loaves of bread, and a portion of beer, brewed in the castle kitchen. On a whim, I packed a lunch basket to carry with me, adding a flask of Clodagh's fragrant fruit wine and a container of her lovely summer preserves. The latest Canute trotted protectively by my side. I refused Colonel Anketell's intent to accompany me. A fiercely determined Captain Bond would not demur and trailed behind as we descended the torchlit darkness of the now long repaired dungeon steps. I knew thirty or so prisoners now lodged in the dungeon. We kept them as potential bargaining chips. In trading favors with those who now held us captive. Colonel Butler was, of course, our most valuable trading chip. And, because of his high rank, was held alone in the first, most brightly lit cell.

Colonel Lawrence, seated on a rough stool, in the dim light of the torches on the walls, indeed guarded the cell of Colonel Butler. He appeared to be engaged in a half-hearted game of chance with our hostage through the bars that separated them. He jumped up from his stool a bit guiltily at my arrival. This familiarity with our enemy, however innocent, nevertheless annoyed me. I did not speak to him, giving only a curt nod.

On the other side of the bars, Colonel Butler, with deliberate laze, also stood. He stood very tall. His charm was palpable. He flashed a dazzling smile. His voice, when he spoke, held a deliberate hint of mockery.

Colonel Lawrence winced at his dicing companion's temerity and had the grace to stare stonily at his shoes.

"Welcome to my home, Lady Mary Bankes," Colonel Butler said.

A flush warmed my cheeks. I heard myself stammering. "I trust you are treated well," I said, with what I hoped was cool dignity.

An unmistakable hint of amusement flashed in his eyes.

"I have truly enjoyed your hospitality."

Damn the man, I felt suddenly nervous. Charm or no, a faint resentment prickled over me.

My ever-loyal Canute, tuned in to my mood, emitted a low warning growl aimed at the prisoner.

"You are fortunate this porridge I have brought for your noon meal has a bit of meat. A sizeable herd of cattle that would have sustained us at a higher level of comfort was most scurrilously stolen away."

There was no mistaking the glint of a grin that again flickered across my enemy's face.

"By those we once called friends and neighbors," I could not help adding. I stopped, appalled at the stammer that again shook my voice.

"You must be sure to give your king the thanks of the citizens of Wareham for a most tasty Royal roast." My tormenter's grin widened.

Colonel Lawrence beside me shuttered his face even further at this exchange and would not look at me. Captain Bond, on my other side, maintained his formal, eyes straight ahead, military stance.

A nervous prickle shuddered over me. I was more than ready to retreat from this dismal dungeon. I was not sure, in retrospect, why I had come.

"Let me know if there is more I can do to attend to your comfort," I concluded in my iciest tone, the stammer, thankfully, now held in check.

Colonel Lawrence grabbed a torch from the wall and accompanied us mutely back up the steep stairs. Canute could not help unleashing another low warning growl as we turned away.

The ever brazen Colonel Butler called after us. "It was a pleasure to meet you, Lady Mary Bankes. Come again, any time."

Colonel Lawrence lit our way in somber silence. The susurrant hiss of the flare accompanied the thuds of our shoes in the narrow stair. He did not speak. He was no longer the buoyant, jaunty young leader who had once inspired such confidence in me.

I took pity on him. "We have missed you," I ventured.

"I am no longer in the chain of command," was his stony response. "It would not be proper for me to impose."

"Little Arabella, especially, misses you."

"I am sorry for that," was his only, guarded, reply.

The next morning following breakfast the older girls entertained Arabella by taking her for a walk. Baby William played with his toys at my feet as I set about planning my day. Colonel Anketell and Captain Bond both appeared at my door in obvious distress urgently requesting an audience. I seated them in front of the fire that dampened the morning chill.

"I am so sorry to disturb you, Lady Mary," Colonel Anketell apologized. The ever ramrod straight Captain Bond was visibly distressed but deferred to the more senior officer.

"There was a most serious defection from the dungeon sometime in the early hours just after midnight! Colonel Lawrence unlocked the cell of Colonel Butler and appears to have led him out through one of the castle's sally ports. I am sorry to report Colonel Lawrence himself, has also deserted, along with several other trusted guards." I could not hold back my tears.

"How many others that we trust has Colonel Butler corrupted with his clever way with words?" I wondered. My toddler son threw a block at the hapless Colonel Anketell, who he apparently blamed for making his mother cry.

In retrospect, I am convinced the elaborate plan that soon unfolded depended much on getting my longtime friend, Colonel Lawrence, out of the way early on—hence his premature, heartbreaking defection at the hands of Colonel Butler. I could not help forgiving him a little bit. He and his family had suffered such dreadful losses in this never-ending war.

Several days later, I again met with Colonel Anketell and Captain Bond. Baby William, my fierce defender, was safely out of the way in the care of his big sisters. Our worries grew more intense. Colonel Anketell brought with him a somewhat nondescript Royalist officer I recognized only vaguely. Lieutenant Colonel Thomas Pittman. I later learned he came to us as an officer who previously served King Charles in Ireland under the Earl of Inchiquin—famous for burning the homes, crops, and livestock of any Catholic Irish who refused to convert to the Anglican church. Needless to say, the Earl of Inchiquin, notwithstanding his Royalist credentials, was not someone admired by my late darling husband. The Inchiquin association alone would have been warning enough about his character had I only known of it earlier. There was one other warning bell that should have alarmed us all, but, in my own defense, no one mentioned it to me until after the dreadful deed was done. Lieutenant Colonel Pittman was one of the Royalist guards who served in the Corfe Castle dungeon during the brief tenure and corrupting influence of the now infamous Colonel Butler.

The reason for the current urgent gathering of my military defenders was the already stretched too thin staff of the Royalist forces that protected Corfe Castle. Now additionally diminished by those who had deserted their posts in the company of the glib-tongued Colonel Butler. Morale was at an all-time low. Our troops were exhausted. They increasingly fell asleep at their posts. They universally feared for the welfare of their families.

Lieutenant Colonel Pittman himself requested our audience and presented a most tempting, almost too good to be true proposal. He had a brother, a Royalist soldier, who was known to be worrisomely ill and was held prisoner by the Parliamentarians. Among the thirty or so yet imprisoned in the Corfe Castle dungeon was a prominent local Parliamentarian. A most valuable bargaining chip. Lieutenant Colonel Pittman suggested that Colonel Anketell approach the Parliamentarian leader, Colonel John Bingham, with this proposal. If Lieutenant Colonel Pittman were compassionately and safely allowed to leave the castle to secure the release of his ailing brother and return him to his family, we would in exchange release the high-value Parliamentarian prisoner we now held in the castle dungeon.

What would really happen, Lieutenant Colonel Pittman proposed, was that he would quickly gallop to a Royalist enclave in Somersetshire, seventy miles away. He would obtain a garrison of new Royalist forces to augment and reinforce the already beleaguered Royalist forces inside the castle walls. He would return three days hence under cover of darkness. At midnight he would signal when he was at a designated sally gate on the east side of the castle. It was unguarded by the enemy. Colonel Anketell would stand by to unbar the gate.

Of course, this devious scheme was a complete lie. Set up by my arch-foe, the ever-glib Colonel Butler, while he enjoyed the "hospitality" of the Corfe Castle dungeon. And was also guarded by the despicable, traitorous, Lieutenant Colonel Pittman. And, of course, the Parliamentary leader, Colonel John Bingham, who now besieged Corfe Castle, was in on the plot from the very beginning.

In reality, Lieutenant Colonel Pittman went straight to the Parliamentary garrison then at nearby Weymouth, where he acquired more than one hundred Parliamentary forces, many of whom had been to the castle in happier times. They knew, firsthand, the layout of the upper wards of the castle. He even recruited fifty more volunteers (hopeful looters?) along the way on his march back to Corfe Castle on that terrible night. He knocked at the designated sally gate.

Colonel Anketell, waiting, as previously arranged, opened it. The recruited Parliamentarians treacherously turned their easily identifiable uniform coats inside out to conceal their identities and falsely pose as Royalists. The unsuspecting Colonel Anketell let fifty of the enemy in before he barred the sally gate. He had by then grown suspicious.

The now belligerent Lt Col Pittman shouted rudely at his former commanding officer, Colonel Anketell.

"These brave soldiers risked their lives to come to the castle's defense," he argued. "To deny them entrance now puts them at perilous risk of falling into the hands of the Parliamentarians. It is unthinkable to make them stand by without shelter on such a cold night."

Colonel Anketell stood firm, but it was already too late. We were lost. We always considered the Upper Ward where I lived with my children and most trusted maidservants to be impregnable. It was ceremonially guarded under this second siege by only my loyal Captain Bond and his four ever-faithful men. One of them always stood outside our chambers round the clock while the other stalwarts catnapped close by.

I was taken completely unaware. A little past midnight I could scarcely gather my thoughts when a ramrod straight Captain Bond roused me from my slumber. Tears glistened in his eyes. Several men I had never seen before stood behind him with muskets at his back. I heard shouts and the sounds of fierce battle in the Lower Ward. The enemy was inside our compound.

"There is no time to tarry," Captain Bond urged. "We must hurry to the Parliamentary Commander, Colonel Bingham. He is not an evil man. We must persuade him not to allow the slaughter of our villagers."

A solemn Clodagh, sorrow sparkling in her green-blue eyes, materialized behind me. Standing behind her were Elizabeth with a terrified, tiny Arabella clinging to her hand. Joanna held Baby William in her arms. Charlie the charmer fiercely clutched sister Jane's hand. She had not had time to attach her ever-present bow to her back.

Captain Bond motioned for me to bend down so he could whisper in my ear. "Do not forget. There are twenty high-value Parliamentary prisoners in the Corfe dungeons. I do not believe their guards are yet in harm's way. You could easily negotiate the lives of these prisoners for a promise of safe passage for your family and for our villagers. I assure you, Colonel Bingham is known in our surrounding communities as being a man of honor and compassion. He descends from a family long admired in this area."

That is how I came to square my shoulders, lift my chin and turn in my nightdress to the men who pointed their muskets at us.

"Take us to Colonel Bingham," I ordered. I grabbed a cloak from my wardrobe as we left.

Captain Bond lifted his hand. He turned to our captors. "I have one last urgent request. Please send someone with me to tell Colonel Anketell to initiate an immediate cease-fire order. There must be no further bloodshed on either side." I could not hold back the tears that filled my eyes as I watched him march away from me with muskets aimed at his back. His back, as always, remained unbendingly straight.

It was the 27th day of February 1646. Colonel Bingham was indeed gracious. He seemed actually much relieved to grant the terms of my surrender. He ordered his men to stand down.

"Can you and your family and your servants pack a few of your personal belongings into your carriages and be ready to depart the castle by dawn?" he asked. I would, at that point, have been happy to just run away in my nightclothes. We did not have room in our carriages to gather much as we rushed away and prepared to leave. A few family portraits, a few changes of clothing, our London servants, and that was it. I was sure we would not be allowed to take anything of value that might fund the treasury of the new Parliamentarian government that would soon rule us all.

Clodagh and Elizabeth and I paused before the cupboard with the solid silver, hugely expensive, unwanted plate my husband had presented to me. Our eyes met as we considered our options. There were none. It was Elizabeth who decided. She stealthily made several quick trips in the dark to dump the entire treasure down a nearby well. She and her sisters similarly gathered and tossed away the lovely jewels my husband had gifted to "his girls" over the years. At least that small treasure would not be available to fund the Parliamentarians who now sought to destitute us.

All too soon streaks of a dreary February dawn lightened the dark sky. A courteous Colonel Bingham waited for us at the castle gate. An assembly of his soldiers stood at attention, massed in a formation. He asked me to alight from the carriage with my entourage. And then, in a formal ceremony, with great solemnity and words of praise that brought tears to my eyes, he executed a graceful bow and presented me for a final time with the keys to Corfe Castle. "In recognition of your valor and courage at a most difficult time for all who love England," he said. And then he presented to me the ancient Great Seal of Corfe Castle that depicted the now absent ravens who had stood watch over Corfe Castle over the past centuries.

We turned from this touching ceremony to enter our carriages. A volley of musket fire from a distant tower shattered the peace. A suddenly stern and forbidding Colonel

Bingham ordered us to stop. Were we yet to be massacred? Colonel Bingham dispatched a large group of armed and ready subordinates to investigate. They were gone for what seemed an eternity. The only sound was the wailing of our frightened eighteen-month-old, Baby William. At last Colonel Bingham's troops returned with two of our Royalist soldiers who manned a distant wall. They did not get the orders to cease-fire. They shot two (non-military) marauders who, hearing Corfe Castle would soon fall, scaled a wall in an attempt to get an early start in looting our home.

Upon hearing these facts, Colonel Bingham graciously accepted this loss of life. He kept his part of the bargain we had struck. He sent us on our way and preserved the lives of the 140 villagers and soldiers then within the castle who served my family with such fierce loyalty for so long. Two of my men and one of the Parliamentarians died in this final struggle. The remaining Parliamentary prisoners we held in the castle dungeon were set free. During the forty-eight days of this final siege only eleven men lost their lives.

Toddler William began to fuss. We had been encouraging him about "big boy" potty etiquette but were not quite there yet. I asked daughter Joanna if she would check his diaper. She looked at me guiltily. "I am pretty sure he may be a bit uncomfortable," she confessed.

"I could not bear to throw all our pretty jewels away. I hid a few handfuls in William's diaper in case we were searched before we left."

I did not know where else to go for the moment, so I headed first to "home." To Eastcote Manor in Ruislip. To my mother. To Mair-Mair. To start a new life in a new world. In our carriage, Charlie the charmer cuddled on my lap. Clodagh, beside me, comforted frightened sprite Arabella. Joanna faced us, clinging to Baby William. She squeezed between her big sisters, Elizabeth and Jane. Our tears dropped on the heads of the little ones. We turned our faces and watched Corfe Castle disappear. "It will be all right, Mother," sweet Charlie the charmer whispered in my ear. And he was right. Eventually.

AUTHOR ENDNOTES, CHAPTER TWENTY-FOUR:

Sally Port

This is the back door to the castle and there are the remains of several along the curtain wall. It seemed a waste of time opening the front door every time someone wanted a couple of fish from the medieval fish ponds in the field below. If you look carefully you might be able to make out the edge of the pond, a low bank that runs parallel with the trees below.

A sally port was an easy place to defend. A guard stood above the steps where you are now and when the enemy opened the door at the bottom of the steps the guard simply chopped his head off! If you wanted to shut it tight in time of battle, rocks, old carts and anything heavy was simply pulled up to block the door.

This sally port was discovered when the area was excavated in the 1990s to lay the new pitch paving path. The wall beside the sally port was thought to be 12th century but during the excavation the archaeologists found Civil War pottery beneath the wall. This suggests that the wall had been built after the Civil War. Later the archaeologists realized that a large area of the West Bailey had been turned into a garden by the vicar of Corfe Castle in the 1760s and the wall had been rebuilt to suit his plans. By the way, a certain wall is a wall hung between two towers!

 National Trust

⊗ **Corfe Castle**

* *Extracted from sign posted by the National Trust*

Well

Thomas Bond, writing a history of the castle in 1882, notes that this was a 'great deepe walle and halfway down the mound below the Gloriette there was a spring called St Edwards Fountain.' This suggests that the well was about 100ft deep. The water drains through the chalk rock of the mound so it would have been safe to drink – no-one could have been poisoned it!

The water from the well was used for the buildings within the Inner Bailey, the Keep, the kitchens and the Gloriette. King John bathed once a fortnight and was thought to be very clean. Queen Elizabeth took a bath once a year 'whether she needed it or not'!

During the Civil War Sir John Bankes, owner of the castle, supported King Charles I. He died in 1644 leaving Lady Bankes to defend the castle. She was an extremely wealthy lady and she and her children were fined by the Parliamentarians for their support of King Charles. To pay the fines she sold sheep, land, horses, her jewellery and other precious items.

There is a rumor that when Lady Bankes thought the castle would be taken she threw all her jewels down the well and they have never been recovered. We think it is more likely that she hid them in her underwear when she left the castle!

National Trust

● **Corfe Castle**

* *Extracted from sign posted by the National Trust*

AFTERWORD

Some modern historians now disclaim the four centuries old legend that Lady Mary was present at the second siege of Corfe Castle. Based on household accounts notionally in her 400-year-old handwriting, they theorize she was more probably already back in London bargaining to recover some of the lost family fortunes Parliament seized following the death of Sir John.

When the second siege ended, Colonel Bingham wrote to William Lenthall, the Speaker of the House of Commons:

> *'After extraordinary dutie some slayne and many wownded, God hath strangely delivered the Castle of Corfe into our hands.'*

The response of Parliament to this "victory" was to order that the castle be blown up. The massive blasts of gunpowder began only after Lady Mary's former neighbors thoroughly plundered it. Costly tapestries were carried away along with furniture from the days of Sir Christopher Hatton and current valuables and belongings of the Bankes family. The infamous Sir Walter Erle and even the dauntless Colonel John Bingham, himself, were among the ransackers who helped themselves to precious carpets, costly furnishing, and everything movable in the halls, galleries and private chambers of the castle. More than a few mansions in today's Dorsetshire display stone and timber that once graced Corfe Castle. Those tasked to destroy Corfe Castle eventually gave up. The booming explosions of gunpowder terrorized the Villagers for months. The earth rocked as the towering walls blew apart. There was not enough gunpowder in all of England to topple it all down. To date no one has found the treasure legend says was hastily dumped in a well. Skeletal remains of the towering walls of Corfe Castle guard the Village of Corfe Castle below.

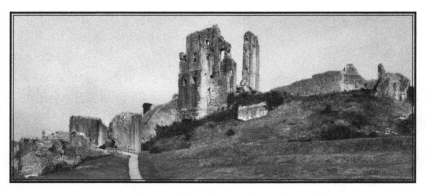

Corfe Castle today, photo by author

Wives of the Royalists were generally allowed to keep their lands and belongings. Such was not the fate of Lady Mary as a "combatant." When she returned to the home of her family in Ruislip, Parliamentary leaders stripped her of all her property and lands. She was, however, the effective head of her family until her young sons came of age. She fiercely fought the confiscation of the family estates. The demoralizing bargaining continued throughout the later 1640s. Finally, it was all settled. She paid fines of £2600. Upon payment of these penalties, she received a special pardon forgiving all her acts of war and treason committed after May 1642.

In 1645, the husband of Lady Mary's oldest daughter, Alice, Sir John Borlase, was imprisoned by order of Oliver

Cromwell, for war crimes. After a year of imprisonment, he was released when his family paid a fine of £2400.

On 25 December 1647 large crowds gathered in Canterbury to protest against the Parliament order that everyone must observe Christmas Day as an ordinary day with no celebration. The protesting throngs (now illegally) decorated the streets with holly and called (to no avail) for a church service to be held for Christmas. (Gambling, wassailing, caroling, mumming, and plum pudding were, of course, all forbidden.)

King Charles I furtively fled and hid in the aftermath of devastating defeat but was ultimately caught and beheaded by the Parliamentarians on 30 Jan 1649.

From 1649 on—prior to the Protectorate—England, Ireland and later Scotland were governed as a Republic by the "Council of State" and the "Rump Parliament." The Act declaring England to be a Commonwealth, which established England, together with "all the Dominions and Territoryes thereunto belonging" as a republic was passed on 19 May 1649, following the beheading of Charles I in January of that year.

Also in 1649, a Parliamentarian army led by Oliver Cromwell invaded Ireland and by 1653 had "conquered" the island. The horrendous slaughter that ensued overwhelms. Here are Cromwell's own chilling words regarding the devastating bloodshed and enslavement of the people of Ireland. Convinced that he was "divinely ordained" (Where have we heard those words before?) as an instrument of retribution against those of the Roman Catholic faith, he personally wrote this of Drogheda in his report to Parliament:

> *"In the heat of action, I forbade them to spare any*
> *that were in arms in the town, and, I think, that night*
> *they put to the sword about 2,000 men. Divers of the*

officers and soldiers being fled over the Bridge into the other part of the Town, where about one hundred of them possessed St Peter's steeple... The next day, the other two Towers were summonsed... When they submitted, their officers were knocked on the head, and every tenth man of the soldiers killed, and the others shipped [as slaves] to the Barbadoes... The last Lord's Day before the storm, the Protestants were thrust out of the great church called St Peter's and they had a public Mass there; and in this very place near one thousand Catholics were put to the sword, fleeing thither for safety. I believe all the friars were knocked promiscuously on the head but two; the one of which was Fr Peter Taaff... whom the soldiers took and made an end of; the other was taken in the round tower, under the repute of lieutenant, and when he understood that the officers in the Tower had no quarter, he confessed he was a friar; but that did not save him."

Some modern historians describe these appalling losses in Ireland as an ultimate form of ethnic cleansing.

Estimates suggest that as a result of the Civil War England lost 4 percent of its population and Scotland 6 percent, while Ireland suffered a loss of 41 percent.

The crowded conditions and lack of cleanliness of the military camps in England and Scotland intensified the loss of life during the war. Dysentery, cholera, scarlet fever, typhoid, and plague headed the death-dealing list of shared disease. The marching troops "drank stinking water," sometimes dipped from shallow indentations left by horse hooves. The soldiers, often soaked by rain, soon became filthy and infested with lice. The slightest injury often became a serious infection with fatal results.

Following the beheading of King Charles I, Parliament ruled England as a Commonwealth. Oliver Cromwell, however, ultimately dissolved the ensuing "Rump" and "Barebones" sessions of Parliament. While he declined to be named king, he was inaugurated on December 16, 1653, as Lord Protector of the Commonwealth of England, Scotland, and Ireland under the authority of a Constitution drawn up by a group of army officers. "The Protectorate," as Cromwell's government is known, continued only for a short time after his death on Sept. 3, 1658. His son, Richard, briefly succeeded him, but resigned on May 25, 1659. Parliament resumed power but served merely as a brief precursor to the "Restoration" of King Charles II under a "constitutional monarchy."

Many young Englishmen followed Charles II into exile on the European Continent while Cromwell ruled. These privileged youth visited the courts of crowned heads, soaked up culture, and met the great artists of the day. Among these wealthy young men were Lady Mary's oldest sons, John and Ralph, followed later by son, Jerome. Books from those tours signed by John and Ralph are yet in the library at Kingston Lacy. Her oldest children possibly encouraged a similar tour for "baby" William after her death. Not much is known about son, Charles, other than he still lived at the time of Lady Mary's death. If you believe the words on her monument that was commissioned more than nine years after she died.

When her eldest son, John Bankes (1626-56), returned from his "Grand Tour," he came into his inheritance at the age of twenty-four. In 1656 John died unmarried at the age of thirty. The estate then passed unexpectedly to his next surviving brother, Sir Ralph Bankes (1631-77) who, like his late father, was a lawyer at Grays Inn. When King Charles II assumed the throne in 1660, Sir Ralph was knighted in recognition of the family's contributions and trials in the Civil War. Ralph was named a "Gentleman of the Bedchamber" to King Charles II. The king also restored to Sir Ralph historic positions of power and influence in Dorset. The most significant of his local roles was as Hereditary Admiral of the Isle of Purbeck, a position which had been attached to the owners of Corfe Castle since Elizabethan times.

In Parliament, young Sir Ralph Bankes found himself sitting near the infamous Sir Walter Erle, who had so fiercely sought to destroy his mother and sisters. Sir Ralph suggested that "Old Watt" reimburse him for the valuable items he had taken from Corfe Castle. Four-hundred-year-old records show that while Sir Walter confessed that five or six cartloads of timber and masonry from the demolished castle might have come into his hands, he "…denied that Bankes should expect restitution."

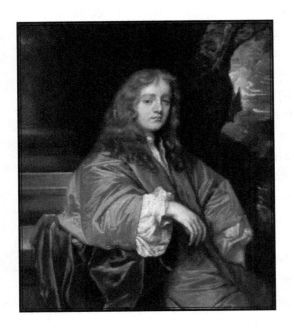

Sir Ralph Bankes by Sir Peter Lely, Photo Credit:National Trust Images

In 1661, coincidentally on the day of his mother's unexpected death, Sir Ralph married Mary Brune, the wealthy daughter of another Dorset landowner. It was, of course, an arranged marriage. Incongruously, her deceased father was a colonel in the Parliamentary Army that provoked the destruction of Corfe Castle. Sir Ralph's new Lady Mary brought him an income of about £1,200 a year—a then luxurious inheritance. With this he built a lavish new home on his Dorset estate to replace the demolished Corfe Castle.

Sir Ralph's friend, Sir Roger Pratt, designed a then innovative home which became a model for a stylish country house in the late 1600s. The design was specifically echoed in High Hall, Pamphill, which was built soon after Kingston Lacy, was completed by Sir Ralph's youngest sister, Arabella, and her husband, Samuel Gilly.

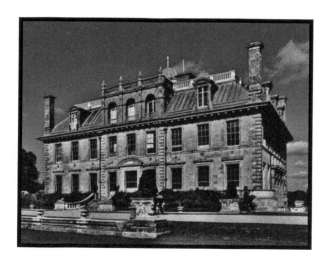

Kingston Lacy, photo credit, Shutterstock

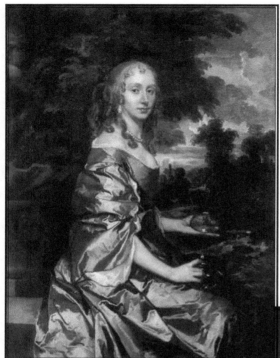

Arabella Bankes, Mrs. Gilly, by Sir Peter Lely, National Trust

Jerome Bankes by Massimo Stanzione, Photo Credit: National Trust Images

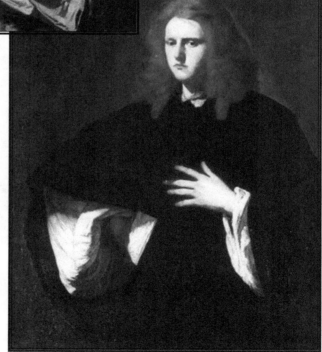

Oldest daughter, Lady Alice (Bankes) Borlase, upon the death of her husband, Sir John Borlase, first Baronet, in 1672, visited Bourbon, France, for a health cure at the famous waters. She ultimately stayed in France, converted to Roman Catholicism, and became well-known for her good works among the poor in Paris.

Corfe Castle remained in the ownership of the Bankes family for three and a half centuries, going through times of plenty and times of not so plenty. Generations later, in 1982, a great-grandson, Ralph Bankes, gave the castle to the National Trust of the United Kingdom along with the family's extensive holdings in Purbeck and their mansion at Kingston Lacy near Wimborne and its adjoining land. The Bankes estate was one of the most generous gifts in the Trust's history.

Epilogue

*What we know about William Bankes
and his "possible?" escape into the "New World"*

The Link to the Worldwide All Bankes/Banks DNA and
Compilation Web Site contains the following statement about
William Bankes, the youngest son of Sir John and Lady Mary
Bankes: "His (William Bankes') nuncupative will [an alleged
oral will] was recorded in the prerogative court of Canterbury
in 1670 by his brother Sir Ralph Bankes. (LDS library reel
92300). The full text is as follows:

> *"Memorandum [a standard term beginning a
> nuncupative will]– an oral, unsigned deathbed will
> that William Bancks late att Rome in the parts beyond
> the seas deceased being the month of March in the year
> of our Lord God attending to the computation of the
> Church of England one thousand six hundred sixty
> and nine seized with a sickness whereof he shortly
> after (viz.) on or about **the first day of Aprill in the
> year of the Lord one thousand six hundred and seventy
> died die in his sickness** whilst he was of perfect mind
> and memory. Being asked by one Edward Altham if
> he had any thoughts to make a will and dispose of
> his goods and estates in case it would please God to
> call him into another world, make and declare his last
> will and testament noncupatum or by word of mouth
> as followes or to the effect (viz.) I do leave my goods*

and ffortune indifferently to my three brothers And what I doe possess and have here in Rome where he then lay sick I doe bequeath to you (Speaking to and meaning the said Edward Altham) if you will retain it excepting my Perewigg which I will leave to my uncle Borlase if he will have it and also two Rings one of which I bequeath to Mr. Barthon Chambers servant to said Mr. Borlase and my uncle And the other to Mr. Woodroffe. And my Dictionary and Grammar and my other books I doe leave to this young Englishman who assisteth me and attends to me in my sickness (meaning one George Brome an Englishman who attended him in his sickness) and was then by him with an intent that what he see declared should stand for and be his last will and testament that in the presence and hearing of said Edward Altham and George Brome."

AUTHOR'S NOTE: Edward Altham, who allegedly recorded this oral "deathbed will" was the son of Lady Mary's Uncle Edward Altham and Aunt Joane. Edward (the son) at that time lived in Rome and had embraced the Roman Catholic faith (much to the dismay of his mother, the ever imperious 'Her Ladyship.') William Bankes was related to the Borlase family through both his older sisters, Alice and Joanna, possibly even living with one or both of their extended families at various times in his formative years. These two facts would authenticate that this particular William Bankes would indeed have been the son of the late Sir John and Lady Mary Bankes. The date of this apparent oral will indicates he was about twenty-six when he "died." He would have been about seventeen when his mother died in 1661. Is it at all significant that this oral will is recorded as having been made on April Fool's Day? A well-established day of pranks in English history dating back to Chaucer's Canterbury Tales in 1392 and before? The timing of the establishment of the monument to Lady Mary is also curious. As indicated in the Prologue to this tale, Lady Mary's monument also eternally "sets in stone" the "fact" of William's death (without children) after the date of his mother's death. Curiously, William's oldest brother, John, original heir to the Bankes fortune, who also died without children, is not listed at all with her other children on Lady Mary's Monument.

If William in fact died on April Fool's Day 1670, Lady Mary's monument could not have been constructed until more than nine years after her own death. Why did her then eldest son, Ralph, wait so long to create this sentimental tribute to his mother? Could something have happened in young William's life that made it necessary to eternally record and formally announce to any possible adversaries that he was "dead"? And to also renounce any claim he might have had as a youngest son to any share of the remaining family fortune? So the family could at last "legally" finalize the complicated process of getting their financial affairs in order in the turmoil following the Civil War? The earliest possible time frame for creating Lady Mary's monument curiously coincides with the date of this unsigned "oral will."

There is yet another odd "coincidence" occurring simultaneously in the "New World," specifically, in Mantapike, Virginia. What if, by 1669 (a year before his supposed death) William was no longer even in Europe, but had already made his way to the "New World?"

It is well documented that a William Bankes, born around 1644, died in Mantapike in Stephens Parish in King and Queen County, Virginia, United States of America, on 10 November 1709. Historical documents confirm the direct lineage of many US families to this particular William Bankes. But was this William Bankes indeed the youngest son of the Sir John Bankes who had owned Corfe Castle? The following additional research notes might establish a highly probable if not conclusive, link.

"RESEARCH NOTES ON WILLIAM BANKES AND MANTAPIKE
by William Ross Banks, Captain, US Navy, retired *[now deceased]*.

The study of Mantapike and its owner, William Bankes, reinforces the traditional linkage between the Bankes of Corfe Castle and the Bankes of Elbert. For those who have not had the personal opportunity to carry out research on the matter, these brief notes may help to better understand the story as it now appears.

William Bankes's origins, his travels en route to Virginia, and his acquisition of Mantapike represent inseparable parts of a riddle whose solution, as we piece it together today, will not yet withstand the full test of legal evidence. Recent circumstantial evidence lends support to longstanding traditions in the American branch of the Banks family—at the same time, it casts doubt on some earlier published conclusion which had never been challenged or subjected to careful scrutiny.

Involved in the riddles of William Bankes and Mantapike are the recorded history of 17th century England, the political climate and impact of the Puritan Revolution, the fortunes and treatment of the younger sons and brothers of the English peerage and landed gentry, and the fragmentary legal records of colonial Virginia where the Banks family first settled in North America.

In 1632 King Charles I appointed a Council of Superintendents over Virginia—among the several commissioners on that council were Sir Dudley Digges, and [Sir] John Bankes, Esquire. Both of these men served the king in positions of great responsibility until their deaths. Undoubtedly there was more than a passing, impersonal acquaintance since Sir Dudley was Knight and Baronet, and Master of the Rolls from approximately 1619 until 1639, while Sir John [also a Knight] served as Attorney General to the Prince of Wales from 1630 to 1640 and was then elevated to the post of Lord Chief Justice to the Common Pleas, which office he held until his death in 1644.

Sir Dudley's second son, Colonel Edward Digges, emigrated to Virginia and settled in Warwick County in about 1650. Edward Digges was later to become Colonial Governor of Virginia, but our interest primarily concerns the land he held. Land patent records show that his holdings include land in that part of Gloucester County which is now King and Queen County. The entry in the Patent Book reflects:

> "Edward Diggs, Gent. 700 acres of land called Mantopoyick, Gloucester Co., 18 Apr 1653. on N. side of Maattapony River, running from a small creek by the river S. Ely to Mattoones Creek …"

Other records indicate that Edward Digges probably did not live on this land, since he first lived at a place called Denbigh, on the James River, and subsequently at "Bellefield," his seat on the York River. Because of certain blank pages later in the Land Patent records, which will be addressed later, one can conjecture that Mantopoyick was being held in "safekeeping" for some future transfer to a friend or family connection from England.

At Sir John Bankes's death, he was survived by his wife,

Lady Mary, and several children, the youngest of whom was William, born at Corfe Castle, in Dorset in 1644. We know little of William's early life, however, he attended Eton until about 1663 and was indentured for King's College, Oxford, for 1663, but records show he never entered. Instead it appears he traveled extensively on the continent, and on the basis of an alleged nuncupative "will" recorded in 1670, it has been stated that he died in Rome, young and unmarried...research by an eminent genealogist gives reason to believe the will could have been a fraud, and may have been intended to "solve some problems" with the Bankes estate in England and to clear the way for William to anonymously depart the English scene for America.

Turning back to the colonial land records in Virginia, we find in Old Volume 5 of the patent records that pages 33 and 34 are left blank except for several names in the margin, with space being left to record the patents at a later time. One of the marginal notes is "Wm. Bankes es, 861 acres." These pages appear to be for part of 1661, the year after the Restoration in England. We find nothing further in the land patent records until agentry made in 1690, which describes a patent to William Bankes of 1079 acres of land in St. Stephen's Parish, New Kent County. (Note: King and Queen County was formed from a part of New Kent County in 1691). The patent specifically states that a 700-acre portion of the land was anciently called "Mantapike" [Mantopoyick] and was that which Edward Digges originally patented on 18 April 1653 and was assigned by him to Adam (?) Holland who in turn assigned it to William Bankes. The other three hundred seventy-nine acres consisted of some newly granted King's land together with an "overplus" of land found by resurvey to have been included in the original patent. Although the patent was recorded on 20 April 1690, it contains a statement within the text to indicate that it was to appear dated as of 1669. **Thus, William Bankes possibly came into the possession of 'Mantapike' at about the same time we encounter the "probably fraudulent will" of William Bankes, the youngest son of Sir John Bankes of Corfe Castle.** There are other records which confirm William Bankes's residence in St. Stephen's Parish prior to 1685.

Here's another observation from a different Bankes family historian in the United States, who speculates, "If William Bankes of Virginia was 'in hiding' in this country as some seem to think, he was here long before the 1669 oral will was made." *Grandpap's Family, Volume II*," by Mary Frances Banks Storey, daughter of Alva Neal Banks and Mae Huddleston Banks, published 1996 by the Amundsen Publishing Company, Decorah, Iowa. [This would not seem inconsistent with the idea that the family conspired to create a fake deathbed will and erected Lady Mary's memorial monument officially documenting William's prior "death" so that remaining portions of the family's complicated estate could at last be divvied up.]

ADDED AUTHOR'S NOTE: The mystery may never be fully resolved. Yet one must surely take notice. The "coincidences" are too compelling to arbitrarily dismiss. Could young William have engaged in some youthful, but serious teenage indiscretion in the two years following his mother's death in 1661 that caused his older siblings to whisk their teenage youngest brother out of possible harm's way? Out of the clutches of emerging English law? And into the comparative safety of Europe or possibly even directly to Virginia? Had they prevailed upon a longtime family friend to help him safely get a "new start" in the "The New World?" Eight years later as a grownup twenty-five-year-old could he have collaborated long distance with his older brother, Ralph, to find a safe way to enable his brothers to legally "inherit" his share of the family estate (and possibly send a portion to him?) Indeed, it seems more than possible that Lady Mary's son was the William Bankes of Mantapike from whom so many US families proudly trace their ancestry. We shall probably never know for sure.

What is not in dispute is that at a time of devastating personal loss Lady Mary Bankes inspired a nation torn by war. She lived a life that mattered, even in her darkest days, and in the face of most dire peril. Who could not delight in her wonderful sass and pizzazz in breaking so many then restrictive rules about the "proper conduct for a lady" and getting away with it? As indeed a most proper and traditional "Lady" her devotion to her husband, passion for her family, and love for her community are legendary. Yet her "unladylike" daring and courage in fiercely facing down overwhelming opposition also inspire. May her legend continue to embolden generations to come.

FINAL AUTHOR'S NOTE: In 2013 I traveled to England with my late husband's brother and wife and their daughter. A jovial young driver picked us up at the airport and chauffeured us to the Village of Corfe Castle. Along the way, he questioned the reason for this "off the beaten path" destination. When told of our interest in Lady Mary's story and her courage in doing battle with "that villain Cromwell's forces," he cheerfully argued with us. "Ah, but Cromwell was a true champion of the people," he assured us. "If it were not for Cromwell, the common people in England would not have the freedoms and privileges we now enjoy." A refreshing reminder that in weighing the merits of any account of history, the observer must take into proper account from which of many possible perspectives the tale is told.

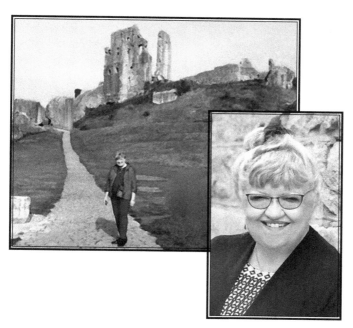

ABOUT THE AUTHOR

Who better to tell this mostly true tale from 400 years ago of military daring by a "lady" than retired United States Air Force Colonel, **Linda Sindt**? An early trailblazer in toppling barriers to upward mobility for today's military women, Linda says, "Lady Mary's voice demands to be heard. While her husband was away trying to talk sense into England's King 400 years ago, she boldly defended her home—Corfe Castle."

Linda's prior literary claim to fame is writing compelling position papers on often controversial subjects and persuading her General-ranked Pentagon bosses to sign them. The Keys to Corfe Castle is her first novel.

Check out her author's website at www.lindasindt.com

"The Keys to Corfe Castle" is Linda's first novel

10% of the author's royalties will go to the Pancreatic Cancer Action Network in memory of her husband to promote pancreatic cancer research. Anyone facing this dreadful disease can check out their website (https://www.pancan.org/) for help and support – and opportunities to create a world in which all pancreatic cancer patients will thrive.

The Military Women's Memorial in Arlington, VA, https://womensmemorial.org will also share 10 % of the author's royalties in special tribute to the inspiring military exploits of Lady Mary Hawtrey Bankes.

Bibliography

17th Century The British Association of Urological Surgeons. *https://www.baus.org.uk/museum/82/17th_century* accessed 3/21/19

Ackroyd, Peter, 2014. "Civil War." London, Macmillan

Alchin, Linda. "Elizabethan Recusants and Recusancy Laws." *www.elizabethan-era.org.uk.* accessed 10/31/21

Alchin, Linda. "Elizabethan Era." *www.elizabethan-era.org.uk.* accessed 11/3/2016

Alchin, Linda. "Elizabethan Wedding Customs." *http://www.william-shakespeare.info/elizabethan-wedding-customs-htm.* accessed 16 May 2012

Alpha History. "1633: Women Actors Are 'Notorious Whores.'" *https://alphahistory.com/pastpeculiar/1633-women-actors-notorious-whores-prynne.* accessed 10/31/2021

Alsop, Chris. "Hallowed Ground: Corfe Castle." *https://www.historynet.com/hallowed-ground-corfe-castle-england.htm.* accessed 11/6/2019

Altham, Emmanuel, John Pory, Issak De Rasieres. "Three Visitors to

Early Plymouth." Applewood Books, 1997

Altham, Emmanuel. "Yale Indian Papers Project." *https://news.yale.edu/2014/12/24/yale-indian-papers-project-brings-native-american-research-21st-century.* accessed 4/18/2018

Anthony, Evelyn. "Charles the King." 2005, Great Britain, Museum Press.

Archives Hub. "Altham Family Correspondence." *https://archiveshub.jisc.ac.uk/search/archives/30f8642c-f4cc-3799-a60b-13c1c21b175b.* accessed 5/19/2020

At the Archives. "Barbados Emigration and Immigration." *https://atthebarbadosarchives.wordpress.com/2010/.* accessed 28 Sep 2019

Bankes, The Right Honorable George. "The Story of Corfe Castle and

Many Who Have Lived There." London, J. Murray.

Banks, Ray H. "Compilation Project for All Bancks, Bankes, Banks Persons of the British Isles." *https://wc.rootsweb.com* accessed 3 Mar 2013

Baylor Magazine. "How the King James Bible Changed the World." Baylor University, Baylor Magazine, Summer 2011.

BBC. "Civil War & Revolution." *https://www.bbc.co.uk/history/british/civil_war_revolution.* accessed 20 Aug 2019

BBC. "Reformation." *https://www.bbc.co.uk/.* accessed 8 June 2018

BBC History Magazine. "Dressing to Impress in the 17th Century." *https://jyfmuseums.org/blog/dressing-to-impress-in-the-17th-century.* accessed 21 Mar 2019

BBC History Magazine. "Elizabeth I's Wars with England's Catholics — History Extra." *https://www.historyextra.com/period/tudor/Elizabeth-is-warring-with-englands-catholics.* accessed 31 Oct/2021

BBC History Magazine. "Love & Marriage in Tudor England." *https://www.historyextra.com/period/tudor/love-and-marriage-in-tudor-england.* accessed 11 Jul 2018

BCW Project, 1621-52. "Prince Maurice Moritz." *https://bcw-project.org/biography/prince-maurice.* accessed 9 June 2017

BCW Project. "Bishops' Wars." *https://bcw-project.org/military/bishops-wars.* accessed 5 Sep 2019

BCW Project. "Custom Demised: The Kissing Bush or Bunch." *https://bcw-project.org/military/bishops-wars.* accessed 31 Dec 2012

BCW Project. "George Villiers, First Duke of Buckingham." *https://bcw-project.org/biography/george-villiers-1st-duke-of-buckingham.* accessed 31 Oct 2021

BCW Project. "Oliver St. John, c. 1598 — 1673." *https://bcw-project.org/biography/oliver-st-john.* accessed 19 Apr 2020

BCW Project. "Soldiers of the Civil War." *https:// bcw-project-org.* accessed 9 Nov 2019

BCW Project. "William Prynne, 1600 — 1669." *https:// bcw-project-org.* accessed 24 Aug 2019

Benson, George Vere, John Bankes. "Dictionary of National Biography, 1885-1900, Vol. 3." *en.wikisource.org.* accessed 25 Aug 2019

Bible Research. "Roman Catholic Bible Versions." *www.bible-researcher. com/cath-intro.html.* accessed 28 Jul 2018

Biographical Sketches of Memorable Christians of the Past. "Charles I of England and Scotland, King and Martyr." *https://justus.anglican.org/ resources/bio/.* accessed 22 Oct 2017

Biographical Sketches of Memorable Christians of the Past. "William Laud, Archbishop and Martyr, 30 Jan 1649." *https://justus.anglican.org/ resources/bio/.* accessed 19 Apr 2020

Biographies.net. "Sir Robert Jenkinson, 1st Baronet." *www.biographies.net.* accessed 7 Sep 2019

Bodleian Library, University of Oxford. "Papers of Sir John Bankes." *www.bodleian.ox.ac.uk/* accessed 18 Aug 2019

Bodleian Library, University of Oxford. "Parliament in Oxford." *www. bodleian.ox.ac.uk/.* accessed 18 Nov 2019

Bond, Thomas. "History and Description of Corfe Castle in the Isle of Purbeck, Dorset." Stanford, 1883.

Borders, William. "A 40-Million Gift of British History to the National Trust." New York Times, 4 March 1982.

Borman, Tracy. "James I and Witchcraft." *https://tudortimes.co.uk/guest-articles/james-i-and-witchcraft-1.* accessed 6 Jan 2015

Bowlt, Colin. "The Ruislip Church House Almshouses, Middlesex." *https://www.lamas.org.uk/images/documents/Transactions60/211-224 Ruislip Church House.pdf.* accessed 1 May 2018

Brabcova, Alice. "Marriage in Seventeenth Century England: The Woman's Story." *https://www.phil.muni.cz/angl/thepes/thepes_02_02.pdf.* accessed 10 May 2018

Britannica. "Sidney Algernon." *www.britannica.com/biography.* accessed 10 May 2018

Britannica. "Bonham's Case, British History." *www.britannica.com/event/ Bonhams-Case.* accessed 1 Nov 2021

Britannica. "Samuel Cooper." *https://www.britannica.com/biography/ Samuel-Cooper.* accessed 12 May2921

Britannica. "Oliver Cromwell." *https://www.britannica.com/biography/ oliver-cromwell.* accessed 2 Feb 2013

Britannica. "Culverin." *www.britannica.com/technology/culverin.* accessed 31 October 2021

Britannica. "James I." *https://www.britannica.com/biography/James-I-king-of-England-and-Scotland.* accessed 31 Oct 2021

Britannica. "John Hampden, English Political Leader." *www.britannica. com.* accessed 18 Apr 2020

Britannica. "Long Parliament." *www.britannica.com.* accessed 19 Apr 2020

Britannica. "Puritanism." *www.britannica.com* accessed 10 May 2018

Britannica. "Roundhead." *www.britannica.com.* accessed 19 April 2020

Britannica. "William Prynne, English Pamphleteer." *www.britannica.com.* accessed 25 June 2019

BitishBattles.com. "The Battle of Edgehill." *www.britishbattles.com/english-civil-war.* accessed 12 June 2015

British Heritage. "Treachery and Valor in Corfe Castle." *https:// britishheritage.com/treachery-valor-in-corfe-castle.* accessed 12 June 2018

Linda Sindt

British History Online. "Early Modern Oxford." *https://www.british-history.ac.uk/vch/oxon/vol4/pp74-180.* accessed 18 Nov 2019

British History Online. "The Star Chamber on Printing, 1637." *https://www.british-history.ac.uk/rushworth-papers/vol3/pp306-316.* accessed 20 Aug 2019

British History Online. "Corfe Castle." *https://www.british-history.ac.uk/rchme/dorset/vol2/pp52-100.* accessed 16 Sep 2019

Britroyals. "King Charles I (1625-1649)." *www.britroyals.com.* accessed 29 July 2019

Brookes, Christopher W. "Sir John Bankes (1589 – 1644)." Oxford University Press, 2018.

Browne, Jill. "Twelfth Night at the Banqueting House." *https://londonheritagehotspots.com/twelfth-night-at-the-banqueting-house-1617.* accessed 7 Jan 2018

Brown, Michael H. "An Introduction to the Geneva Bible." *www.puritanpublications.com,* accessed 1 Nov 2021

Burke, John. "A Genealogical and Heraldic History of the Commoners of Great Britain and Ireland, Vol. 3." *http://luminarium.org/sevenlit/james/jamesbio.html.* Colburn, London, 1836. accessed 23 March 2019

Butler, Martin. "The Court Masque and Political Culture." Cambridge 2009.

Campbell, Heather, Senior Editor. "John Bastwick, Religious Zealot." *www.brittanica.com.* Encyclopedia Brittanica. accessed 24 Aug 2019

Christmas Traditions in 17th Century England and Virginia. "Christmas in 17th Century England and Virginia." *www.historyisfun.org/jamestown-settlement/a-colonial-christmas/christmas-traditions/.* accessed 10 Feb 2018

Christmas Symbols. "Wassailing." *www.santasnet.wassailing.htm.* accessed 15 May 2018

Churchill, Nick. "Queen of the Castle." *www.dorsetlife.co.uk.* Dorset Life, Feb 26, 2017. accessed 1 Nov 2021

Churchill, Nick. "Keeper of the Castle Exposed?" *https://www. nickchurchill.org.uk/keeper-of-the-castle-exposed/.* accessed 1 Nov 2021

"Civil War and Revolution." *www.bbc.co.uk.* accessed 20 July 2021

Cody, David. "The Anglican Church." *www.victorianweb.org/religion/ denom1.html.* accessed 1 Nov 2021

Cole, Mary Hill. "James VI and I (1566-1625)" *https://encyclopediavirginia. org/entries/james-vi-and-i-1566-1625.* accessed 10 Feb 2018

Colonial America Reference Library. "John Rolfe." The Gale Group, 2000.

Connolly, Sharon Bennet. "The Short Life and Sad Death of Edward the Martyr." *www.historytheinterestingbits.com/2016/08/27/the-short-life-and- sad-death-of-edward-the-martyr.* accessed Aug 27, 2016

Cooper, Elizabeth. "The Life & Times of Thomas Wentworth, Earl of Strafford & Lord-Lieutenant of Ireland, Volume I." Tinsley, London 1874.

Conservapedia. "King James Bible." *https://www.conservapedia.com/King_ James_Bible.* accessed 17 Dec 2017

"Cross-dressing in Twelfth Night." The Globe Education Trust, London, 2016.

Crosthwaite, J. Fisher. "The Life and Times of Sir John Bankes, Attorney-General and Lord Chief Justice." London 1872.

Curtis, Ken, PhD. "The Story Behind the King James Bible." *www. christianity.com.* accessed 30 June 2018

Daily Mail. "Bringing Corfe Castle Back to Life: Digital Reconstruction." *www.dailymail.co.uk/sciencetecharticle-3539618/Bringing-Corfe-Castle-life.* accessed 17 Aug 2018

Deetz, Patricia Scott and James Deetz. "Plymouth Town Early Descriptions, 1620−1628." W.H. Freeman, New York, 2000.

DeMarc, Virginia. "Sexuality in the Seventeenth Century." Grantville Gazette, Chattanooga, TN, 19 Oct 2015.

Dismore, Jane. "Pocahontas in England." *https://www.historytoday.com/ author/jane-dismore*. accessed 24 May 2016

Dixon, Simon. "Seditious Works in Special Collections: the Case of William Prynne." *https://staffblogs.le.ac.uk/specialcollections/tag/william-prynne*. University of Leicester Library Special Collections. accessed 17 Aug 2019

Doe, Martha. "Virginia and the Puritan Ban on Christmas." *www. timetravel-britain.com*. accessed 30 Jul 2015

Dorney, John. "The First Day of the 1641 Rebellion." *www.theirishstory. com*. accessed 13 Sep 2019

Dorset Ancestors. "Lady Mary Bankes, the Mistress of the Castle." *www. dorset-ancestors.com*. accessed 12 Oct 2012

Dorset Ancestors. "Corfe Castle—Its Chequered History of Owners and Occupiers." *www.dorset-ancestors.com*. accessed 27 April 2011

Dorset Life. "Dressing to Impress in the 17th Century." *www.historyextra. com*. accessed 21 Apr 2019

Dorset Magazine. "Rebuilding Corfe Castle." *http://www.dorsetlife.co.uk*. accessed 22 July 2018

Durston, Chris. "The Puritan War on Christmas." History Today Volume 35, Issue 12, December 1985.

Egloff, Nancy. "Christmas in 17th Century England and Virginia." *www. historyisfun.org*. accessed 30 July 2015

Egloff, Nancy. "The Puritan Ban on Christmas." *www.historyisfun.org*. accessed 30 July 2015

Elder, Gregory. "When Christmas was banned in 17th Century England." *www.redlandsdailyfacts.com*. accessed 18 Dec 2013

Elizabethan World Reference Library. "Daily Life in the Elizabethan Era." *https://www.encyclopedia.com/.../daily-life-elizabethan-era*. accessed 10 May 2018

Ellis, Steven. "Turning Ireland English." *https://www.bbc.co.uk/history/british/tudors/elizabeth_ireland_01.shtm.* accessed 9 Feb 2018

Encyclopedia of Irish History and Culture. "Religion: 1500 – 1690." *www.encyclopedia.com.* accessed 1 Nov 2021

"Elizabethan Wedding Customs." *www.william-shakespeare.info.* William Shakespeare Site Map. accessed 22 Oct 2017

ElizabethanEra.Org. "Elizabethan Recusancy Laws." *www.elizabethan-era.org.uk.* accessed 14 Oct 2019

Encyclopedia.com. "Daily Life in the Elizabethan Era." *www.encyclopedia.com.* accessed 10 May 2018

Encyclopedia Virginia. "Gabriel Archer." *www.encyclopediavirginia.org.* accessed 6 May 2018

English Law. "Dr. Bonham's Case." *http://law.jrank.org/pages/6484/English-Law-DR-BONHAM-S/CASE-html.* accessed 17 May 2018

Explaining the English Civil Wars. "The Warrior Women of the English Civil War." *https://earlofmanchesters.co.uk/the-warrior-women-of-the-english-civil-war.* accessed 14 Oct 2019

Family Search Wiki. "Clergy of the Church of England." *https://www.familysearch.org.* accessed 8 June 2018

The Famous People. "King James I, Timeline & History." *https://study.com/academy/lesson/king-james-i-timeline-history-quiz.html.* accessed 9 June 2019

Ferris, John P. "Edward Lawrence of Creech Grange, Dorset." *www.historyofparliamentonline.org.* accessed 14 Nov 2019

Festing, Gabrielle. "Unstirred History: Portraits of Some Famous Women in the 16th, 17th, and 18th Centuries." Forgotten Books, London, 2019.

Linda Sindt

Finley, Gavin. "Puritans Rise to Power in the Early 1600s and Assume a Dominant Role in the English Parliament." *www.endtimepilgrim.org*. accessed 4 June 2019

Fleming, Hanna. "The Puritan War on Christmas." History Today, volume 15, London 1985.

Fletcher, Anthony. "Growing Up in England, the Experience of Childhood." Yale University Press London 1985.

Flood, Alison. "Inflame Her to Venery with Wanton Kisses." *www. theguardian.com/books*. The Guardian. accessed 7 June 2017

Fraser, Antonia. "Cromwell." Grove Press New York, 1973.

Fraser, Antonia. "Faith and Treason, the Story of the Gunpowder Plot." Doubleday New York, 1996.

Fraser, Antonia. "King Charles II." Weidenfeld, London, 1979.

Fraser, Antonia. "The Weaker Vessel." Knopf, New York, 1984.

"Cross-dressing in Twelfth Night." The Globe Education Trust, London, 2016.

Gospel Assembly Free. "Who Was King James?" *www.gospelassemblyfree. com/facts/kingjames.htm*. accessed 9 June 2019

Grace, Maria. "Rectors and Vicars and Curates...Oh My!" *https:// randombitsoffascination.com/2012/01/18/rectors-and-vicars-and-*. accessed 2 Nov 2021

Gray's Inn. "Benchers." *www.graysinn.org.uk*. accessed 29 July 2019

Gray's Inn. "King James Bible." *www.graysinn.org.uk*. accessed 19 June 2019

Gregg Pauline. "King Charles I." University of California Press, Los Angeles, 1981.

Hardy, Emmeline. "The Story of Corfe Castle." University Press, London, 1983.

Harmonious Music. "Renaissance Wedding Music." *www. harmoniousmusic.com.* accessed 10 May 2018

Harris, J. Rendell. "The Origin and Meaning of Apple Cults." University Press, London, 1919.

Havran, M.J. "Sources for Recusant History Among the Bankes Papers in the Bodleian." *https://www.cambridge.org/core/journals/british-catholic-history/article/sources-for.* accessed 16 Sep 2015

Hawtrey, Frances Molesworth. "The History of the Hawtrey Family." George Allen, Charing Cross Road, London 1903.

Hawtrey, Louisa. "Brave Dame Mary, or the Siege of Corfe Castle." Society for Promoting Christian Knowledge, London, 1873.

Hern, Candace. "Regency World, Riding Habits." *https://candicehern.com/regencyworld/riding-habits-overview.* accessed 21 Jun 2018

Historical Articles, History, Law, Royalty. "The Trial of John Hampden for Not Paying Ship Money." *www.lookandlearn.com.* accessed 25 Aug 2019

History Is Fun. "Christmas Traditions in 17th Century England." *https://www.historyisfun.org/jamestown-settlement/a-colonial-christmas/christmas-traditions.* accessed 10 Feb 2018

History Learning Site. "Life in England Under Oliver Cromwell." *https://www.historylearningsite.co.uk/stuart.* accessed 2 Feb 2013

History of England from the Celts Through 20th Century England. "England Under James the First." *www.england-history.org./england-under-james-the-first.* accessed 2 Feb 2013

History of England from the Celts Through 20th Century England. "England Under Charles the First." *www.england-history.org./england-under-charles-the-first.* accessed 10 Feb 2018

History of England from the Celts Through 20th Century England. "England Under Charles the Second." *www.england-history.org./england-under-charles-the-second.* accessed 26 Mar 2013

Linda Sindt

History of England from the Celts Through 20th Century England. "England Under Oliver Cromwell." *www.england-history.org./england-under-oliver-cromwell.* accessed 11 Apr 2019

History Extra. "Love and Marriage in Tudor England." *https://www.historyextra.com/period/tudor/love-and-marriage-in-tudor-england.* accessed 11 July 2018

History of Parliament Online. "Sir Walter Erle (1586-1665) of Charborough, Dorset." *https://www.historyofparliamentonline.org.* accessed 16 Oct 2019

History on the Net. "English Civil War (1642-1651)" *www.historyonthenet.com.* accessed 14 Oct 2014

History Timeline/Historic Jamestowne. "Capt Bartholomew Gosnold, Capt Gabriel Archer, and Others Voyage to the New England Coast." *https://historicjamestowne.org/history/timeline.*

History Today. "Clarendon's History of the Rebellion." *www.historytoday.com.* accessed 10 Dec 2019

Jordan, Don and Michael Walsh. "White Cargo: The Forgotten History of Britain's White Slaves in America." New York University Press, New York, March 1, 2008.

History Hit. "Oliver Cromwell and the New Modern Army." *www.historyhit.com.* accessed 10 Dec 2019

History of Ireland. "Captains Hunger, Toil, Cold and Sickness." *https://www.historyireland.com/early-modern-history-1500-1700/the-dead-sick-wounded-of-the nine years-1594-1603.* accessed 8 Feb 2018

History of Parliament Online. "John Bankes (1589 – 1644), of Gray's Inn, Later of Corfe Castle, Dorset." *http://www.historyofparliamentonline.org.* accessed 29 July 2019

History of Parliament Online. "Sir Walter Erle, 1586 – 1665." *http://www.historyofparliamentonline.org.* accessed 20 Aug 2019

History of Parliament Online. "Ralph Hawtrey (1570 – 1638) of Eastcote Hall, Ruislip, Middlesex." *http://www.historyofparliamentonline.org.* accessed 27 Apr 2018

History of Parliament Online. "Sir William Masham, 1ˢᵗ Baronet." *http://www.historyofparliamentonline.org.* accessed 27 April 2018

History of Parliament Online. "The Parliament of 1614." *http://www.historyofparliamentonline.org.* accessed 17 Nov 2018

History on the Net. "English Civil War Timeline." *https://www.historyonthenet.com/english-civil-war-timeline.* accessed 16 Sep 2019

History Today. "The Last Dodo." *www.historytoday.com.* accessed 7 May 2018

Hobson Woodward. "Namontack's Fate: The Last Voyage of the First Powhatan Envoy to England." *www.worldcat.org/oclc/747949316.* accessed 7 May 2018

Imperial Society of Knights Bachelor. "History of Knighthood." *https://www.iskb.co.uk/history.* accessed 9 June 2018

Irish America. "The Irish of Barbados." *www.irishamerica.com.* accessed 28 Sep 2019

Irish Eyes of Virginia. "The Nine Years War 1594-1603." *www.irisheyesofva.com/9_years_war.pdf.* accessed 8 Feb 2018

James, Sydney V., Jr. "Three Visitors to Early Plymouth." Applewood Books, Carlisle, MA 1963

Jamieson, Lee. "Cross Dressing in Shakespeare Plays." *https://www.thoughtco.com/cross-dressing-in-shakespeare-plays-2984940.* accessed 16 Apr 2018

Johnova, Lucie. "Patterns of Crossdressing in Shakespeare's Comedies." Charles University Prague *https://www.phil.muni.cz/angl/thepes/thepes_02_09.pdf.*
accessed 24 March 2019

Johnson, Ben. "A Tudor Christmas." *www.historic.uk.com/HistoryUK/HistoryofEngland/A-Tudor-Christmas/.* accessed 10 Feb 2018

Johnson, Caleb. "Emmanuel Altham to Sir Edward Altham March 1623." *www.MayflowerHistory.com.* accessed 2 Nov 2021

Johnson, Caleb. "Emmanuel Altham to Sir Edward Altham September 1623." *www.MayflowerHistory.com.* accessed 2 Nov 2021

Johnson, Caleb. "Emmanuel Altham to James Sherley May 1624." *www. MayflowerHistory.com.* accessed 2 Nov 2021

Jokinen, Anniina. "Henry, Prince of Wales." *http://www.luminarium.org/ encyclopedia/princehenry.htm.* Luminarium, 30 Nov 2006.

Jones, Gareth H. "Sir Edward Coke." *https://www.britannica.com/ biography/Edward-Coke.* accessed 28 Nov 2018

Jones Paul Anthony. "30 Excellent Terms from a 17th Century Slang Dictionary." *www.mentalfloss.com* accessed 18 May 2019

Jrank Articles. "English Law — Dr. Bonham's Case." *https://law.jrank.org/ pages/6484/English-Law-DR-BONHAM-S-CASE-html.* accessed 17 May 2018

Kershaw, Samuel. "The Papers of William Laud and Others." Wayland Library, 17th Century.

Kreis, Steven. "Lecture 7, The English Civil War, The History Guide." Cambridge 2002.

Krstovic, Elena, Ed., and Marie Lazzari. "Literature of the English Revolution — Introduction." Literary Criticism (1400 — 1800). *http://www. enotes.com/topics/literature-english-revolution#critical-essays-introduction.* accessed 15 Aug 2019

Kupperman, Karen Ordahl. "The Jamestown Project." Belknapp Press, Massachusetts, 2007.

Lambert, Tim. "A Brief History of Drinks and Beverages." *http://www. localhistories.org.* accessed 29 July 2018

Lambert, Tim. "Daily Life in 17th Century England." *http://www. localhistories.org.* accessed 20 May 2018

Lambert, Tim. "Daily Life in England in the 1600s." *http://www. localhistories.org.* accessed 20 May 2018

Lambert, Tim. "Life for Women in the 17th Century." *http://www. localhistories.org.* accessed 27 July 2015

Lambert, Tim. "A History of 17th Century England." *http://www. localhistories.org.* accessed 13 Nov 2016

Landed Families of Britain and Ireland. "Bankes Family of Kingston Lacy." *http://landedfamilies.blogspot.com.* accessed 19 Apr 2020

Landed Families of Britain and Ireland. "Altham of Mark Hall, Oxhey Place and Timbercombe." *http://landedfamilies.blogspot.com.* accessed 14 Mar 2014

Lark, Jane. "The Tale of the 'Mad Cavalier,' Prince Rupert." *https:// janelark.blog/2012/10/21/the-tale-of-the-mad-cavalier-prince-rupert-.* accessed 23 May 2018

Lax, Amy. "The Seathwaite Connection. Some Aspects of the Graphite Mine and Its Owners." National Trust Archaeological Review, 1988-1989.

Levinson, Bernard M., and Joshua A Berman. "The King James Bible, at 400." *https://www.sbl-site.org/assets/pdfs/ LevinsonBermanKJV400HistoryChannel.pdf.* accessed 23 May 2018

Levy, Joel. "How the King James Bible Came to Be." *http://time. com/4821911/king-james-bible-history.* accessed 23 May 2018

Lewis, Yvonne. "Enthusiastic Collectors: The Bankes Brothers European Shopping in the 1640s." *https://referisg.wordpress.com/2016/03/14/ enthusiastic-collectors-the-bankes-brothers.* accessed 3 Nov 2011

Life in Elizabethan England 1558-1603. "A Compendium of Common Knowledge." *www.elizabethan.org/compendium/index.html.* accessed 19 Apr 2019

Look and Learn. "Charles I Betrays Thomas Wentworth, Earl of Strafford." *www.lookandlearn.com.* accessed 14 Sep 2019

Luminarium Encyclopedia Project. "Anne of Denmark." (1574–1619) *www.luminarium.org/encyclopedia/annedenmark.htm.* accessed 23 March 2019

Linda Sindt

Mabillard, Amanda. "Contemporary References to King James I in Shakespeare's Macbeth." *shakespeare-online.com/plays/macbeth/jamescompliments.html.* accessed 20 Nov 2011

Mad Monarchist, "Monarchist Profile: Lady Mary Bankes." *https://madmonarchist.blogspot.com/2017/11/monarchist-profile-lady-mary-bankes.html.* accessed 27 June 2018

Martin, Madeleine. "History of Hygiene: Bathing, Teeth Cleaning, Deodorizing." *https://www.historyundressed.com/2008/07/history-of-hygiene.* accessed 12 Oct 2000

Maryland Institute for Technology in the Humanities. "History of the Masque Genre." *http://www.mith.umd.edu.* accessed 10 Dec 2000

Mathew, David. "James I, King of England and Scotland." *https://britannica.com/biography/James-I-king-of-England-and-Scotland.* accessed 18 Nov 2018

McCarson, Debbie. "What Type of Foods Did They Eat in 1600s England?" *https://classroom.synonym.com/type-foods-did-eat-during-1600s-england-19733.html.* accessed 27 April 2019

McCartney, Martha W. "Virginia Immigrants and Adventurers, 1607–1635: A Biographical Dictionary of Early Virginians." Genealogical Publishing, 2007, Maryland.

McCrum, Robert. "How the King James Bible Shaped the English Language." *https://www.theguardian.com/books/2010/nov/21/king-james-bible-english-language.* accessed 18 Nov 2018

McQueeney, Kerry. "Ye Olde Stinke Bomb." *www.dailymail.co.uk.* accessed 17 July 2012

Mendle, Michael. "The Ship Money Case, the Case of Shipment, and the Development of Henry Parker's Parliamentary Absolutism." Cambridge Core, Cambridge, September 1989.

Metcalfe, Charles. "A Book of Knights Bannaret, Knights of Bath, and Knights Bachelor." Harvard University, Harvard, 1885.

Molesworth, Florence Hawtrey. "The History of the Hawtrey Family." G.Allen, London 1903.

Moremus, David. "The Real Pocahontas." *http://pocahontas.morenus.org/.* accessed 16 May 2018

Mortlock, Stephen. "Death and Disease in the English Civil War." The Biomedical Scientist, 1 Jun 2017.

Mummers Museum. "Mummers 101." *https://mummersmuseum.com.* accessed 26 Apr 2018

Nantwich Museum. "English Civil War — Cannons and Mortar, an Overview." *www.nantwichmuseum.org.uk.* accessed 10 Nov 2019

National Park Service. "Pocahontas: Her Life and Legend." *www.nps.gov.* accessed 3 May 2019

National Trust. "Bankes Family Bible, Relating to Sir John and Dame Mary Bankes." *https://app.dorsetcouncil.gov.uk/bankes-archive/bankes-family-bible-relating-to-sir.* accessed 9 June 2019

National Trust. "Beyond the Portrait: Revealing the Woman Within." *https://www.nationaltrust.org.uk.* accessed 29 June 2018

National Trust. "Corfe Castle." Acorn Press 2003.

National Trust. "The Defiance of Mary Bankes." *www.nationaltrust.org.uk.* accessed 25 Jan 2021

National Trust. "Kingston Lacy." 1994.

National Trust. "Kingston Lacy Illustrated List of Pictures." *https://www.nationaltrust.org.uk.* accessed 8 July 2008

National Trust. "Mary Hawtrey, Lady Bankes," *https://www.nationaltrust.org.uk.* accessed 27 June 2018

National Trust. "Sir Christopher Hatton and an Age of Adventure." *https://www.nationaltrust.org.uk.*

National Trust. "Unlocking the Archive of the Bankes Family of Kingston Lacy." *https://www.nationaltrust.org.uk/kingston-lacy/features/unlocking-the-bankes-archive.* accessed 18 Sep 2016

Linda Sindt

Nichols, A. Bryant. "Captain Christopher Newport." Newport News, Virginia, 2007.

Noah, William H., and David L. Brown. "Geneva Bible History." *jesus-is savior.com/Bible/geneva_bible.htm.* accessed 27 Apr 2019

Norman, Andrew. "Corfe Remembered." Halsgrove House, 2017, Great Britain.

Norman, Andrew. "By Swords Divided, Corfe Castle in the Civil War." 2003, Great Britain.

Past Peculiar. "1633: Women Actors Are 'Notorious Whores.'" *www. alphahistory.com.* accessed 239 July 2019

People Pill. "Walter Erle: English Politician, Biography." *www.peoplepill. com.* accessed 20 Aug 2019

Perkins, T., and H. Pentin. "Memorials of Old Dorset." Forgotten Books, London, Jan 1, 1907.

Pilgrim Hall Museum. "Beyond the Pilgrim Story." America's Museum of Pilgrim Possessions 2012.

Plant, David. "Biography of George Villiers, First Duke of Buckingham." British Civil Wars Project, March 6, 2003.

Plant, David. "Biography of Sir Thomas Wentworth, 1st Earl of Strafford." *https://bcw-project.org/biography/thomas-wentworth-earl-of-strafford.* accessed 9 June 2017

Plimoth Plantation. "Raising Children in the Early 17th Century." *https://plimoth.org.* accessed 29 June 2018

Plowden, Alison. "Women All on Fire." Sutton Publishing Limited, Gloucester, 1998.

Poole Museum Society. "Lady Mary Bankes and the Fall of Corfe Castle." *www.poolemuseumsociety.wordpress.com.* accessed 4 April 2018

Powhatan Tribe. "Powhatan Tribe: Facts, Clothes, Food and History." *https://www.warpaths2peacepipes.com/indian-tribes/powhatan-tribe,htm.* accessed 4 April 2018

Prothero, G.W. "Constitutional Struggle in England (1625-40)." *http://localhistories.org/tudorxmas.html*. Unknown Binding London 1906. accessed 9 June 2017

Purkiss, Diane. "The English Civil War." Harper Collins, United Kingdom 2006.

Queen Mary University of London. "Who Were the Nuns." *https://wwtn.history.qmul.ac.uk/counties/details.php?uid=LA004&county-Essex*. accessed 9 June 2018

Raymond, Joad. "Pamphlets and Pamphleteering in Early Modern Britain." Cambridge University Press, Cambridge 2003.

Recusant Rolls (Catholic). "Timeline of Roman Catholic Persecution and Tolerations." *https://www.genguide.co.uk/source/recusant-rolls-catholics/3*. accessed 15 April 2018

"Recusants and the Recusancy Laws — Elizabethan Era." *elizabethanenglandlife.com/recusants-and-the-recusancy-laws.html*. accessed 8 Nov 2021

Reese, Christine Noelle. "Burton, Bastwick and Prynne and the Politics of Memory." *www.americanhistorypodcast.net*. Pennsylvania University, Pennsylvania 2007. accessed 14 Sep 2019

Reformed Reader. "Introduction to the Geneva Bible." *www.reformedreader.org/gbn/igb.htm*. accessed 11 Nov 2018

Rejects and Revolutionaries: The Origins of America. "Execution Speech of the Earl of Strafford." *www.americanhistorypodcast.net/execution-speech-of-the-earl-of-strafford/*. accessed 6 Nov 2021

Rickard, J. "The Battle of Edgehill, 23 October 1642." *http://www.historyofwar.org/articles/battles_edgehill.html*. accessed 6 Nov 2021

Riddell, William Renwick. "The Death of King James I — A Medico-Legal Study." Journal of Criminal Law and Criminology, Vol. 19, Issue 1 May, Article 4.

Rigg, James McMullen. "Christopher Hatton (1540 – 1591)" *https://en.wikisource.org*. accessed 8 June 2019

Robinson, Bruce. "The Human Reformation." *https://www.bbc.co.uk/history/british/tudors/human_reformation_01.shtml.* accessed 8 June 2018

Rountree, Helen C. "Pocahontas (d. 1617)" Encyclopedia Virginia, Virginia November 30, 2015.

Rushworth, John. "The Star Chamber on Printing 1637." *http://www.british-history.ac.uk/rushworth-papers/vol3/pp306-316.* accessed 19 Aug 2019

Russell, Michael. "Sir Walter Erle (1586 – 1665) Knight of Charborough." Fordington, March 2009.

Sabotage Bureau. "The Pamphleteers." *https://sabotagebureau.org/wp-content/uploads/2012/11/ThePamphleteers.pdf.* accessed 7 June 2019

Salmon John. "Christopher Newport (1561 – after August 15, 1617)." *https://encyclopediavirginia.org/author/johnsalmon.* Encyclopedia Virginia, accessed 7 June 2016

Schnepper, Rachel. "Yuletide's Outlaws." New York Times, New York 2012.

Schoonover, David. "Lady Borlase's Receiptes Booke." University Press, Iowa, 1998.

Select Surnames. "Select Banks Surname Geneaology." *http://www.selectsurnames3.com/banks.html.* accessed 22 July 2018

Shakespeare Christmas. "How the Elizabethans Celebrated Christmas." *www.shakespeare-online.com/biography/shkchristmas.html.* accessed 21 May 2018

Shakespeare Globe Trust. "Cross-Dressing in Twelfth Night." *2016. playingshakespeare.org/sites/default/files/public/attachments/Cross-Dressing in.* accessed 6 Nov 2021

Shakespeare's Inns of Court. "The Royal Palace and Inns of Court." *www.shakespeare-online.com/theatre/theroyalpalaces.html.* accessed 19 May 2016

Smith, George P. II. "Dr. Bonham's Case and the Modern Significance of Lord Coke's Influence." *htttps://scholarship.law.edu/scholar/794/.* accessed 18 May 2019

Smithsonian National Museum of the American Indian. "Marking the 400th Anniversary of Pocahontas's Death." *https://www.smithsonianmag.com/blogs/national.* accessed 8 July 2018

Smithsonian.com. "The Origins of the King James Bible." *https://www.smithsonianmag.com/smart-news/origins-of-the-king-james-bible.* accessed 23 Jan 2018

Snell, Melissa. "English Court of Star Chamber: A Brief History." Thought Company, March 13, 2018.

Snyder, Howard A. "Jesus and Pocahontas." Cascade Books, Eugene, OR, 2015.

Sparkes, Abigail. "The Life and Death of William Laud." *www.historic-uk.com.* accessed 31 July 2019

Speel, Bob. "Monuments in St. Martin's Church." *www.speel.me.uk/chlondon/ruislipch.htm.* Ruislip, Middlesex. accessed 8 July 2018

St. Edwards, Corfe Castle. "St. Edward, King & Martyr, the Parish Church of Corfe Castle, Dorset." *www.stedwardscorfecastle.co.uk.* accessed 4 Aug 2019

St. Mary at Latton. "Harlow — Our Church History. The History at St. Mary at Latton Church." *http://www.st-mary-at-latton.org.uk/history.htm.* accessed 28 Apr 2018

Storey, Nary Frances Bankes. "Grandpap's Family, Volume II." Amundsen Publishing Company 1996.

Stoyle, Mark. "No Christmas Under Cromwell? The Puritan Assault on Christmas." *http://www.historyextra.com/feature/no-christmas-under-cromwell-puritan-assault-christmas-during-1640s-and-1650s.* University of Michigan. accessed 19 Dec 2014

Study.Com. "King James I: Timeline & History." *https://study.com/academy/lesson/king-james-i-timeline-history-quiz.html.* accessed 9 June 2019

The Stuarts, The English Civil War. "King Charles I." *https://www.britainexpress.com/History/Early_Stuarts_and_the_Civil_War.htm.* accessed 22 Jan 2018

Tagore, Sourindo, Mohun. "The Orders of Knighthood, British and Foreign." *https://archive.org/details/ordersknighthoo01tagogoog*. accessed 6 Nov 2021

Thomas, Melissa. "Theatre Culture of Modern England." *http://www2. cedarcrest.edu/academic/eng/lfletcher/henry4/papers/mthomas.htm*. accessed 21 May 2018

Thrush, Edward and John P. Ferris, editors. "Bankes, John (1589-`644) of Gray's Inn, London; later of Corfe Castle." *https://www. historyofparliamentonline.org/volume/*.accessed 6 Nov 2021

Thrush, Edward and John P. Ferris, editors. "The Parliament of 1614." *https://www.historyofparliamentonline.org/volume/1604-1629/survey/ parliament-1614*. History of Parliament. accessed 6 Nov 2021

Thurnall, Harry Joseph. "King James I's Palace, Royston." *https://artuk. org/discover/artworks/view_as/grid/search/keyword:royston-museum--region:*. accessed 9 June 2018

Trueman, C.N. "Thomas Wentworth, Earl of Strafford." *https://www. historylearningsite.co.uk/stuart-england/thomas-wentworth-earl-of-strafford*. accessed 15 Mar 2017

Tudor Place. "Hunting in Tudor England." *www.tudorplace.com.ar/ Documents/hunting.htm*. accessed 5 Aug 2018

Tusser, Thomas. "Five Hundred Points of Good Husbandrie, ed. 1580. English Dialect Society." 1878.

UK Genealogy Archives. "Altham of Timbercombe." *https://ukga.org*. accessed 26 Apr 2019

United Kingdom Genealogy. "Bankes Miscellanea." *www.uk-genealogy. org.uk*. accessed 12 June 2017

Unlocking the Bankes Archives. "Letter from King Charles I to Sir John Bankes." *https://www.nationaltrust.org.uk/kingston-lacy/features/unlocking-the-bankes-archive*. accessed 25 Oct 2019

Virtual Museum Time Corridor. "17th Century Harvey to van Leeuwenhoek." *https://www.baus.org.uk/museum/82/17th_century*. British Association of Urological Surgeons, Limited. accessed 21 Feb 2019

Watching, Thinking & Praying. "Henry VIII, The Divine Right of Kings and the Church of England." *https://watchthinkpray.blogspot.com/2010/01/henry-v111-divine-right-of-kings-and.html.* accessed 11 Jan 2010

Waterhouse, Edward. "A Declaration of the State of the Colony and Affaires in Virginia, 1622." *https://collections.folger.edu/detail/waterhouse-edward-colonist-a-declaration-of-the.* Library of Congress. accessed 9 Oct 2016

Watkin, Pamela. "A Kingston Lacy Childhood." Dovecote Press, Stanbridge, Winborne Minster, Dorset, 1986.

Weatherwax, Esmeralda. "Pocahontas in England." New English Review, 2007.

Wentworth, Thomas Earl of Strafford. "In His Own Defense." The World's Greatest Orations. *www.Bartleby.com.* accessed 14 Aug 2020

Wikipedia. "1630s in England." *https://en.wikipedia.org/wiki/1630s_in_England.* accessed 28 June 2018

Wikipedia. "Algernon Sidney." *https://en.wikipedia.org.* accessed 10 May 2018

Wikipedia. "Anti-Catholicism in the United Kingdom." *https://en.wikipedia.org.* accessed 20 Apr 2019

Wikipedia. "Assizes." *https://en.wikipedia.org.* accessed 10 Nov 2019

Wikipedia. "Battle of Edgehill." *https://en.wikipedia.org.* accessed 1 Feb 2013

Wikipedia. "Battle of Yellow Ford." *https://en.wikipedia.org.* accessed 25 Jan 2018

Wikipedia. "Brilliana, Lady Harley." *https://en.wikipedia.org.* accessed 27 May 2019

Wikipedia. "Catholic Church in England and Wales." *https://en.wikipedia.org.* accessed 19 Jan 2018

Wikipedia. "Charles I of England." *https://en.wikipedia.org.* accessed 1 Jun 2017

Linda Sindt

Wikipedia. "Christopher Newport." *https://en.wikipedia.org*. accessed 20 April 2019

Wikipedia. "Church of England." *https://en.wikipedia.org*. accessed 26 Jan 2018

Wikipedia. "Church of St. Mary the Virgin, Harlow." *https://en.wikipedia.org*. accessed 8 July 2018

Wikipedia. "Commission of Array." *https://en.wikipedia.org*. accessed 6 Nov 2021

Wikipedia. "Corfe Castle." *https://en.wikipedia.org*. accessed 4 Sep 2013

Wikipedia. "Creech Grange." *https://en.wikipedia.org*. accessed 6 Nov 2019

Wikipedia. "Demi-Cannon." *https://en.wikipedia.org*. accessed 10 Nov 2019

Wikipedia. "Divine Right of Kings." *https://en.wikipedia.org*. accessed 10 Jun 2017

Wikipedia. "Dorothy Spencer, Countess of Sutherland." *https://en.wikipedia.org*. accessed 10 May 2018

Wikipedia. "Dr. Bonham's Case." *https://en.wikipedia.org*. accessed 17 May 2018

Wikipedia. "Edward Coke." *https://en.wikipedia.org*. accessed 18 Nov 2018

Wikipedia. "Edward the Martyr." *https://en.wikipedia.org*. accessed 20 Aug 2019

Wikipedia. "English Civil War." *https://en.wikipedia.org*. accessed 10 June 2017

Wikipedia. "Felim O'Neill of Kinard." *https://en.wikipedia.org*. accessed 4 Dec 2018

Wikipedia. "Geneva Bible." *https://en.wikipedia.org*. accessed 5 July 2018

Wikipedia. "George Villiers, 1st Duke of Buckingham." *https://en.wikipedia.org*. accessed 28 Apr 2019

Wikipedia. "Greyhound." *https://en.wikipedia.org.* accessed 11 June 2017

Wikipedia. "Henry Burton (theologian)." *https://en.wikipedia.org.* accessed24 Aug 2019

Wikipedia. "Henry Frederik, Prince of Wales." *https://en.wikipedia.org.* accessed 19 Nov 2018

Wikipedia. "History of the Puritans Under James I." *https://en.wikipedia.org.* accessed 10 May 2018

Wikipedia. "Irish Rebellion of 1641." *https://en.wikipedia.org.* accessed 29 Sep 2019

Wikipedia. "James VI and I and the English Parliament." *https://en.wikipedia.org.* accessed 10 May 2018

Wikipedia. "James VI and I and Religious Issues." *https://en.wikipedia.org.* accessed 10 May 2018

Wikipedia. "Jenny Geddes." *https://en.wikipedia.org.* accessed 4 Sep 2019

Wikipedia. "John Bankes." *https://en.wikipedia.org.* accessed 30 July 2019

Wikipedia. "John Hampden." *https://en.wikipedia.org.* 19 Aug 2019

Wikipedia. "John Hoskins." *https://en.wikipedia.org.* accessed 29 Jun 2018

Wikipedia. "Keswick, Cumbria." *https://en.wikipedia.org.* accessed 15 Apr 2018

Wikipedia. "King James Version." *https://en.wikipedia.org.* accessed 10 Feb 2018

Wikipedia. "Laudianism." *https://en.wikipedia.org.* accessed 29 May 2015

Wikipedia. "Long Parliament." *https://en.wikipedia.org.* accessed 25 Sep 2019

Wikipedia. "Mary Queen of Scots." *https://en.wikipedia.org.* accessed 20 Jul 2019

Wikipedia. "The Memorable Masque of the Middle Temple and Lincoln's Inn." *https://en.wikipedia.org.* accessed 19 May 2018

Linda Sindt

Wikipedia. "Mummer's Play." *https://en.wikipedia.org.* accessed 26 Apr 2018

Wikipedia. "Music in the Elizabethan Era." *https://en.wikipedia.org.* accessed 13 Feb 2018

Wikipedia. "New Model Army." *https://en.wikipedia.org.* accessed 7 Nov 2019

Wikipedia. "Nine Years' War (Ireland)." *https://en.wikipedia.org.* accessed 25 Jan 2018

Wikipedia. "Oath of Allegiance of James I." *https://en.wikipedia.org.* accessed 15 Apr 2018

Wikipedia. "Oliver Cromwell." *https://en.wikipedia.org.* accessed 2 Feb 2013

Wikipedia. "Oliver St. John." *https://en.wikipedia.org.* accessed 15 Apr 2020

Wikipedia. "Personal Relationships of James VI and I." *https://en.wikipedia.org.* accessed 11 Nov 2018

Wikipedia. "Pocahontas." *https://en.wikipedia.org.* accessed 7 Jun 2019

Wikipedia. "Popish Recusants Act of 1605." *https://en.wikipedia.org.* accessed 5 Apr 2018

Wikipedia. "Pride's Purge." *https://en.wikipedia.org.* accessed 10 Jun 2017

Wikipedia. "Puritans." *https://en.wikipedia.org.* accessed 23 Apr 2018

Wikipedia. "Reader (Inns of Court)." *https://en.wikipedia.org.* accessed 10 Jun 2018

Wikipedia. "Samuel Cooper." *https://en.wikipedia.org.* accessed 12 May 2021

Wikipedia. "Ship Money." *https://en.wikipedia.org.* accessed 1 Aug 2019

Wikipedia. "Sir John Borlase, 1st Baronet." *https://en.wikipedia.org.* accessed 22 Oct 2019

Wikipedia. "Sir Robert Jenkinson, 1ˢᵗ Baronet." *https://en.wikipedia.org.* accessed 9 June 2018

Wikipedia. "William Masham, 1ˢᵗ Baronet." *https://en.wikipedia.org.* accessed 9 Jun 2018

Wikipedia. "Slow Match." *https://en.wikipedia.org.* accessed 2 Nov 2019

Wikipedia. "Spanish Match." *https://en.wikipedia.org.* accessed 11 Nov 2018

Wikipedia. "Tomocomo." *https://en.wikipedia.org.* accessed 11 Jun 2018

Wikipedia. "Thomas Wentworth, 1ˢᵗ Earl of Strafford." *https://en.wikipedia.org.* accessed 7 Mar 2017

Wikipedia. "Twelfth Night Holiday." *https://en.wikipedia.org.* accessed 21 May 2018

Wikipedia. "Twelfth Night or What You Will." *https://en.wikipedia.org.* accessed 11 Jun 2018

Wikipedia. "The Vision of Delight." *https://en.wikipedia.org.* accessed 20 May 2015

Wikipedia. "The Wars of the Three Kingdoms." *https://en.wikipedia.org.* accessed 5 Sep 2019

Wikipedia. "William Harvey." *https://en.wikipedia.org.* accessed 20 Mar 2019

Wikipedia. "William Laud." *https://en.wikipedia.org.* accessed 31 Jul 2019

Wikipedia. "William Prynne." *https://en.wikipedia.org.* accessed 15 Aug 2019

William Shakespeare Site Map. "Elizabethan Wedding Customs." *http://william-shakespeare.info/elizabethan-wedding-customs.htm.* accessed 22 Oct 2017

Winchester University History. "Lady Mary Bankes and the Siege of Corfe Castle." *https://nu-history.com/2016/04/10/lady-mary-bankes-and-the-siege-of-corfe-castle.* accessed 22 Jul 2018

Wollaston, Victoria. "Bringing Corfe Castle Back to Life: Digital Reconstruction." *https://www.dailymail.co.uk/sciencetech/article-3539618*. accessed 21 July 2018

Woodward, Hobson. "The First Powhatan Envoy to England." Thesis: dissertation: e-book, October 22, 2017

WorldCat. "Autographed letter signed: [Plymouth, Mass.], to his brother Sir Edward Altham, [1623 Sept]." *http://www.worldcat.org/title/autograph-letter-signed-plymouth-mass-to-his-brother-sir-edward-altham-1623-sept/oclc/668251540*. accessed 8 Feb 2016

World's Famous Orations, Volume III. "In His Own Defense, by Thomas Wentworth, Earl of Strafford (1593-1641)." *www.bartleby.com*. Great Books Online. accessed 24 Jan 2021

Yale Indian Papers Project. "Emmanuel Altham, 1600." *https://yipp.yale.edu/bio/bibliography/altham-emmanuel-1600*. accessed 8 Apr 2018

YourIrish.com. "The Irish Rebellion of 1641 Direct from Ireland." *www.yourirish.com*. accessed 13 Jan 2019

CPSIA information can be obtained
at www.ICGtesting.com
Printed in the USA
BVHW091109120822
644430BV00001B/1